Fourth Maccabees and the Promotion of the Jewish Philosophy

Fourth Maccabees and the **Promotion** of the **Jewish Philosophy**

Rhetoric, Intertexture, and Reception

David A. deSilva

CASCADE *Books* · Eugene, Oregon

FOURTH MACCABEES AND THE PROMOTION
OF THE JEWISH PHILOSOPHY
Rhetoric, Intertexture, and Reception

Cascade Books
An Imprint of Wipf and Stock Publishers
199 W. 8th Ave., Suite 3
Eugene, OR 97401

www.wipfandstock.com

PAPERBACK ISBN: 978-1-7252-7068-8
HARDCOVER ISBN: 978-1-7252-7069-5
EBOOK ISBN: 978-1-7252-7070-1

Cataloguing-in-Publication data:

Names: DeSilva, David Arthur, author.

Title: Fourth Maccabees and the promotion of the Jewish philosophy : rhetoric, intertexture, and reception / David A. deSilva.

Description: Eugene, OR: Cascade Books, 2020. | Includes bibliographical references and indexes.

Identifiers: ISBN 978-1-7252-7068-8 (paperback). | ISBN 978-1-7252-7069-5 (hardcover). | ISBN 978-1-7252-7070-1 (ebook).

Subjects: LCSH: Bible—Maccabees, 4th—Criticism, interpretation, etc. | Fourth book of Maccabees—Criticism, interpretation, etc. | Codex Sinaiticus (Biblical manuscript). | Greek literature—Jewish authors—History and criticism. | Judaism—History—Post-exilic period, 586 B.C.-210 A.D. | Bible—Apocrypha—Criticism, interpretation, etc. | Rhetoric, ancient. | Philosophy, ancient.

Classification: DS1825.2 D741 2020 (print). | DS1825.2 (ebook).

Manufactured in the U.S.A.   10/27/20

To Gene Heitman and Carol Treadwell

Contents

Acknowledgments

I am grateful to the publishers of the various journals in which these essays first appeared during the long course of my fascination with 4 Maccabees (spanning 1995–2016) for their permission to reproduce them here, with only slight modifications. Chapter 1 first appeared as "The Author of 4 Maccabees and Greek *Paideia*: Facets of the Formation of a Hellenistic Jewish Rhetor," *Bulletin for Biblical Research* 26.4 (2016) 501–531 (copyright © 2016 by the Pennsylvania State University Press). Chapter 7 was first published as "The Human Ideal, the Problem of Evil, and Moral Responsibility in *4 Maccabees*," *Bulletin for Biblical Research* 23 (2013) 57–78 (copyright © 2013 by the Pennsylvania State University Press). These articles are included here by kind permission of The Pennsylvania State University Press. Chapter 2 was first published as "The Noble Contest: Honor, Shame, and the Rhetorical Strategy of 4 Maccabees," *Journal for the Study of the Pseudepigrapha* 13 (1995) 31–57. Chapter 4 first appeared as "'And Not a Drop to Drink': The Story of David's Thirst in the Jewish Scriptures, Josephus, and 4 Maccabees," *Journal for the Study of Pseudepigrapha* 16.1 (2006) 15–40. These articles are included here by kind permission of SAGE Publications, Inc. Chapter 3 first appeared as "Using the Master's Tools to Shore Up Our House: A Postcolonial Analysis of 4 Maccabees," *Journal of Biblical Literature* 127 (2007) 99–127, and is reproduced here by kind permission of the Society of Biblical Literature. Chapter 5 was first published as "The Perfection of 'Love for Offspring': Greek Representations of Maternal Affection and the Achievement of the Heroine of 4 Maccabees," *New Testament Studies* 52 (2006) 251–268, and is included here by kind permission of Cambridge University Press. Chapter 8 was first published as "'An Example of How to Die Nobly for Religion': The Influence of 4 Maccabees on Origen's *Exhortatio ad Martyrium*," *Journal for Early Christian Studies* 17 (2009) 337–355. Chapter 9 first appeared in substantially shorter form as "Ambrose's Use of 4 Maccabees in *De Jacob et Vita Beata*: Some Correctives," *Journal of Early Christian Studies* 22 (2014) 287–293. These are both included by kind permission of Johns Hopkins University Press and the North American Patristics Society. Chapter 10 was first published as "The Sinaiticus Text of 4 Maccabees," *Catholic Biblical Quarterly* 68 (2006) 47–62, and is included here by kind permission of the Catholic Biblical Association of America. Finally, chapter 6 incorporates material from my book, *4 Maccabees: Introduction and Commentary*, and is included here by kind permission of Koninklijke Brill NV. Finally, it is my pleasure to dedicate this volume to two important members of my family, Mr. Eugene Perry Heitman, Sr., and Mrs. V. Carol Treadwell, parents to my wife of thirty years, Donna Jean deSilva.

Abbreviations

Ancient Texts

Aeschylus

Ag.	*Agamemnon*

Anaximenes

Rhet. ad Alex.	*Rhetorica ad Alexandrum*

Aristotle

Eth. Eud.	*Eudemian Ethics*
Eth. Nic.	*Nicomachean Ethics*
Pol.	*Politica*
Rhet.	*Rhetoric*
Virt.	*Virtues and Vices*

Apocrypha

Tob	Tobit
Jdt	Judith
Macc	Maccabees
Wis	Wisdom of Solomon

Cicero

Tusc.	*Tusculun Disputations*

Cyprian

Exh.   *Exhortation to Fortunatus*

Demosthenes

Or.   *Orations*

Dio Chrysostom

Or.   *Orations*

Diodorus Siculus

Bib. Hist.   *Bibliotheca historica*

Diogenes Laertius

Vit.   *Vitae Philosophorum (Lives of the Eminent Philosophers)*

Epictetus

Diatr.   *Diatribai (Dissertationes)*
Ench.   *Encheiridion*

Euripides

Frag.   *Fragmenta*
Tro.   *Troades*
Hec.   *Hecuba*

Gregory of Nazianzus

Or.   *Oration*

Herodotus

Hist.   *Histories*

Homer

Il.   *Ilias*
Od.   *Odyssea*

Hyperides

Or.   *Orations*

Iamblichus

Vit. Pyth.   *De vita pythagorica*

Josephus

Ag. Ap.   *Against Apion*
Ant.   *Antiquitates Judaicae (Jewish Antiquities)*
B.J.   *Bellum Judaicum (Jewish War)*

Juvenal

Sat.   *Satirae*

Let. Aris.   *Letter of Aristeas*

Lucian

Tyr.   *Tyrannicide*

LXX   Septuagint

Lysias

Or.   *Orations*

MT   Masoretic Text

Origen

Exh.   *Exhortatio ad Martyrium*

Philo

Det.   *Quod deterius potiori insidari soleat*
Leg. All.   *Legum allegoriae*
Migr.   *De migration Abrahami*
Mos.   *De vita Mosis*

Opif.	*De opificio mundi*
Prob.	*Quod omnis probus liber sit*
Spec. leg.	*De specialibus legibus*

Plato

Apol.	*Apologia*
Gorg.	*Gorgias*
Menex.	*Menexenus*
Resp.	*Respublica*

Pliny the Younger

Ep.	*Epistulae*

Plutarch

Am. prol.	*De amore prolis*
Lib. ed.	*De liberis educandis*
Mor.	*Moralia*
Mul. Virt.	*Mulierum virtutes*
Plac. Philos.	*De placita philosophorum*
Superst.	*De superstitione*
Tranq. an.	*De tranquilitate animi*
Virt. mor.	*De virtute morali*

Pseudo-Philo

LAB	*Liber antiquitatum biblicarum*

Quintilian

Inst.	*Institutio Oratoria*
Rhet. Her.	*Rhetorica ad Herennium*

Seneca

Ben.	*De beneficiis*
Constant.	*De constantia sapientis*
Ep.	*Epistulae*

Helv.	*Ad Helviam*
Marc.	*Ad Marciam de consolatione*
Polyb.	*Ad Polybium de consolatione*
Prov.	*De providentia*

Sophocles

Ant.	*Antigone*
Oed. tyr.	*Oedipus tyrannus*

Stobaeus

Ecl.	*Eclogae*

Tacitus

Hist.	*Historiae*

T. Job.	*Testament of Job*
T. Levi	*Testament of Levi*
T. Reub.	*Testament of Reuben*

Thucydides

Hist.	The Histories

Xenophon

Mem.	*Memorabilia*

Modern Works

AB	Anchor Bible
ANRW	*Aufstieg und Niedergang der römischen Welt*
BETL	Bibliotheca Ephemeridum Theologicarum Lovaniensium
BTB	*Biblical Theology Bulletin*
CBQ	*Catholic Biblical Quarterly*
CEB	Common English Bible
ESV	English Standard Version
GBSNTS	Guides to Biblical Scholarship: New Testament Series

ICC	International Critical Commentary
JBL	*Journal of Biblical Literature*
JECS	*Journal of Early Christian Studies*
JJS	*Journal of Jewish Studies*
JSNT	*Journal for the Study of the New Testament*
JSNTSup	Journal for the Study of the New Testament Supplement
JSP	*Journal for the Study of the Pseudepigrapha*
JTS	*Journal of Theological Studies*
LCL	Loeb Classical Library
MSU	Mitteilungen des Septuaginta-Unternehmens
NICNT	New International Commentary on the New Testament
NRSV	New Revised Standard Version of the Bible
NTS	*New Testament Studies*
OTL	Old Testament Library
PG	Patrologiae Graeca, edited by J.-P. Migne. 162 vols. Paris, 1857–1866
PL	Patrologia Latina, edited by J.-P. Migne. 217 vols. Paris, 1841–1855
SBLDS	Society of Biblical Literature Dissertation Series
SBLMS	Society of Biblical Literature Monograph Series
SNTSMS	Society for New Testament Studies Monograph Series
TDNT	*Theological Dictionary of the New Testament*. Edited by Gerhard Kittel and Gerhard Friedrich. Translated by Geoffrey W. Bromiley. 10 vols. Grand Rapids: Eerdmans, 1964–1976
VC	*Vigiliae christianae*
VT	*Vetus Testamentum*
WBC	Word Biblical Commentary
WUNT	Wissenschaftliche Untersuchungen zum Neuen Testament

Introduction

Why should anyone invest himself or herself in reading, let alone studying in minute detail, the book we call 4 Maccabees? This is a question with which I have been long familiar, as I have had to answer it dozens of times over the course of the last twenty-five years after first answering the question, "What are you working on these days?"

The first part of my answer concerns what this particular text reveals about the quality and nature of the interaction of Judaism and Hellenism in the first century of the common era. Even though we are close to celebrating the fiftieth anniversary of Martin Hengel's landmark work on *Judaism and Hellenism*, many of my students (and even a number of scholars whose work I have critiqued or who have critiqued my own work) continue to look upon Judaism—and especially *pious* Jews—as standing apart from all things Greek as if from something unclean. Faithful Jews think "Hebraically" and not "Hellenistically." It still surprises many in the classroom and in the pews that the majority of faithful Jews throughout the Diaspora knew their Scriptures in Greek and *only* in Greek. In the author of 4 Maccabees, we find a man who has excelled in Greek composition and rhetoric, who has provided for himself a more-than-passing acquaintance with Greek philosophical ethics and Greek drama, speaking in the most Greek modes to promote the most Jewish way of life. Here is a man who has developed fully Greek rationales for remaining true to the Jewish way of life, who has thought about for himself and now proclaims to others the significance and value of his ancestral Law and the kind of life it shapes in terms that any non-Jew could understand (if not accept). Fourth Maccabees thus provides a witness to the possibility of being fully Hellenized in terms of knowledge, cultural literacy, and training in the arts of communication while remaining fully dedicated to promoting continued, unyielding commitment to the

Jewish way of life—the possibility of being fully acculturated while resisting assimilation in any and every sense.

The second part of my answer concerns what 4 Maccabees reveals about the way Paul's contemporaries or near-contemporaries—who did *not* have a life-changing encounter that distanced them significantly from the convictions and pursuits of the first part of their careers—thought about the Jewish Law. In light of popular Christian (and particularly Protestant Christian) tendencies to view the Law as impossible in its demands—a crushing burden that drives people either to hypocrisy or despair—it is most illumining and even refreshing to encounter a book that portrays the Law of Moses as a divinely-given good without qualification. The author of 4 Maccabees preaches with an evangelistic fervor about the value and benefits of the Torah-driven life. It is not only *possible* to live in line with the Torah (2:6). It is also the way of life most suited to our created natures and to God's plan for how we will realize our best selves in the here and now (2:21–23; 5:25–26). It is the educative discipline by means of which we become well-formed and mature moral agents (1:15–17; 5:23–24) and the training program whereby we gain the moral muscle needed to escape the domination of our passions and desires (1:31–2:14). It strengthens human and humane feelings without allowing one to be *overcome* by feelings and turned away from the just and right course of action by them at any point (13:19–27; 14:13–20). A text like 4 Maccabees provides, in this way, an important corrective to theologically-rooted prejudices against a Torah-centered piety—not that 4 Maccabees is likely to make Christian theologians discard Galatians or Romans, but it is likely to make them read them (and their treatment of the Law of Moses) in a far more nuanced fashion.[1]

The third part of my answer (if my interlocutor has not yet walked away) concerns the impact of this book—one that seems so remote to modern readers—on Christian martyrology and ethics during the second through fifth centuries, to which it was seen to have immediate relevance. In the face of increasingly hostile persecution and, in particular, trials before governors and other representatives of the imperial power that typically ended in grisly forms of execution, Christian leaders turned for their own inspiration and that of their charges to the story of the Jewish martyrs who chose death for the sake of piety over release at the cost of apostasy as found in both 2 Maccabees and 4 Maccabees. After Constantine I and

---

1. I have considered elsewhere the possibility that 4 Maccabees is suggestive for the ways in which the rival Jewish Christian missionaries who came to Paul's converts in the province of Galatia might have presented Torah-observance in precisely the attractive manner that threatened to win Paul's converts over to their understanding of what trusting Jesus opened up for the Gentile convert (*Galatians*, 19–22).

Licinius issued the Edict of Milan declaring Christianity a tolerated religion, Christian leaders continued to draw inspiration from 4 Maccabees and its author's assurance that the piety-infused mind could successfully master the impulses, cravings, and emotions that threatened a consistent commitment to virtue. Neither the political situation of the global Church nor the ethical situation of humanity has advanced to such a state as to render either contribution of this ancient text superfluous in the modern world.

This volume contains ten essays written on 4 Maccabees over the course of what I hope is only the first half of my career (1995–2016). Each contributes in some way to the reader's appreciation of one of these three focal points concerning the abiding value of this text. In the first part ("Rhetorical Situation and Strategic Response"), I focus more fully on the question of the author's relationship to his Jewish identity and community, on the one hand, and his Hellenistic-Roman context on the other. The first chapter ("The Author of 4 Maccabees and Greek *Paideia*: Facets of the Formation of a Hellenistic Jewish Rhetor") represents an attempt to reconstruct the kind of educational background that would have produced a communicator like the author of 4 Maccabees. I look first for signs of elementary and secondary training in his work, exploring points of contact between the skills developed by the curriculum of exercises known as the "Progymnasmata" (elementary exercises in composition) and the skills exhibited in 4 Maccabees. I examine also the author's level of mastery of Greek language, philosophical ethics, and literature against scholarly reconstructions of secondary and tertiary curricula, on the one hand, and consider, on the other hand, how he was likely to have come by his significant facility in his own Jewish tradition and practice.

In the second and third chapters, I examine the use to which the author has put his education. In "Honor and Shame as Argumentative Topoi in 4 Maccabees," I consider the correspondences between 4 Maccabees and the kind of oratory and rhetorical aims addressed by epideictic and deliberative speeches (and, specifically, how considerations of the honorable and the shameful are used to position the author's audience vis-à-vis their commitment to their ancestral way of life. In "Fourth Maccabees as Acculturated Resistance Literature," I employ a "postcolonial optic" more forthrightly to examine 4 Maccabees as a specimen of resistance literature—specifically, as a work whose author has used his facility in the tools and knowledge of the dominant culture to carve out a space for his own subaltern culture and model strategies for sustaining a minority cultural identity in the midst of a dominant and majority culture that fairly aggressively promotes assimilation.

In the second part ("The Rhetorical Contributions of Intertexture"), I examine how the author has used both Greek and traditional Jewish resources to advance his goals for his audience. Chapter 4 ("The Strategic Retelling of Scripture in 4 Maccabees: David's Thirst [4 Macc 3:6–18]") examines four accounts of a particular episode in the life of David and the correspondences between the various authors' redaction or re-invention of that episode to better support each author's particular goals for the story—in the case of our author, the demonstration that, while intense sensations cannot but be felt, they need not lead one to intemperate or unjust actions. Chapter 5 ("Engagement with Greco-Roman Intertexture: Conversations about Maternal Affections") examines the correspondences between the presentation of the love that the mother of the seven brothers felt for her sons (and the pains she endured as they were tortured) and discussions about "affection for offspring" in Aristotle and Plutarch and, then, the correspondences between the laments of bereaved mothers in Euripidean tragedy and the lament that the author crafts for the mother—"had *she* been of cowardly disposition" (4 Macc 16:5). This provides a case study in the author's use of Greek cultural knowledge to advance his claims concerning the superiority of training in the Jewish way of life (the Torah-prescribed life) for the attainment of the ideals prized by the dominant Hellenized culture. A third essay (chapter 6, "'Father Knew Best': Intertextuality and Argumentation in 4 Macc 18:6–19") investigates the string of examples and brief quotations from the Jewish scriptures that the author incorporates into the mother's second speech as the "epitome" of the instruction her husband passed along to their sons before his own death with a view to laying bare the implicit argumentation advanced by the *sequence* of material, even in the general absence of explicit inferential conjunctions and particles.

In the third and final part ("The Legacy of 4 Maccabees"), I give attention to the ongoing contributions of 4 Maccabees to theological reflection in general and the early church's responses to pastoral needs in particular. Chapter 7 ("The Human Ideal, the Problem of Evil, and Moral Responsibility in 4 Maccabees") explores the responses that this text gives to the perennial questions of human existence: What does it mean to be fully human? What are the origins of the evils that invade human lives? How will good be restored—and justice done—where we see unjust suffering? In chapters 8 ("Fourth Maccabees and Early Christian Martyrdom: The Influence of 4 Maccabees on Origen's *Exhortatio ad Martyrium*") and 9 ("Ambrose's Use of 4 Maccabees in *De Jacob et Vita Beata*"), I trace out the impact of 4 Maccabees on two early Christian texts that exemplify the twin interests of the early church in this text noted above. Finally, in chapter 10 ("Beyond the Eclectic Text of 4 Maccabees: Reading 4 Maccabees in Codex Sinaiticus"),

I inquire into how readers of 4 Maccabees as represented in a particular, fourth-century Christian manuscript will experience the text differently than readers of the reconstructed, eclectic text (or translations based on the same). It is, incidentally, also a testimony to the importance of 4 Maccabees for the early Church that it should have been included in Codex Sinaiticus (as well as Codex Alexandrinus) in the first place.

I have been drawn again and again to 4 Maccabees because the author and his work demolish stereotypes—the stereotype of the Second Temple Period Jew who eschews rather than deeply engages Greek culture without yielding his or her own way of life for a moment; the stereotype of the Second Temple Period Jew laboring under "the curse of the Law"; the stereotype of the extrabiblical text that exercises little or no influence and is little or nothing valued by the Church in its formative centuries. As one who is primarily a scholar of the New Testament, I have found the study of 4 Maccabees to be indispensable for my primary work because it teaches me again and again to think about Christian origins and early Christian literature more clearly and honestly, because it teaches me to do so apart from these stereotypes.

Part 1

Rhetorical Situation and Strategic Response

1

The Author of 4 Maccabees
and Greek *Paideia*

Facets of the Formation of a
Hellenistic Jewish Rhetor

The author of 4 Maccabees famously praises education in and practice of the Jewish Torah as the kind of παιδεία (4 Macc 1:15–17; 5:23–24) that produces people of the highest moral caliber, people who embody the Greek ideal of the virtuous and honorable person—the person of καλοκἀγαθία (1:10; 3:18; 11:22; 13:25; 15:9) and ἀρετή (1:8, 10; 7:22; 9:8, 18, 31; 10:10; 11:2; 12:14; 13:24, 27; 17:23), the person who walks in line with the cardinal virtues of justice, courage, moderation, and prudence (1:18; 5:23–24). But what was the author's *own* experience of παιδεία? What training—aside, no doubt, from being educated in and formed by the practice of the Torah—contributed to the formation of this skilled preacher and orator? This study seeks out the "effects" visible in the text known as 4 Maccabees that plausibly point to a "cause," namely the Jewish author's experience of a formal education reflective of the curriculum typical of Greek education in the Hellenistic and Roman periods. It seeks to create a profile of the author in terms of his level of education as a case study in the degree to which one member of an ethnic subculture was formed by the kind of training associated with the formation of citizens of a Greek city while still remaining explicitly committed to the convictions, practices, and cultural knowledge of his ethnic subculture.

Mastery of the Greek Language

The author of 4 Maccabees has had enough training in Greek grammar and syntax to demonstrate absolute mastery of the language. He does not write as one who has acquired Greek as a second language. His Greek is free from Semitisms, the exception being "giving glory" (δόξαν διδοὺς) in 1:12, a Septuagintalism and an echo of Jewish liturgical expression.[1] His writing exhibits the complex subordination of clauses rather than the paratactic sentence structure typical of those who lack facility in Greek or have acquired it imperfectly as a second language.[2] His text includes a striking number of *hapax legomena* (e.g. μιαροφαγῆσαι, 5:3; ἀντιρρητορεύσαντα, 6:1; περιαγκωνίσαντες, 6:3; παθοκρατεῖσθαι, 7:20; προσεμειδίασεν, 8:4; ἀντεφιλοσόφησα, 8:15) many of which may be neologisms as they reflect common patterns of formulating new compound words, demonstrating again his level of facility in Greek.[3] He also uses poetic forms (like προυφάνησαν for προεφάνησαν in 4 Macc 4:10), and makes frequent use of the optative mood against the general trend of moving away from such forms in favor of the subjunctive mood.[4] Dupont-Sommer could therefore justly claim that "Our author expresses himself in Greek and he thinks in Greek."[5] The level of his language suggests that he had not only successfully undertaken primary and secondary studies in grammar, but also engaged in extensive reading of Greek literature, such that its subtleties were internalized through broad acquaintance with its exemplary writers. This is not to suggest that the author is himself a model stylist, by any means, but rather that he has learned to imitate a broad array of linguistic skills and syntactic structures from model stylists.

Mastery of Elementary Exercises in Composition

The author gives evidence of having been trained in the elementary exercises in composition that were introduced toward the end of secondary education and the beginning of tertiary education.[6] The details concerning these elementary exercises survive in several training manuals (*Progymnasmata*),

1. Townshend, "Fourth Book," 667; A. Dupont-Sommer, *Quatrième Livre*, 57; Stowers, "4 Maccabees," 845.

2. Breitenstein, *Beobachtungen*, 177–78.

3. Dupont-Sommer, *Quatrième Livre*, 57–58. Breitenstein (*Beobach-tungen*, 28 n.2) lists 26 *hapax legomena*.

4. Dupont-Sommer, *Quatrième Livre*, 59; Breitenstein, *Beobachtungen*, 53–56; on vocabulary and style, see further Dupont-Sommer, *Quatrième Livre*, 57–66.

5. Dupont-Sommer, *Quatrième Livre*, 57 (my trans.).

6. Marrou, *Education in Antiquity*, 238–41.

notably those of Aelius Theon (a rhetor from Alexandria active in the late 1st century) and Hermogenes (a rhetor from the late 2nd-century CE).[7] These manuals incidentally correspond quite closely to the descriptions of the elementary exercises found in Quintilian, *Inst.* 2.4, suggesting a certain universality in regard to this portion of the curriculum at least from the Eastern Mediterranean as far West as Italy. The skills and forms of writing learned at this stage would become the building blocks of prose composition and, thence, declamation for the course of a speaker's lifetime. Fourth Maccabees reflects just such a foundation.

Narrative

The most basic exercise in the *Progymnasmata* is the recounting or invention of a fable in the style of Aesop and others. The author of 4 Maccabees makes no use of fables in this particular text, so we have no direct evidence that this would have been part of his curriculum, though we also have no reason to doubt it.[8] Nevertheless, the first elementary exercise that has made a discernible contribution to the author's skill set is the "narrative" (διήγημα), the ability to recount an episode (whether mythical, fictitious/dramatic, historical, political or private) with clarity, conciseness, and credibility.[9] Hermogenes distinguishes between the creation of a narrative episode (a διήγημα, the schoolbook exercise) concerning "one thing" (i.e., event) and a narration (a διήγησις), referring to a longer narrative work concerned with "many things." One gets the impression from Hermogenes' analogous distinction between a "poem" (ποίημα) like the "Making of the Shield" (*Il.* 18), "Descent into the Underworld" (*Od.* 11), or "Killing the Suitors" (*Od.* 22) and a "poetic work" (ποίησις) like the *Iliad* or the *Odyssey* that the ability to craft a narration (a διήγησις) is essentially the ability to craft a series of related narratives (διηγήματα) and bind them together into a larger whole.[10]

Fourth Maccabees contains extensive narration which represents a skillful deployment of the more basic skills of writing episodes ("narratives"), vivid description ("ecphrasis"), and ethopoeia ("speech in character"). As an individual narrative—and one that remains disconnected from

7. Translations are readily found in Kennedy, *Progymnasmata*, 1–88.

8. We should not surmise that, as a Jewish author, he would have had no use for the fable in general. Even the apocalyptist who wrote 4 Ezra invented a fable in the course of his writing (i.e., the fable of the forest and the waves of the sea in 4 Ezra 4:13–19).

9. Hermogenes, *Preliminary Exercises* 2.4 (Kennedy, *Progymnasmata*, 75); Theon, *Exercises* 5.79 (Kennedy, *Progymnasmata*, 29).

10. Hermogenes, *Preliminary Exercises* 2.4 (Kennedy, *Progymnasmata*, 75).

the longer narration created by the martyr episodes—we might consider the author's retelling of the story of David's thirst (4 Macc 3:6–18). The episode has all the essential elements of a narrative identified by Theon: the person (David); the action done by the person (suffering an irrational craving, yet nevertheless pouring out the drink as a libation); the place where the action was done (army encampment); the time at which it was done (evening, after a long day of battle); the manner of the action (the various actions of the narrative); and the cause of these things (natural thirst from heavy exertion, the workings of irrational desires, piety). According to Theon's rubric ("a complete narration consists of all of them and of things related to them and one lacking any of these is deficient"), the author would have scored high marks.[11] A close comparison of this narrative and the classical sources on which it is based (2 Sam 23:13–17; 1 Chron 11:15–19) also shows the author's creativity in regard to his retelling of the episode, shaping it to serve the argumentative ends to which he puts the story.[12]

The author also shows his ability both to abridge and to expand narratives in his retelling of the narration of his source. He conflates characters and developments in order to state more concisely episodes that are of secondary importance to his oration (providing an abridged version of 2 Macc 3:1–6:17), while amplifying and embellishing that part of the story that is most germane to his topic (providing expansive retellings of the episodes constituting 2 Macc 6:18–7:42). The episode of David's thirst is also a noteworthy expansion of the story as known from the older, classical texts.

Ecphrasis

Within his creation of narratives, the author of 4 Maccabees also exhibits facility in ecphrasis, the vivid description of a scene. A good ecphrasis "should almost create seeing through the hearing."[13] The scene could be static, as in the ecphrasis of the Shield of Achilles in *Iliad* 18.478–608, or dynamic, as in the depiction of an action. The author of 4 Maccabees gives significant attention to bringing the scenes before the eyes (and other senses) throughout his work. His engagement in ecphrasis is particularly evident when his material is compared with that of his source.

---

11. Theon, *Exercises* 5.78; Kennedy, *Progymnasmata*, 28.

12. See chapter 4 below.

13. Hermogenes, *Preliminary Exercises* 10.23 (Kennedy, *Progymnasmata*, 86); this is also stressed in Theon, *Exercises* 7.119 (Kennedy, *Progymnasmata*, 47): "The virtues of an ecphrasis are as follows: most of all, clarity and a vivid impression of all-but-seeing what is described."

> David was then in the stronghold; and the garrison of the Phi-
> listines was then at Bethlehem. David said longingly, "O that
> someone would give me water to drink from the well of Bethle-
> hem that is by the gate!" (2 Sam 23:14–15, NRSV)

> David was attacking the foreigners all day long, killing many
> of them with the help of his nation's soldiers. When evening
> came, he returned to the royal tent, drenched with sweat and
> completely exhausted. Now the whole army of his nation was
> encamped around him, and all the others were having supper.
> The king, however, was extremely thirsty. Even though there
> were plentiful springs of water in the camp, he was unable to
> satisfy his thirst from them. Instead, he was utterly possessed
> by an irrational desire for the water in the camp of the enemy.
> (4 Macc 3:7–11)[14]

Here the author of 4 Maccabees carefully describes the scene, provides a
credible motive for David's thirst (the "cause" being an important feature
of the exercise in "narrative"), and adds vivid details about the king's being
"drenched with sweat and completely exhausted" from a day in battle and
about the layout of the camp and its surrounding terrain.

> The Three broke through the camp of the Philistines, and drew
> water from the well of Bethlehem that was by the gate, and they
> brought it to David. (2 Sam 23:18)

> Two strong, young soldiers, embarrassed for the king on ac-
> count of his desire, put on their armor, grabbed a pitcher, and
> went out behind enemy lines. They sneaked past the guards at
> the gate and began searching through the whole camp. They
> found the spring and boldly carried off a drink for the king. (4
> Macc 3:12–14)

Again the author (aside from also supplying a motive) creates a more vivid
picture of the soldier's preparation and movements through the enemy
camp on the way to their objective.

> But David would not drink of it; he poured it out to the Lord. (2
> Sam 23:18, NRSV)

> But David, even though he was on fire with thirst, understood the
> terrible danger that this drink, being of equal value to the blood of
> the men who risked their lives to fetch it, posed to his soul.

---

14. Translations from 4 Maccabees are my own unless otherwise noted.

The author adds the vivid detail of David being "on fire with thirst" as he performs his pious act of honoring God with the drink as a libation (incidentally also representing the king's speech in the original as a paraphrase in the form of David's mental deliberations).

Of course, it is the scenes of torture wherein the author's facility in ecphrasis fully and famously emerges.[15] Despite the amount of space devoted to Eleazar in 2 Maccabees, that author said very little about the nature of his torments: "he . . . went up to the rack of his own accord, spitting out the flesh" (2 Macc 6:19); "he went at once to the rack" (2 Macc 6:28); "when he was about to die under the blows" (2 Macc 6:30). Compare to this the author of 4 Maccabees' portrayal of Eleazar's torments:

> The soldiers who were standing by hauled him off to the instruments of torture. First, they tore off the old man's clothes, though he remained decently clad in his mindfulness of God. They tied his arms behind him and began to flog him from both sides while a herald kept calling out, "Obey the king's orders!" But Eleazar, that noble-minded and virtuous man, experiencing the truth in his name, was not shaken from his resolve. He seemed to experience the tortures as if in a dream. The old man kept his eyes raised toward heaven, while the whips tore into his flesh, shredded his sides, and released fountains of blood. His body fell to the ground because of the unendurable pain, but he kept his mind upright and unbending. One of the pitiless guards rushed up to him and started kicking him in his side to make him stand up again. But Eleazar bore up under the pains, rose above the attempts at coercion, and endured the tortures . . . His face drenched in sweat and gasping for air, he amazed even the torturers by his unyielding spirit. (4 Macc 6:1–9, 11)

The author of 2 Maccabees is more generous with details concerning the sufferings of the first few sons than he was in regard to Eleazar. After the seven were subjected first to "torture with whips and thongs" (2 Macc 7:1),

> The king fell into a rage and gave orders to have pans and caldrons heated. These were heated immediately, and he commanded that the tongue of their spokesman be cut out and that they scalp him and cut off his hands and feet, while the rest of the brothers and the mother looked on. When he was utterly helpless, the king ordered them to take him to the fire, still breathing, and to fry him in a pan. The smoke from the pan

---

15. Dupont-Sommer, *Quatrième Livre*, 63–65 especially highlights 9:19–20; 10:5–8; 15:14–21 as examples of ecphrasis.

spread widely, but the brothers and their mother encouraged
one another to die nobly. (2 Macc 7:3–5, NRSV)

After this the author again becomes more sparing. Regarding the second, he
relates that "they tore off the skin of his head with the hair" (7:7) and that "he
in turn underwent tortures as the first brother had done" (7:8). Regarding
the third, we are told only that "When it was demanded, he quickly put out
his tongue and courageously stretched forth his hands" (7:10). No details are
given in 2 Maccabees of the manner of tortures applied to the fourth through
seventh sons (except the vague statement in regard to the latter that "the king
. . . handled him worse than the others," 2 Macc 7:39).

The author of 4 Maccabees has clearly exercised his ingenuity in his
descriptions of the varied tortures experienced by the first six brothers
(9:10—11:27), once again giving significant attention to the level of detail
that would qualify these episodes as exhibiting ecphrasis:

> They spread fiery coals below him. They fanned the flames and
> tightened the wheel even more. By this point, the wheel was cov-
> ered in blood, the burning coals were being extinguished by the
> drippings, and chunks of flesh were falling off the axles of the
> machine. Even with all the ligaments of his bones severed, the
> high-minded, Abrahamic young man did not cry out. (9:19–21)

> They put on iron gloves equipped with sharp claws and bound
> the young man to the torture device . . . The leopard-like beasts
> ripped out his muscles with their iron claws, tore his flesh all the
> way up to his chin, and scalped him. (9:26, 28)

> They used instruments to pull his hands and feet out of joint and
> pried his arms and legs out of their sockets. Then they broke his
> fingers, arms, legs, and elbows. For all this, they weren't strong
> enough to break his resolve, so they put away their tools and
> tore off his scalp in the Scythian way—using their fingernails.
> Then they dragged him to the wheel. As they were pulling his
> spine apart, he saw his own flesh falling off his bones and his
> blood flowing out. (10:5–8)

> The guards tied him up and dragged him to the "catapult." They
> forced him down onto his knees, bound him to the machine,
> and fitted iron clamps on his thighs. They began to work the
> wheel, drawing him backwards around a wedge until he was
> curled back all the way like a scorpion. With all his bones
> pulled out of joint, gasping for air and racked by pain in his
> body, he said . . . (11:9–12)

> When he said this, they marched him up to the wheel. They
> stretched him tight upon him until his back broke, and they
> roasted him from underneath with fire. They skewered his back
> with sharp spits heated in the fire, piercing his ribs and burning
> through his organs. (11:17–19)

The author's motive in employing ecphrasis in these scenes of torture is, of
course, to assist the shuddering audience to begin to fathom what is truly
possible for them to withstand where piety and virtue are at stake, and
thus to understand the depth of virtue and moral firmness that training in
the Torah nurtures.

The mother is a major character in 2 Maccabees as in 4 Maccabees, but
the former tells only of her bravery (2 Macc 7:20), her encouragement of her
sons in general (2 Macc 7:21–23), her encouragement of her last surviving
son (2 Macc 7:25–29), and her death ("Last of all, the mother died, after
her sons," 2 Macc 7:41). Here the author of 4 Maccabees shows his greatest
inventiveness, for every detail concerning the mother's sufferings is his own
creation. He accomplishes this chiefly by combining the seven episodes narrated in 9.10–12.19 into a single, accumulated experience, presenting before
the readers/hearers the scenes that the mother herself witnessed and the
impact that these scenes had upon her:

> She looked on as her children's flesh was eaten up by fire, their
> fingers and toes scattered all over the ground, the flesh of their
> faces down to the chin torn off like masks. How terribly that
> mother was being tested, experiencing pains far worse than the
> labor pains she suffered for them! . . . You did not cry out when
> you looked into each one's eyes, transfixed upon their own ago-
> nies, or when you saw on their faces the signs of approaching
> death. You did not burst into tears when you saw the burnt flesh
> of one child piling up on the burnt flesh of the others, severed
> hands upon severed hands, severed heads beside severed heads,
> remains piled up on remains, nor when you gazed out at the
> crowd of spectators that had gathered to witness your sons' suf-
> ferings. The children's voices calling out to their mother from
> the midst of their agony held her attention more powerfully
> than the Sirens' singing or the song of swans capture their hear-
> ers' attention. How many, how great, then, were the torments
> that this mother suffered, while her sons were being tortured by
> the wheels and hot irons! (15:15–16, 19–22)

The author also creates a window into the mother's inner turmoil through
a vivid and figurative depiction of "her soul . . . as a courtroom" wherein

"many frightfully persuasive voices were speaking out—Nature, family, parental love, and the instruments of torture set out for her children. This mother held two ballots in her hand: the first sentenced her children to death, the second brought deliverance for them" (15:25–26).

The author of 4 Maccabees may thus be justified in his confidence in his ability to bring scenes powerfully before the eyes and impact the audience's senses through ecphrasis: "We shudder even now as we merely hear about the trials of these young men. They, however, looked on; they heard the word of threat directed against their own selves; they had to endure these sufferings firsthand, even the agonies of being burned by fire" (14:9). Indeed, audiences still squirm when attentively reading or hearing the text.

Elaboration of a Chreia or a Maxim

The exercise known as elaboration or *ergasia* was particularly important in terms of teaching students the basic gamut of argumentation.[16] After a brief introduction to or commendation of the saying or its originator, the student offers a statement of the chreia or maxim and then proceeds to support the saying (or the appropriateness of the action in "action chreiai") with a rationale for the saying or action, an argument from the contrary, an argument from analogy, an historical example, and a supportive quotation from ancient authority before offering a concluding statement or exhortation. There would be little incentive for a mature speaker to reproduce a complete schoolbook elaboration in the course of a larger speech (though some authors have been found to include this, as, for example, Heb 12:5–11).[17] Nevertheless there are several passages in 4 Maccabees where the author appears to have used the beginning of the elaboration pattern as a means of "getting his start" in regard to new sections.

The opening paragraph exhibits something of this pattern: 1:1–2 states the maxim upon which the author intends to elaborate, amplifying the importance of this subject for his hearers (the equivalent of a brief word of praise or other commendation); 1:3–4 offers an expanded restatement of the maxim; 1:5 introduces an objection that allows a statement from the contrary ("reason does not master *those* passions") and a restatement of the position in the

---

16. Hermogenes, *Preliminary Exercises* 3.6–4.10 (Kennedy, *Progymnasmata*, 77–78; compare *Rhet. Her.* 4.43.56–4.44.57). Theon does not treat this exercise as systematically, although the basic elements are also present in his treatment of the chreia and the thesis (*Exercises* 3.101–102, 11.121–125; Kennedy, *Progymnasmata*, 19–23, 55–59).

17. DeSilva, "How Greek Was the Author of 'Hebrews,'" 651–55, offering some correctives to the earlier analysis in Mack, *Rhetoric*, 77–78.

positive ("but reason masters *these* passions"). Similar patterns may be seen at transitions from martyr narratives to encomiastic reflections on the martyrs. 4 Maccabees 6:31–33 follows the pattern of a statement of the thesis (6:31), statement from the contrary (6:32), and two restatements of the thesis with embedded rationales (6:33, 34). 4 Maccabees 13:1–3 provides a statement of the thesis, argument from the contrary (using a mixed contrafactual conditional sentence), and restatement of the thesis.

One can readily find the author using other building blocks taught in the "elaboration" exercise throughout his oration. Central is his use of historical example: Joseph (2:2–3); Moses (2:17); Aaron (7:11–12); Jacob (2:19–20); David (3:6–18); Abraham and Isaac (13:12; 16:20); Daniel (16:21); the three youths (13:9; 16:21); and the martyrs themselves (1:7–8; 6:1–35; 7:16–23; 8:1; 9:10–13:5; 14:11–12; 15:11–28; 16:1–4). He also employs, with surprising reserve, quotations from ancient authority (2:5–6; 17:19; 18:14–19). He does not appear to utilize true *arguments* from analogy, though he does employs a rich variety of analogies *qua* simile or metaphor, which may often function as compressed arguments from analogy (agriculture: 1:29; government: 2:22–23; athletics: 3:5; 6:10; 11:20; 12:14; 14:5; 15:29; 16:16; 17:11–16; nautical images: 7:1–3, 5; 15:31–32; military images: 7:4, 24; 11:22, 27; 13:13, 16; architecture: 13:6–7; 17:3; musical and dramatic images: 13:8; 14:3, 7–8; judicial images: 15:25–28; 16:16; astronomical images: 17:5; cultic images: 6:28–29; 17:21–22). Rationales and other signs of enthymematic-argumentative reasoning in 4 Maccabees are too numerous to list.

Common-places (*topoi* or *koinoi topoi*)

The exercise involving "common-place" is not an element of demonstration (for example, that so-and-so committed murder) but rather of elaboration (so-and-so being [allegedly] a murder, what more can be said about so-and-so). The elaboration depends more upon the type than the particular instance, with the particular instance (so-and-so) being painted in all the colors of the type (murderer).[18] According to Hermogenes, elements of amplification might include a proem (a generalization about the type), presentations of the contrary (e.g., in the case of a murderer, the provisions of the law for the safeguarding of life or the virtues of saving a life) to make the case at hand seem all the more vicious (or virtuous, if common-place is used to praise), comparisons, etiology (how the subject came to be the person now before us, whether good or bad), relevant maxims, appeals to emotions (e.g.,

18. Hermogenes, *Preliminary Exercises* 6.12 (Kennedy, *Progymnasmata*, 79); see also Theon, *Exercises* 6.106 (Kennedy, *Progymnasmata*, 42–43).

arousing indignation or emulation), and final topics (the legal, the just, the beneficial, the possible, the appropriate).[19] Theon directs the student to amplify the common-place by dwelling upon the moral choice of the doer, the magnitude of the action, the consequences to others and themselves, comparison, analysis of the parts of the crime or achievement, arguments from opposites (if the opposite action merits honor, this action merits punishment or shame), and opinions of ancient authorities.[20]

The author's presentation of the brothers and their love for one another, of the mother and her affection for her children, and even of the martyrs in general might be seen to develop facets of common-places. The portrait of harmonious siblings, loving mothers, and brave philosopher-sages had become quite well established, even stereotyped, by the time of the composition of 4 Maccabees.[21] Here we will dwell only on the author's presentation of Antiochus IV as a tyrant—a type so well known it is even listed by Theon as an example.[22]

Lucian of Samosata provides a snapshot of the stereotypical tyrant in "The Downward Journey, or, the Tyrant." The charges on which the tyrant Megapenthes is arraigned before Minos for eternal judgement (*Tyr.* 26) are almost all applied to Antiochus IV in 4 Maccabees. He uses his position to enrich himself (4:16–17); he corrupts boys, here not sexually, but morally (4 Macc 8:12–14), trying to lead them away from the way of life so carefully instilled in them by their parents (cf. 4 Macc 18:10–19);[23] he exudes pride and haughtiness (4 Macc 4:15; 5:7, 9–11; 9:30; 12:11–14); he uses enticements to undermine resistance (4 Macc 8:7; 12:5);[24] he is savage in his invention of

---

19. Hermogenes, *Preliminary Exercises* 6.12–14 (Kennedy, *Progymnasmata*, 80–81).

20. Theon, *Exercises* 6.107 (Kennedy, *Progymnasmata*, 44–45).

21. Seen especially in regard to the author's presentation of the first two types in comparison with Plutarch's treatises "On Brotherly Love" (*De fraterno amore*) and "On Affection for Offspring" (*De amore prolis*).

22. "Topos (*topos*) is language amplifying something that is acknowledged to be either a fault or a brave deed. It is of two kinds: one is an attack on those who have done evil deeds, for example, a tyrant, traitor, murderer, profligate; the other in favor of those who have done something good: for example, a tyrannicide, a hero, a lawgiver" (Theon, *Exercises* 6.106; in Kennedy, *Progymnasmata*, 42–43). On the depiction of Antiochus as a stereotypical tyrant, see Heininger, "Der böse Antiochus," 50–53.

23. Heininger ("Der böse Antiochus," 52) reminds us, however, that the brothers' handsome appearance does not escape Antiochus's notice (4 Macc 8:3–5).

24. This trait emerges earlier in Lucian's satire (*Tyrant* 11).

tortures (4 Macc 10:16; 11:23; 18:20);[25] he overturns the long-respected laws and customs of the lands he rules (4 Macc 5:27).[26]

Amplification of this common-place proceeds more along the lines prescribed by Theon in his exercises than those prescribed by Hermogenes. The author speaks of the consequences of Antiochus's tyranny, not least in his destruction of a state of stable order and peace under Onias III (3:20 versus 4:16) and in his execution of nine virtuous people (not to mention the other martyrs passed over briefly in 4 Macc 4:23–25). In the voice of the youngest brother, the author engages in something like amplification based on a consideration of the parts of the crime that Antiochus IV has perpetrated in this arena: he has disregarded the common humanity that ought to bind him with his subjects, such that he can brutalize them without feeling (12:13); he has similarly disregarded the greater power of Providence that ought to mitigate arrogance and excess in the exercise of power (12:11). Elevating his own authority to the highest level, the tyrant treats piety and obedience to laws long regarded to be divine as something worthy of torture and punishment, when it ought rather to be honored, making himself the "enemy of virtue" rather than its enforcer, as a good ruler would be (9:15; 11:4–6). In this regard, we may find elaboration not only from the topic of moral choice, but also from the topic of the opposite: if a good ruler would honor the pious Judeans for their commitment, Antiochus must be a vicious ruler indeed for punishing them for the same. The attention the author gives to Antiochus's motives for action also contribute to the amplification of his tyranny, all the more as he is repeatedly shown to be driven by his passions—his unmeasured, emotional responses to the stimuli in Judea (8:2; 9:10–11).

Encomium and Syncrisis

An encomium involved "an exposition of the good qualities of a person or thing, in general or individually" or "language revealing the greatness of virtuous actions and other good qualities belonging to a particular person."[27] It

---

25. On the use of torture by tyrants, who rely on force rather than legitimate authority, see Seneca, *De ira* 2.23.1; Thucydides, *Hist.* 6.57.4; Aristotle, *Athenian Constitution* 18.4; Diogenes Laertius, *Vit.* 9.26, 58–60; Cicero, *Tusc. disp.* 2.52; Lucian, *Phalaris* 11–12; *Tyrant* 26; Heininger, "Der böse Antiochus," 50–51.

26. On this last trait, see Dionysius of Halicarnassus, *Roman Antiquities* 4.41.2; Xenophon, *Mem.* 4.6.12; Lucian, *Tyrannicide* 10). The restoration of law that follows the death of tyrants also notably follows the martyrs' defeat of Antiochus (18:4).

27. Hermogenes, *Preliminary Exercises* 7.14 (Kennedy, *Progymnasmata*, 81); Theon, *Exercises* 9.109 (Kennedy, *Progymnasmata*, 50).

was a particularly useful exercise, as public speakers could count on giving full-fledged encomia throughout their careers. The author of 4 Maccabees, indeed, considers himself to be writing a text that is part "demonstration" of a thesis (ἐπιδείχνυσθαι, 1:1; ἀπόδειξιν, 3:19) and part encomium, offering a "praise" of the highest virtues (ἔπαινον, 1:2) and "praising" the nine martyrs who embodied the verity of the thesis (ἐπαινεῖν, 1:10).

If the subject of the encomium was a person, Theon directed the student to develop any laudatory traits under several headings. A person's "external goods" or qualities would be praised first, including "good birth, . . . education, friendship, reputation, official position, wealth, good children, a good death." This would be followed by the "goods of the body," which include "health, strength, beauty, and acuteness of sense," and by "ethical virtues," which are the "goods of the mind and the actions resulting from these; for example, that a person is prudent, temperate, courageous, just, pious, generous, magnanimous, and the like." Attention is then given to "fine actions," which are "those done for others rather than ourselves; and done for the sake of the honorable, not the expedient or the pleasant; and in which the toil is that of the doer but the benefit is common; and through which the populace experiences benefits and which are done for benefactors and even more for those who are dead." Noble actions include those "actions . . . beyond what was characteristic of his age." These "actions and successes" are to be discussed in such a way as exemplifies the specific virtues possessed and evidenced in action by the subject, even being arranged under the headings of the virtues.[28]

The author of 4 Maccabees includes many of these elements as he praises the martyrs (as well as recounts their trials in ways that redound to their credit). We learn of Eleazar's good birth (as a member of the priestly line, 7:6, 12), his education (5:23–24), his reputation (5:18; 6:18), and his official position and altruistic use of his office (7:6, 8). The author praises the soundness of Eleazar's mind for its steadfastness in virtue in the face of torrents of pain (6:7; 7:1–5) and the strength of his body, renewed in youthful vigor by "right thinking," despite his physical age (5:31; 7:13–14). Eleazar is thus praised for "actions . . . beyond what was characteristic of his age."[29] He is a model of the virtue of courage, particularly in the form of endurance (6:5, 9–11, 13, 17); of justice, honoring the commitments of the ancestors and the demands of piety (5:20–21, 29, 33–34); and of living

28. Theon, *Exercises* 9.110, 112 (Kennedy, *Progymnasmata*, 50–52).

29. The Greek here (ἡλικία) is as ambiguous as the English translation: age as "period of life" or age as "epoch." Marrou (*Education*, 273) understands this as "period of life," to judge from his representation of this topic as "old head on young shoulders" in his outline of Theon's prescriptions for an encomium.

and dying consistently with the values that he had praised throughout his lifetime (5:35–36; 7:9). His death may have been a degrading one in the estimation of Antiochus, but the author speaks of it as a noble death and a crowning deed in a life well lived: it is a death endured to benefit others by providing an example of courage in the face of coercion (6:18–19) and offering to God the obedience that might turn God's wrath against the nation to mercy (6:27–29), contributing thus to the overthrow of the tyrant and purification of the homeland (1:11; 17:20–21; 18:4–5). The seven brothers and their mother are also praised in regard to many of the typical, specific topics of encomia, particular in connection with the virtues that their stalwart resistance unto death demonstrates.[30]

Syncrisis is an exercise in which students perform an extended comparison between one subject and another, chiefly for the purpose of demonstrating the honor of the subject through favorable comparison with another, honored figure. It is closely related to the exercise in encomium since it also "proceeds by use of encomiastic topics" and since "the best source of argument in encomia is derived from comparisons, which you will use as the occasion may suggest."[31] The author of 4 Maccabees does not engage in any well-developed syncrises, but he does use brief comparisons as appropriate within encomium.[32] Thus Eleazar merits comparison with Aaron (7:11–12); the brothers' courage is comparable to that of Isaac, Daniel, and the three young men as they all faced death for the sake of God's commands (13:9–10, 12; 16:20–21); the mother shows fortitude equal to that of Abraham (14:20; 15:28) and also of Daniel and the three (16:3). These brief syncrises work in two ways: they show that the subjects of the encomium have not "fallen short of the fair fame of . . . their sires" (Quintilian, *Inst.* 3.7.10), and also that they stand as "part of a long, glorious tradition which showed the extraordinary character" of the citizenry to which they belong—here, notably, the citizenry of the Jewish people.[33]

---

30. See, further, deSilva, *4 Maccabees*, 76–98.

31. Hermogenes, *Preliminary Exercises* 8.19 (Kennedy, *Progymnasmata*, 83); ibid, *Preliminary Exercises* 7.17 (Kennedy, *Progymnasmata*, 82).

32. Hermogenes, *Preliminary Exercises* 8.18 (Kennedy, *Progymnasmata*, 83). See also Theon, *Exercises* 8.111: "It is not without utility also to make mention of those already honored, comparing their deeds to those of the persons being praised" (Kennedy, *Progymnasmata*, 51).

33. See van Henten, "Martyrs as Heroes," 308, on the parallels between 4 Maccabees and Athenian funeral orations.

THE AUTHOR OF 4 MACCABEES AND GREEK *PAIDEIA* 23

Ethopoeia (Prosopopoeia)

The exercise in ethopoeia involves the "introduction of a person to whom words are attributed that are suitable to the speaker and have an indisputable application to the subject discussed; for example, What words would a man say to his wife when leaving on a journey? Or a general to his soldiers in time of danger? Also when the persons are specified; for example, What words would Cyrus say when marching against the Massagetae? Or what would Datis say when he met the king after the battle of Marathon?"[34] The exercise could focus on displaying the character of the speaker (an ethical ethopoeia), the feelings of the speaker (pathetical ethopoeia; "for example, what Andromache would say over the dead Hector"), or both.[35] The speech must be crafted in such a way as to be appropriate to the speaker in regard to many variables—age, social status, occupation, gender, frame of mind, nationality, audience, occasion, and subject.[36]

The author's genius shines through in his ability to create speeches appropriate to his characters. He expands considerably upon his source in this regard,[37] crafting a number of ethopoeiai:

1. A speech by Antiochus urging Eleazar to acquiesce to eating pork (5:6–13).

2. A speech by Eleazar refuting Antiochus's exhortations and arguments (5:16–38).

3. A speech by Antiochus urging the seven brothers to acquiesce (8:5–11, 14).

4. A hypothetical speech in which the seven brothers accept Antiochus's arguments (8:17–26).

5. A speech by the seven brothers rejecting Antiochus's exhortation (9:1–9).

34. Theon, *Exercises* 8.115 (Kennedy, *Progymnasmata*, 47); similarly Hermogenes, *Preliminary Exercises* 9.20 (Kennedy, *Progymnasmata*, 84). Unlike Theon, who treats all such exercises under the heading of "prosopopoeia," Hermogenes observes a distinction between ethopoeia and prosopopoeia: "in ethopoeia we imagine words for a real person, in prosopopoeia we imagine a non-existing person" (Kennedy, *Progymnasmata*, 84).

35. Hermogenes, *Preliminary Exercises* 9.21 (Kennedy, *Progymnasmata*, 85); Theon (*Exercises* 8.117) also recognizes these as principal foci (Kennedy, *Progymnasmata*, 49).

36. Theon, *Exercises* 8.115–116 (Kennedy, *Progymnasmata*, 47–48); Hermogenes, *Preliminary Exercises* 9.21 (Kennedy, *Progymnasmata*, 85).

37. See the comparative tables in Breitenstein, *Beobachtungen*, 92–93.

6. A hypothetical lament by the mother, having been bereaved of her children (16:6–11).

7. A speech by the mother inciting her children on to fidelity in the face of death (16:16–23).

8. A second speech by the mother recalling her own virtue and the lessons her husband taught their children (18:7–19).

The narratives are also strewn with briefer instances of speech-in-character (Antiochus: 12:3–5; Counselors: 6:14–15; Eleazar: 617–23, 27–29; one or another of the brothers: 9:15, 17–18, 23–24, 29–31; 10:2–3, 10–11, 14–16, 18–21; 11:2–6, 12, 14–16, 20–27; 12:8, 11–18; 13:9–18; guards: 6:4; 9:16; 10:13).

It is immediately evident to the reader or hearer that all of these speeches are appropriate to the occasion and situation in which they are imagined being uttered. The author is also careful to make them "age-appropriate" (for example, Eleazar speaks as a man with the majority of life-experience behind him; see 5:31, 33–34, 36; 6:18–20; while the brothers give voice to their awareness of standing much nearer the start of life, and also from within a certain birth order; see 8:20, 26; 9:2, 6, 18; 10:2; 11:14–15, 24). The mother's hypothetical lament would be recognized as a "pathetical" ethopoeia, depicting through speech the emotions of the speaker; the other instances are all largely "ethical" ethopoeiai, reflecting the character of the speakers in the display of their decision-making processes and the values that serve as "final topics" in those processes. Character is also displayed in how the speaker addresses or assesses those to whom he speaks. For example, Antiochus's arrogance is evident in his dismissive attitude toward a foreign way of life that he does not take the trouble to understand (5:7, 9–11).

Several of the longer speeches incidentally reveal the author's facility in crafting basic deliberative speeches (speeches promoting or dissuading from a particular course of action). Standard deliberative topics overlap with the "final topics" of the progymnasmata, as is evident from Theon's advice concerning the creation of a hortatory ethopoeia: "In exhorting, then, we shall say that what we are urging is possible and easy and noble and appropriate; that it is beneficial, just, reverent—and the latter is of two sorts, either toward the gods or toward the dead—; that it is pleasant; that we are not the only ones doing it or the first . . . if dissuading we shall use the opposite arguments."[38] The lists of categories of persuasion (or motives of choice) in advanced handbooks on rhetoric and ethics overlap with this list to various degrees. Aristotle, for example, identified the noble, beneficial, and pleasant

---

38. Theon, *Exercises* 8.116–117 (in Kennedy, *Progymnasmata*, 48–49).

(καλοῦ συμφέροντος ἡδέος) as the considerations that moved people to choose a course of action, while the shameful, harmful, and painful (αἰσχροῦ βλαβεροῦ λυπηροῦ) dissuaded people from a course of action (Aristotle, *Eth. Nic.* 2.3.7–1104b31–32). Anaximenes expanded this list to that which is right (δίκαιον), lawful (νόμιμον), expedient or beneficial (συμφέρον), honorable (καλόν), pleasant (ἡδύς), easy (ῥάδιον), feasible (δυνατόν), and necessary (ἀναγκαῖον; *Rhet. ad Alex.* 1.1421b,21–1422b,12).

In his protreptic deliberative (in Greek, *symbouleutikos,* or "advisory") speeches, Antiochus gives advice (συμβουλεύσαιμ᾽ ἄν σοι, 5:6) relying on the topics of what is pleasant (5:9; 8:5, 8), just (5:9), advantageous (5:11; 8:6–7), and necessary (5:13; 8:14; "necessary" reflects the same Greek root as those words frequently translated as "compulsion" or "coercion" in 4 Maccabees).[39] In their rebuttals—and since Eleazar is really addressing the crowd (ἤρξατο δημηγορεῖν, 5:15) as well as Antiochus, his is also a protreptic speech in favor of remaining steadfast in the Jewish way of life—Eleazar and the seven brothers invoke the topics of the "just" (5:20–21, 29, 34; 9:1b),[40] the "honorable" (5:18, 27–28, 35; 6:18–21; 9:2), the "necessary" (5:16), the "lawful" (5:27; 9:1, 4), and the virtuous, particularly the courageous (5:31–32, 37–38; 6:21; 9:5–6), as well as the advantageous, where advantage is reckoned in terms of eternity (9:8–9). The appeals to examples invoke implicitly the topic of not being the first to be called upon to undertake such a course of action (13:9, 12; 16:20–21). The mother notably appeals to the topic of what is just in her protreptic speech to her sons (repaying their divine Benefactor for the gift of life, 16:18–19; keeping faith with their Benefactor, 16:22). Within his evident facility in the exercise of ethopoeia, therefore, the author also shows himself adept in the confirmation and refutation of a hypothesis, here specifically of deliberative hypotheses, perhaps a sign of higher-level training in rhetoric.[41]

---

39. Antiochus's assurance of forgiveness by the Deity for sins committed under compulsion emerges by analogy with how violations of laws are treated by human authorities, who "punish and exact redress from those who do evil except when it is done under compulsion" (Aristotle, *Eth. Nic.* 3.5.7 1113b24–29; see also *Rh.* 1.10.3, which limits "injustice" to voluntary violations of law).

40. Preserving "ancestral customs and institutions and the established laws" was identified as a component of justice (Aristotle, *Virt.* 5.2), as was honoring one's obligation to his nation (here, by preserving it from disgrace, 5:18; also by keeping faith with the agreements made by one's ancestors, 5:29, 33–34; see *Rhet. Her.* 3.3.4; Aristotle, *Virt.* 5.2; Josephus, *B.J.* 7.8.7 §357).

41. The "hypothesis" differed from the "thesis" in that the latter was general (e.g., whether war was an advantageous or justifiable policy) while the former was specific (e.g., whether we, the Athenians, should go to war with Sparta on this particular occasion). See Hermogenes, *Preliminary Exercises* 11.24–25 (Kennedy, *Progymnasmata,* 87).

Thesis

One of the more advanced of the progymnastic exercises is the proposal and confirmation of a thesis. In this exercise, the student takes up a question, whether theoretical ("whether or not the gods exist," "whether the sky is spherical") or practical ("whether one ought to marry," "whether one should teach rhetoric"), and argues for or against.[42] The subject is "viewed apart from any specific circumstance; for thesis seems to take the place of a general piece of advice, not directed to any specific person but with quite general application to any person."[43]

The position taken (especially in regard to practical theses) is then supported by arguments appealing to the principal "final topics" or "final headings"—those values upon which decisions tend to be made. Among these, Hermogenes lists "justice, advantage, possibility, appropriateness."[44] Theon gives a more extensive sampling, listing arguments "from what is necessary and what is noble and what is beneficial and what is pleasant," as well as "what . . . is possible, . . . is in accordance with nature and according to the common manners and customs of all mankind, is easy, and . . . is just. Then that it is reverent; this is twofold, either pleasing to gods or to the dead. Next that it is necessary, . . . honorable, . . . profitable, . . . contributes to security, . . . that it is pleasant, and that if it is not done it brings regret and it is hard to correct the omission."[45] Refutation of a position comes from the opposites.

Theon instructs the "more advanced student" to further develop supporting arguments using the judgments of "famous men, poets and statesmen and philosophers" as well as proofs from historical examples.[46] The confirmation of a thesis can become quite the advanced exercise, as the student may also "compose amplifications and digressions as the parts of the thesis permit" as well as "make use of emotions and characterizations and exhortations and nearly all the kinds (*ideai*) of discourse."[47] Particularly if the thesis is a "practical" one, "at the end there will be exhortations"

---

42. Hermogenes, *Preliminary Exercises* 11.25 (Kennedy, *Progymnasmata*, 87). On "theoretical" versus "practical" theses, see also Theon, *Exercises* 11.121 (Kennedy, *Progymnasmata*, 56).

43. Hermogenes, *Preliminary Exercises* 11.24 (in Kennedy, *Progymnasmata*, 87); see also Theon, *Exercises* 11.120 (Kennedy, *Progymnasmata*, 55).

44. Hermogenes, *Preliminary Exercises* 11.25–26 (Kennedy, *Progymnasmata*, 87).

45. Theon, *Exercises* 11.121–122 (Kennedy, *Progymnasmata*, 56–57).

46. Theon, *Exercises* 11.122 (Kennedy, *Progymnasmata*, 57).

47. Theon, *Exercises* 11.128.(Kennedy, *Progymnasmata*, 61).

THE AUTHOR OF 4 MACCABEES AND GREEK *PAIDEIA*   27

to allow that thesis to impact one's audience's commitments and practices in meaningful ways.[48]

In terms of its form, 4 Maccabees is straightforwardly the confirmation of a thesis, executed very much in line with (although at a level far beyond) the progymnastic exercise. The opening sentence states the author's position and uses the specific language of demonstration: "I am about to prove (ἐπιδείκνυσθαι) a supremely philosophical principle, namely that God-centered thinking is absolute master over emotions and cravings" (1:1), the descriptor "pious" or "God-centered" (ὁ εὐσεβὴς λογισμός) providing a key element in this thesis.[49]

Historical examples provide the lion's share of proof for the truth of this proposition. Joseph's mastery of lust (2:1–4), Moses' mastery of anger (2:16–18),[50] David's mastery of his craving (3:6–18), but above all the martyrs' mastery of fear, pain, and natural love of life and one another (5:1–17:6) demonstrate that the proposition is "possible" or "feasible," even if not "easy."[51] The author returns to the thesis after recounting each story of martyrdom (6:31–35; 7:16–23; 13:1–5; 16:1–4),[52] exploring also the relevance of each specific example for his thesis (e.g., the ability of pious reason to master the emotions of fraternal affection in 13:19–14:1 or love for offspring in 14:13–20; 15:4–10, sections that include relevant "digressions" developing those particular emotions). From another perspective, the fact of God's

48. Hermogenes, *Preliminary Exercises* 11.26 (Kennedy, *Progymnasmata*, 88).

49. The language of demonstration recurs at important junctures in the work (τὴν ἀπόδειξιν, 3:19; ἀπέδειξα, 16:4).

50. Moses' example is balanced by an "argument from the contrary" focused on Simeon and Levi's failure to control their anger—if they had not been capable of exercising control (if it were not possible for pious reason to master the passions), Jacob would have been wrong to curse their anger (2:19–20).

51. 4 Maccabees 3:19–17:24 provides the "narrative demonstration" (3:19) of the philosophical thesis, which is precisely the function of the martyr stories for which the author prepares the audience in his exordium (1:7–12). See Klauck, "Hellenistiche Rhetorik," 461–64; van Henten, *Maccabean Martyrs*, 69; Stowers, "4 Maccabees," 844–45.

52. Scholars of a previous generation might regard the two parts of 4 Maccabees (i.e., 1.1–3.18 and 3.19–18.24) as originally separate units (a "philosophical discourse" and an "encomium"; so Lebram, "Literarische Form," 82–83) or treat them as functioning essentially independently (so Breitenstein, *Beobachtungen*,132–33; Dupont-Sommer, *Quatrième Livre*, 19). Such views ignore the author's explicit claims about how the discursive and narrative sections will work together (1:12), as well as the obvious signs of the integration of the two parts in passages such as these reprises of the thesis. Scholars who understand the book as a unified whole include Redditt, "Concept of *Nomos*," 262–63; Klauck, *4 Makkabäerbuch*, 648; van Henten, *Maccabean Martyrs*, 69; deSilva, *4 Maccabees: Introduction and Commentary*, 25–28, 46–49; Stowers, "4 Maccabees," 844–45.

commandments concerning covetousness—rendered in Greek more baldly as "you will not desire . . ." (οὐκ ἐπιθυμήσεις, 2:5, 6, reciting Exod 20:17; Deut 5:21)—demonstrates the thesis to be "possible," the unstated premise being that God would not command what is impossible to perform. The author also employs the topic of "appropriateness" in 4 Macc 2:21–23 vis-à-vis the manner of God's design of the human being, this being a Jewish equivalent of the topic of being "in accordance with Nature."

Major constellations of topics, however, fall under the headings of the "noble" or "honorable" and the "advantageous" or "beneficial." The thesis that the author treats is not essentially a theoretical one (though it may seem thus from the statement in 1:1), but rather a practical one: "we should pursue the Torah-nurtured piety that allows our rational faculty to master emotions, desires, and sensations." This is evident above all from the exhortation (appropriate for the development of the "practical thesis") that stands at the climax of the speech, following the author's most effusive praise of the exemplars of the thesis: "Israelite children, all you who have been born from Abraham's stock, obey this Law and give God his due ("exercise piety," εὐσεβεῖτε) in every situation, knowing that God-centered thinking is the master of the emotions, not only of cravings and feelings arising from inside, but also of sufferings inflicted from outside" (18:1–2).

The martyrs' own deliberations (see discussion above under "ethopoeia") align living in line with the thesis with the just course of action (the course that renders to one's benefactors—here, the Divine Benefactor—what is due, and that honors the commitments previously made when doing so becomes costly), the courageous course of action (the course that endures hardship for the sake of virtue or noble ends), and the wise course of action (the course that weighs relative advantages and disadvantages correctly, here in terms of temporary versus eternal losses and gains).[53] The author's encomia upon the martyrs, praising them for their choices, their commitments, and their endurance, function to commend the thesis (qua life-principle) on the basis of the "honorable" in terms of that which leads to a praiseworthy remembrance. The author has indeed skillfully combined many "kinds (ideai) of discourse" (ethopoeia, encomium, digression) in his demonstration of his thesis.

---

53. This last point is especially foregrounded in 13:14–17; 15:2–3, 8, 27.

Contradiction (or Refutation)

Theon lists contradiction (ἀντίρρησις, *antirrhêsis*) at the end of his *Progymnasmata* as an exercise for "advanced students."[54] As its name suggests, this exercise sets the student to creating "a discourse that attacks the credibility of another discourse" by showing the latter to be "unseemly or inexpedient or inopportune" and by formulating arguments in refutation of those in the discourse being undermined.[55] Eleazar's first speech is clearly conceived of as such a refutation, the author referring to it using a neologism fashioned from the name of the exercise: "When Eleazar had in this manner refuted (ἀντιρρητορεύσαντα) the counsels of the tyrant . . ." (4 Macc 6:1).

Eleazar answers the material in Antiochus's discourse point for point. The king had twice called into question the value of Judaism as a viable philosophy ("you do not seem to me to think like a philosopher as long as you embrace the Jewish religion," 5:7; "Wake up from your foolish philosophy!" 5:11). Eleazar refutes the claim by explaining the formational fruit of the Torah-observant life in terms of the virtues of its practitioners (5:22–24). Antiochus claimed that the Jewish Law involves its adherents in acts of injustice against Nature (by rejecting her bounty, 5:8–9). Eleazar refutes this claim by calling attention to the source of the Torah being the Creator of Nature (5:25–26), who is best able to determine what is "suitable" for God's creatures (and thus to prescribe what "alignment with Nature" really looks like). Antiochus appealed to his power to exert compulsion (5:13); Eleazar more nobly retorts that "nothing [is] more compelling than our obedience to the Law," with the result that he will not accept any excuse to transgress (5:16–17). Antiochus urges Eleazar to "take pity on [his] old age" (5:12); Eleazar rejects this appeal as an insufficient excuse to tear down the ancestral law by his own actions (5:33–35). It is thus a complete "refutation," leaving no element of Antiochus's case unanswered, giving evidence that the author had a firm grasp even of this exercise.

Indications of Rhetorical Training beyond the *Progymnasmata*

The author reflects a degree of training that falls beyond the scope of the *Progymnasmata*. Some of these skills may reflect education not "beyond" but rather "outside" these preliminary exercises at the secondary level.

---

54. Theon, *Exercises* 17; Kennedy, *Progymnasmata*, 72.
55. Kennedy, *Progymnasmata*, p. 72.

However, it seems on balance more likely that some of these features do, in fact, reflect post-secondary education.

The author is skilled in the use of several literary devices that might more properly be learned as facets of "style" at an advanced stage of training, though it remains possible that the author learned these inductively from material read at an earlier stage. These include the use of metaphor and simile, particularly in the encomiastic sections of his discourse (e.g., the figure of the ship in a tempest, 7:1–3; 13:6–7; 15:31–32; the athletic contest, 6:10–11; 17:12–16; the besieged city, 7:4; architectural figures, 17:3);[56] the device of apostrophe (5:34–35; 7:6–7, 9–10, 15; 11:20; 14:2–3, 7; 15:1, 13, 16–17, 29–30; 16:14; 17:2, 4–6);[57] the figure of "correction" ("O how bitter that day was, and not bitter," 18:20), the latter phrase correcting first impressions about the carnage and horror with a reminder of the praiseworthy remembrance and the eternal honor and life granted to the martyrs as a result of that day.

Of special interest is the author's familiarity with devices such as the proposed epitaph in 17:9–10 and other topics reminiscent of the Athenian funeral oration (the *epitaphios logos*), a form of encomium not discussed in the *Progymnasmata*.[58] Alongside typical encomiastic elements, these commemorative addresses often highlight the heroes' liberation of the homeland from tyranny or its threat,[59] urge the audience to cherish their own laws rather than submit to the laws of any other group, and contrast the short span of mortal life with the eternal praise that the virtuous receive.[60] The proposition of a suitable epitaph to commemorate the fallen is a defining feature of the genre (see Demosthenes, *Or.* 60.1; Lysias, *Or.* 2.1). Each of these features is apparent in 4 Maccabees as well (1:11; 17:2, 5, 20–21; 18:1–2, 4–5).[61]

More clearly indicative of education at the tertiary level is the author's knowledge of the conventions of "arrangement" in terms of the construction

56. Dupont-Sommer, *Quatrième Livre*, 65; Breitenstein, *Beobachtungen*, 129.

57. Dupont-Sommer, *Quatrième Livre*, 61.

58. Examples include Thucydides, *Hist.* 2.34–46; Lysias, *Or.* 2; Demosthenes, *Or.* 60; Hyperides, *Or.* 6; satirized in Plato, *Menexenus*. See Lebram, "Literarische Form," 82, 84–85; van Henten, "Jewish Epitaph," 58–59; *Maccabean Martyrs*, 64–65.

59. Van Henten and Avemarie, *Martyrdom and Noble Death*, 18, citing Hyperides, *Or.* 6.38–40; Lysias, *Or.* 2.21, 41, 57, 59; Plato, *Men.* 239d–240a.

60. Redditt, "Concept of *Nomos*," 263.

61. The figure of the proposed epitaph appears outside of the genre as well, as for example in Euripides's *Trojan Women* (1188–1191). There, as part of her lament over the executed Astyanax, infant son of Hector, Hecuba says: "what word shall poet inscribe of thee upon thy tomb? 'This child the Argives murdered in times past, dreading him'—an inscription disgracing Greece!"

of a complete speech (i.e., beyond the scope and length of a secondary-level exercise). The opening twelve verses have been shown to possess all the necessary qualities of a formal exordium.[62] The author states his principal theme, providing the "keynotes" of the speech (1:1; cf. Aristotle, *Rhet.* 3.14; 1414b), employs amplification to augment audience attention and contribute to rendering them "willing, attentive, and docile" (1:1b–2; see Quintilian, *Inst.* 4.1.5), and prepares the hearers for the blend of *epideixis* ("demonstration") and *epainos* ("praise," "encomium") that will occupy the remainder of the discourse. He gives an overview of the plan for his discourse, identifying the ways in which his extended examination of historical examples will contribute to the demonstration of the thesis (1:7–11) and supplying a clear segue into the opening of speech's body (1:12). A proper division or enumeration of the points to be addressed by the speech, frequently a formal element of the arrangement of a speech, appears at the outset of the body (1:14).

The author is just as artful in his peroration, typically an opportunity for the orator to let "all the streams of eloquence" pour out (Quintilian, *Inst.* 6.1.51). He provides an accumulation of images designed to make a strong parting impression: the figure of the portrait, "if it were possible" (17:7); the proposed inscription for the martyrs' epitaph (17:8–10); the extended athletic image with the lists of the combatants and the crowning of the victors (17:11–16); and the *enumeratio* of the accomplishments of the martyrs in both religious and political terms (17:20–22; 18:4–5). As is also appropriate to the peroration, a customary place for the arousal of emotions in the hearers, the author also gives attention to rousing pity, admiration, and (as it is a protreptic speech) emulation (e.g., 17:7, 16; 18:1–2, 20–21).

Acquaintance with Philosophical Ethics

The thesis of 4 Maccabees, that "pious reason is supreme master over the passions" (1:1), stands well near the center of Greco-Roman philosophical ethics (thus perhaps justifying his claim that his topic was "supremely philosophical," φιλοσοφώτατον). Plato had spoken of the virtuous person being thus distinguished because his or her soul opposed and withstood the feelings and drives of the body rather than giving way to them (*Phaedo* 93–94). The Hellenistic Jewish author of *Letter of Aristeas* identified "the highest rule" of philosophy to be "to rule oneself and not be carried away by the passions" (*Ep. Aristeas* 221–22). Plutarch would write that ethical virtue consists in reason's subjection of "the emotions of the soul" to itself (*Virt. mor.* 1 [*Mor.* 440D]). The essential goal of ethical philosophy is

---

62. Klauck, "Hellenistiche Rhetorik," 451–65.

"self-mastery," in which "the better part [of a human being] is master of the worse part," while the opposite condition is censurable (Plato, *Resp.* 431A; see also *Gorg.* 491; Cicero, *Tusc.* 2.22.53).

The author shows an awareness of the philosophical debates concerning whether the philosopher's goal is mastery or elimination of the passions (see especially 2:21–22; 3:3–18), aligning himself with the position of Poseidonius, the Peripatetics, and Plutarch (*Virt. mor.* 4 [*Mor.* 442C]) in setting "mastery and guidance" of the emotions as the sage's goal.[63] He is also aware of discussions concerning the limits of reason's ability to master passions, with the result that the individual is not responsible for the "passions" to which the reasoning faculty is itself liable, such as forgetfulness and ignorance (1:5–6; 2:24–3:2).[64] He is knowledgeable also about Greek philosophical discussions concerning the classification of the passions (τὰ πάθη), as well as discussions about the inclinations (τὰ ἤθη) peculiar to the various developmental stages of life.[65] He follows Aristotle's classification of the passions primarily in terms of "pleasure and pain" (Aristotle, *Rhet.* 2.1.8: λύπη καὶ ἡδονή; 4 Macc 1:20: ἡδονή τε καὶ πόνος), even adopting Aristotle's analysis of "anger" as a mixture of the two (Aristotle, *Rhet.* 2.2.1–2; 4 Macc 1:24).

The author is also highly conversant with the philosophical ideal of the wise man or woman as the genuinely "free" person. He has inherited the plot of a tyrant seeking to coerce obedience through torture and execution from his source material (2 Macc 6:18–7:42), but he has thoroughly re-imagined the story as that of a tyrant confronting philosopher-sages, applying argument, enticement, and coercion to defeat the will of the sages while the latter prove the worth of their philosophy by their steadfast resistance to any assaults.[66] In the course of the "narrative demonstration" of his

63. Seneca (*Ep.* 116.1) and Cicero (*Tusc. Disp.* 3.22; 4.57) favored the hardcore Stoic line of striving after ἀπαθεία, the elimination of the experience of emotions and passions from one's life. Plutarch regarded it as "neither possible nor expedient" for reason to uproot the passions entirely, since the passions, properly moderated, can even become allies in the quest for virtue as one accustoms oneself to experience the joys of virtuous choices and turn these into habit (*Virt. mor.* 4 [*Mor* 443D]). The author of 4 Maccabees also would regard the uprooting of the passions to be impossible and inexpedient, since God planted them within the human person to be moderated, not uprooted (4 Macc 2:21–23). See, further, Renehan, "Philosophic Background," 226–27.

64. See, further, deSilva, *4 Maccabees: Introduction and Commentary*, 67–71, 76–77, 104–6. Cicero (*De finibus* 5.13.36) distinguished between voluntary and involuntary virtues. Memory ranks among the latter, and thus forgetfulness would be an "involuntary" defect (so also Philo, *Migr.* 206), whereas the cardinal virtues fall under the power of the will (Breitenstein, *Beobachtungen*, 140).

65. See deSilva, *4 Maccabees: Introduction and Commentary*, 87–90.

66. Historical or fictive versions of this scenario appear in Seneca, *De constantia*; Diogenes Laertius, *Vit.* 9.26–28, 58–59; Cicero, *Tusc. Disp.* 2.22.52; Philo, *Prob.*

thesis, the author introduces a host of commonplaces familiar from Greco-Roman philosophical literature concerning the wise person: philosopher-sages are "free" (4 Macc 14:2; see, e.g., Epictetus, *Diatr.*. 4.1.152); their wills cannot be overcome through enticements, tortures, or exploitation of internal weakness (4 Macc 9:17; 10:4; see Diogenes Laertius, *Vit.* 9.28; 9.59; Epictetus, *Diatr.*. 1.25.21; 3.24.71; 4.1.1, 60–87; Cicero, *Paradoxa* 5.1.34; Seneca, *Constant.* 5.6–6.8); they remain masters of themselves and, therefore, "kings" (4 Macc 14:2; see, e.g., Diogenes, Laertius *Vit.* 7.122; Stobaeus, *Eth.* 2.222); they suffer no injury beyond that which they can inflict upon themselves by acting contrary to virtue (4 Macc 9:7; 13:14; see Plato, *Apol.* 18 [30C]; Epictetus, *Ench.* 53.4; *Diatr.* 1.29.18; 2.2.15; 3.23.21; Plutarch, *Tranq. an.* 17 [*Mor.* 475E]; Seneca, *Constant.* 2.1, 3); they remain invincible (4 Macc 9:18; 11:21, 27; Seneca, *Ep.* 67.16); the hardships they suffer only demonstrate their achievement of virtue (4 Macc 11:12; Seneca, *Constant.* 3.4; 9.3; *Prov.* 5.10; Epictetus, *Diatr.* 1.6.37).

The author is also thoroughly familiar with Greco-Roman ethical conversations about "brotherly and sisterly love" (φιλαδελφία) and "love for offspring" (φιλοστοργία). His digressions on these two subjects (4 Macc 13:19–14:1; 14:13–20; 15:4–10) read like summary statements of Plutarch's treatises on the same, expertly adapted to serve the author's goal of demonstrating the power of Torah-trained piety to overcome even these feelings.[67]

Fourth Maccabees as a whole *most* resembles philosophical protreptic literature along the lines of Seneca's treatise "On the Constancy of the Wise Person" (*De Constantia sapientis*) and Epictetus's discourse on the true Cynic (*Diatr.* 3.22). Seneca's text is a particularly instructive parallel: he also writes in favor of an ethical thesis ("the wise person cannot receive insult or injury") and combines discursive argumentation, historical examples of the principle-in-action (specifically the examples of Stilbo of Megara and Cato the Younger), and encomium on these "perfect men" who render the Stoic philosophy credible by their example. The author of 4 Maccabees holds his ground well alongside Seneca in this regard, writing a comparable *logos protreptikos* promoting continued observance of the Jewish philosophy.

106–107; Epictetus, *Diatr.* 1.19.7–10; 1.29.5–8; 4.1.132–135 and Iamblichus, *Vit. Pyth.* 215–222. The motif persists in the resistance literature of Christian and non-Christian authors of late antiquity (see the discussion of Christian martyrologies in Hilhorst, "Fourth Maccabees," 111–112; and the presentation of the *Acts of the Alexandrian Martyrs* in van Henten and Avemarie, *Martyrdom and Noble Death*, 38–41).

67. See Plutarch, *De fraterno amore* (*Moralia* 478A–492D) and *De amore prolis* (*Moralia* 493A–497E). These are discussed in relation to 4 Maccabees in Klauck, "Brotherly Love"; deSilva, *4 Maccabees: Introduction and Commentary*, 210–24 (see also chapter 5 below).

The author of 4 Maccabees had in previously generations been disparaged as a philosophical dilettante,[68] but closer examination of the author's acquaintance and interaction with the philosophical *koinē* of his period has overturned this verdict, showing the author to be an eclectic philosopher in his own right.[69] The study of philosophy was, in some way and at some stage, a part of his formation, his παιδεία.[70] But at what stages and in what venues did he pursue this study? Here we lack the transparent windows into classical Greek education that are provided, for example, in textbooks like the *Progymnasmata*. The papyrus school texts studied by Teresa Morgan indicate that collections of gnomic wisdom texts were an important resource in Egyptian Greek curricula.[71] The author might well have come by his material about the sage as the truly free person, for example, through exposure to (and reflection upon) gnomic sayings or excerpts from philosophical texts such as "Anytus and Meletus can kill me, but they cannot injure me" (Plato, *Apol.* 18 [30C]; cited frequently as an abbreviated chreia or proverbial saying in, e.g., Epictetus, *Ench.* 53.4; *Diatr.* 1.29.18; 2.2.15; 3.23.21; Plutarch, *Tranq. an.* 17 [*Mor.* 475E]). His knowledge, however, is sufficiently rich and dense in other areas to suggest more formal exposure to philosophical ethics.

A dominant view of tertiary education in the ancient world is that the student would choose between advanced studies in rhetoric or advanced studies in philosophy, with these studies being pursued in different venues:

> It is sometimes, though not always, acknowledged that philosophy may have been available at the higher levels of education; if so philosophy is variously treated as the business of the 'university' stage of education after the 'secondary school' of the rhetor, or as one of two competing disciplines between which pupils may choose. Almost all commentators agree in discussing the teaching of rhetoric or rhetoric and philosophy to the exclusion of all other subjects in the later stages of *enkyklios paideia*.[72]

---

68. Schürer, *History*, 590.

69. Renehan, "Philosophic Background," 232–238.

70. As Renehan ("Philosophic Background," 238) concludes: "The author of *Fourth Maccabees* has indeed studied and used formal philosophical literature."

71. This is, in fact, the largest body of literature cited in papyrus schoolbook exercises; see Morgan, *Literate Education*, 120–44, 313.

72. Morgan, *Literate Education*, 193. See also Marrou, *History of Education*, 283–84, who envisions tertiary education in philosophy as taking place in one of the established philosophical schools or through personal acquaintance with an independent or itinerant philosopher-teacher.

Philosophy could also have been read at the secondary level, where the local curriculum might have included aphorisms or even short excerpts from writers such as Plato, Xenophon, or Aristotle,[73] or as a discipline ancillary to the advanced study of rhetoric "to the extent that these subjects might prove useful."[74] Plutarch's essays on reading poetry and listening to lectures attest to the importance, at least in some circles, of attending to philosophy as part of a literate education.[75]

Ultimately, we cannot say how the author of 4 Maccabees came by the philosophical knowledge that he evidences. It is significant, however, that he exhibits the high level of acquaintance and facility that he does, perhaps all the more if he pursued this study on his own initiative rather than as a part of the curriculum laid out for him during his formative years.

Acquaintance with the Greek Poets

The speech representing the response to her calamities that the mother *could* have uttered, but did not, merits special attention. It, too, is a speech appropriate to the character's role (a mother), age (beyond childbearing years), and situation (tragic bereavement). But it is also clearly modeled after other laments of bereaved mothers known from the poets, particularly Euripidean drama.

> Ah, wretched me (ὦ μελέα) and many times thrice-unhappy, who, having borne seven children, have become a mother of not even one. Ah, seven empty (μάταιοι) pregnancies, and seven profitless (ἀνόνητοι) ten-month periods, and fruitless nursings, and miserable (ταλαίπωροι) breast-feedings! For nothing (μάτην), O children, I endured many pangs for you and the more burdensome concerns of rearing you. Ah, my unmarried children and my married ones without progeny (ἀνόνητοι)! I will not see (οὐκ ὄψομαι) your children nor be blessed with being called "grandmother." Ah, me, a woman with many and beautiful children (πολύπαις καὶ καλλίπαις), now a widow (χήρα) and alone, wailing bitterly! Nor will I have any of my sons to bury me when I die. (4 Macc 16:6–11)

Almost every phrase, every detail, in 4 Macc 16:6–11 has a parallel in a Euripidean lament, suggesting that the author has patterned his character's hypothetical lament after those found especially in *Trojan Women* and *Hecuba* (all

73. Quintilian 1.1.36; Morgan, *Literate Education*, 146.

74. Koester, *History*, 98.

75. Morgan, *Literate Education*, 194.

the more appropriate as Hecuba and the mother in 4 Maccabees were both celebrated as having especially numerous offspring).[76]

The mother's lament begins with the self-referential vocative ὦ μελέα—"O wretched person that I am!"—so common in Greek tragedy (see Euripides, *Tro.* 144, [ὦ μελέαι]; 165 [μελέαι]; 601 [ὦ μελέα]). At the beginning and end of the lament, she draws attention to the dramatic and sudden reversal of fortune that has befallen here as, in a single day, she has gone from having seven children to having "not even one" (16:6), from "having many children" (πολύπαις) to having much to grieve (πολύθρηνος, 16:10). Such sudden reversals are the essence of Greek tragedy, highlighted also by Euripides' bereaved mothers and those who comment upon them (see *Tro.* 101, 474–499, 1203–1206; *Hec.* 55–58, 282–285, 956–960). The author's artful use of language (seen, for example, in the contrasting compound words πολύπαις . . . πολύθρηνος) also elevates this prose above ordinary speech to the level of the poetic and dramatic. Like the mother of the seven, Hecuba uses compounds of—παις in her lament: "I was blessed with children (εὔπαις) once, but now I am both old and childless (ἄπαις)" (*Hec.* 810; cf. 4 Macc 16:10). Cassandra speaks of Achaean women also "dying in widowhood (χῆραι), while others died childless (ἄπαιδες) in their houses, having reared children all for nothing" (*Tro.* 380–381; compare 4 Macc 16.10). Lamenting one's investment in children who die prematurely as "fruitless" and "purposeless" is a common element. Andromache exclaims, "It was for nothing (διὰ κενῆς) that this breast of mine suckled you . . . and all in vain (μάτην) was my labor!" (*Tro.* 758–760; compare 4 Macc 16.8). Similarly, Hecuba laments Polydorus, "born to no purpose (ἀνόνητα)" (*Hec.* 766; compare 4 Macc 16.7, 9). Hopelessness is expressed in terms of what will never be seen because of these untimely deaths: "No hope have I of being seen of them, no, nor of seeing them for evermore (ὀφθήσομαί . . . ὄψομαί ποτε)" (*Tro.* 487–488; compare 4 Macc 16:9). Loss of help in old age (including burial) is another common element (*Tro.* 382, 504–505, 1180–84; compare 4 Macc 16:11).

The author's familiarity with Euripidean tragedy plausibly reflects the prominence of Euripides in his own education, as this classical tragedian was typically featured in the curricula of Greek schools. Helmut Koester writes that Homer and Euripides were the most prominent authors to be studied during the course of secondary education, even as they were well represented in the holdings of public libraries in cities, as well as libraries in gymnasia and schools.[77] This claim has been substantiated by Teresa

---

76. See the list in Klauck, *4 Makkabäerbuch*, 747–48.

77. Koester, *History*, 97, 99; so also Marrou, *Education in Antiquity*, 227–28. Koester

Morgan in her study of papyri classified as school exercises: "Of the roughly 150 other texts by known authors, 97 are extracts from the *Iliad* and the *Odyssey*. The next most popular author is Euripides, with 20 texts. After him come Isocrates with seven (all gnomic, however) and Menander with seven."[78] Formulating a kind of "independent study" for a friend, Dio Chrysostom gives advice that also incidentally highlights the prominence of Euripides as an educational standard:

> So let us consider the poets: I would counsel you to read Menander of the writers of comedy quite carefully, and Euripides of the writers of tragedy . . . The suavity and plausibility of Euripides, while perhaps not completely attaining to the grandeur of the tragic poet's way of deifying his characters, or to his high dignity, are very useful for the man in public life; and furthermore, he cleverly fills his plays with an abundance of characters and moving incidents, and strews them with maxims useful on all occasions, since he was not without acquaintance with philosophy. (*Or.* 18.6–7)

The tragedies of Euripides would also be available ongoingly through the regular performance of the Classical tragedians in the theaters of Greek cities (in preference to new works).[79]

This same text from Dio Chrysostom tells us that, of course, "Homer comes first and in the middle and last" (*Or.* 18.8). The author of 4 Maccabees includes one unmistakable allusion to Homer when he compares the power of the cries of her sons over the mother to the power of the Sirens' song to compel attention and response (15:21), a reference to the story of Odysseus' encounter with these figures (Homer, *Od.* 12.158–200). He also speaks of the death of the oldest brother in terms of the image of the "thread of life": as this martyr was being tortured to death upon the rack, the author fittingly writes that "the saintly youth *snapped* the thread of life" (9:25). The image of the Fates measuring out and cutting the thread of life

---

(*History*, 99) notes that in libraries "in both east and west the same works constituted the standard holdings: the classical Greek authors, with the poets—especially Homer and Euripides—more fully represented than prose writers and philosophers; textbooks; florilegia; and compendia."

78. Morgan, *Literate Education*, 69. A full table of data appears on p. 313. Also interesting are the tabulations of recitations of classical literature in Plutarch as a reflection of the relative importance or prominence of authors in the work of a literate Greek (Morgan, *Literate Education*, 318–19): Euripides ranks third (359 quotations) after Plato and Homer (915 and 889 quotations, respectively), ahead of Herodotus (304 quotations), Hesiod (207 quotations), and Sophocles (140 quotations).

79. Koester, *History*, 99.

to determine the length of life is not peculiarly Homeric, but the poet does speak of the "Spinners'" work in determining a person's fate, figured as a thread (see *Od.* 7.198; *Il.* 24.209).

Formative Education with Regard to the Jewish Ethnic Subculture

Alongside elements of the formative education typically associated with Greek παιδεία, the classic texts of Judaism clearly constituted another major focus of study for the author of 4 Maccabees. His oration is, in part, an encomium on the formative potential of these texts (recommending the reading of these texts as prescriptive for one's thinking and practice) based on the attainment of moral virtue and consistently virtuous practice that result from such nurture—that is, an encomium on Torah as the essential core of παιδεία *qua* moral formation:

> Right thinking, then, is the mind that, forming correct opin-
> ions, prefers the path of wisdom. Wisdom is the knowledge of
> divine and human behavior and their causes. This comes, in
> turn, from the formative education provided by the Law (ἡ τοῦ
> νόμου παιδεία), through which we learn (μανθάνομεν) about the
> divine in a reverent manner and about human affairs in a way
> that gives us the advantage. (1:15–17)

> Our way of life, however, teaches us self-control (σωφροσύνην
> ... ἐκδιδάσκει), with the result that we are not carried away by
> any pleasure or desire. It trains us in courage (ἀνδρείαν ἐξασκεῖ),
> with the result that we willingly endure any suffering. It educates
> us about justice (δικαιοσύνην παιδεύει), with the result that we
> give each person what is his or her due in all our dealings. It
> educates us in genuine religion (εὐσέβειαν ἐκδιδάσκει), with the
> result that we worship the only God that truly exists and show
> God due respect.[80] (5:23–24)

One of the striking features of this author's work is that he uses the fruits of the Greek elements of the παιδεία he has himself received solely to rec-ommend the more particularistic παιδεία of immersion in the classic texts of Judaism and the practice of the way of life they prescribe and model as the path to attaining the (Greek) ideal of the virtuous person: the person of καλοκἀγαθία and ἀρετή who exhibits the cardinal virtues of "rational

---

80. Eleazar also addressed the Torah, in an apostrophe, as his "educator" (παιδευτὰ νόμε, 5:34).

thought, justice, courage, and self-control" (φρόνησις καὶ δικαιοσύνη καὶ ἀνδρεία καὶ σωφροσύνη, 1:18).[81]

The author of 4 Maccabees is fully conversant in the narrative and legal materials of the Pentateuch, references to which are interwoven throughout his opening discussion of how observance of the Torah's specific commands works to restrain the impulses of particular passions. Its dietary regulations are proof of the Jews' self-control (1:31–35, referring in a general way to Lev 11:4–23, 41–42; Deut 14:4–21); the tenth commandment restrains desire in general and, indeed, proves the feasibility of self-mastery (2:5–6, referring specifically to Exod 20:17; Deut 5:21); the regulations concerning lending and harvesting curb greed (2:8–9, referring specifically to Ex 22:25; 23:10–11; Lev 19:9–10; Deut 15:1–2, 9; 23:19–20); it sets obedience to God above the affections natural to human relationships, whether love (2:10–13, referring in a general way to prescriptions such as Deut 13:6–11) or enmity (2:14–15, referring to the specific rules of Exod 23:4–5; Deut 20:19–20, 24). The specific regulations of Torah outline a form of ἄσκησις (4 Macc 13:22) comparable to that which was practiced by the Spartans or prescribed by Epictetus and Galen for the mastery of particular vices or weaknesses of character.[82] He refers to the examples of Joseph and Moses as proof of the power of reason to master both lust and anger (2:1–3, 17–18, referring to the stories of Gen 39:7–12 and Num 16:1–35) and to Jacob's censure of Simeon and Levi as proof from the contrary that they ought to have been able to master anger as well (2:19, reciting Gen 49:7 and referring to Gen 34:1–31). The nature of his references to these texts and stories, incidentally, also presumes a high degree of familiarity with the Pentateuch on the part of his audience. The author looks beyond the Pentateuch at one point prior to his "narrative demonstration" of his thesis, and that is to the story of David's thirst, which he develops at length as an example of pious reasoning's power to oppose intensely burning, but irrational, desires (3:6–18, retelling the story found in 2 Sam 23:13–17; 1 Chr 11:15–19).

The author's knowledge of the whole spectrum of the canon of classic Jewish texts is evident in his treatment of the martyrs' stories, particularly where he invents speeches for the martyrs and where he expands

---

81. καλοκἀγαθία: 1:10; 3:17–18; 11:22; 13:25; 15:9; ἀρετή: 1:8, 10; 7:21–22; 9:8, 18, 31; 10:10; 11:2; 12:14; 13:24, 27; 17:12, 25. With the standard list of the four cardinal virtues in 1:18 compare 5:23–24, where the virtues highlighted are σωφροσύνην τε . . . καὶ ἀνδρείαν . . . καὶ δικαιοσύνην . . . καὶ εὐσέβειαν, as in Xenophon, *Mem.* 4.6. Philo (*Mos.* 2.215–16; *Prob.* 80) and the author of the *Letter of Aristeas* (144–160) similarly focus on the educative and ethically formative functions of Torah, justifying the distinctive rules and practices of the Jewish subculture by the ethical fruits produced in the lives of its conscientious practitioners. See, further, deSilva, *4 Maccabees*, 59–74, 80–85.

82. Renehan, "Philosophic Background," 235–36.

encomiastically on their achievements. The author is particularly interested in culling examples of people making decisions and choosing often unpleasant (or, at least, self-denying) courses of action for the sake of piety. Thus the figures of Abraham and Isaac (13:12, 14:20; 15:28; 16:20, referring to the episode of Gen 22:1–19), Daniel (16:3, 21; 18:13, referring to Daniel 6), and Hananiah, Azariah, and Mishael (13:9, 16:3, 21; 18:12–13, referring to Daniel 3) are prominent, especially in the exhortations that the martyrs give to one another. The author also has Eleazar refer to the historic oaths by which the wilderness generation committed themselves to the covenant (5:29, referring to Exod 24:3, 7; Josh 24:18, 21, 24). He similarly has the mother refer, among other lessons taught the sons by their father, to Abel and Joseph as exemplifications of the persecution that befalls the righteous (18:11, referring to Gen 4:1–10; 39:1–23), as well as to Phinehas, an example of zeal for the Torah leading to eternal recognition (18:12, referring to Num 25:1–9, the story in which his "zeal" was quintessentially expressed). The author refers in his own voice to Aaron's courageous rush into the thick of the plague to save the people as a point of comparison with Eleazar (7:11–12, referring to Num 16:41–50 and possibly Wis 18:20–25) and to Noah's endurance of the flood as a point of comparison with the metaphorical flood endured by the mother (15:31–32, referring to the story of Genesis 6–9). Specific texts from Isaiah, Psalms, Proverbs, Ezekiel, and Deuteronomy are recited as a means of reinforcing the conviction that fidelity to God, though potentially costly in this life, leads to the experience of eternal reward beyond death (17:19; 18:14–19, reciting Deut 33:3; Isa 43:2; Ps 34:19; Prov 3:18; Ezek 37:2–3; Deut 30:20; 32:39). The author's reading and study extends beyond the "classics" to more contemporary Jewish literature as well, most notably 2 Maccabees, his most pervasive resource.[83]

This raises a question concerning the more precise nature of the author's own formation. As a teenager, did he execute his progymnastic exercises in a secondary school alongside non-Jewish teenagers from his city, reading Euripides with them and then reading Torah in the synagogue, an ancillary Jewish school, or at home? Or did the Jewish community of his city create its own educational institutions patterned after, and using the curriculum of, the Greek institutions, but moving the core texts of the Jewish subculture to the center of the curriculum (still alongside the classic "canon" of Greek education)?

---

83. See Dupont-Sommer, Quatrieme Livre, 26–32; Hadas, Third and Fourth Maccabees, 92–95; Klauck, 4 Makkabäerbuch, 654; deSilva, 4 Maccabees: Introduction and Commentary, xxx–xxxi; against Freudenthal, Flavius Josephus, 72–90, and Deissmann, "Vierte Makkabäerbuch," 156, who argued that the authors of 2 and 4 Maccabees worked independently on the basis of the lost work of Jason of Cyrene.

His oration does not give us the basis for a clear answer. One wonders, however, to what extent his depiction of the seven brothers' formation is a projection of his own experience (or, at least, a projection of a paradigm familiar to him from his own community). Reflecting upon his heroes' upbringing, he imagines their "brother-loving souls" growing more exceedingly "through nurture and daily habit and other educative formation (τῆς ἄλλης παιδείας) and our training in the Law of God" (καὶ τῆς ἡμετέρας ἐν νόμῳ θεοῦ ἀσκήσεως, 13:22). What distinguishes "other educative formation" here from "our training in the Law of God"? One is tempted to see in the former whatever degree of education a Jew might receive through the typical venues available to all of the more elite and affluent residents of a Greek city and in the latter the particularly Jewish enculturation available through more private venues.

The author lays significant stress on the education the seven brothers received at home from their father, as related in the second speech crafted for the heroine of the oration (18:10–19). The author envisions the home as the primary locus of training in the practices, stories, and convictions of the Torah and the Jewish canon (here in the sense of "classic texts for cultural knowledge and practice"). The third brother may reflect the same locus as he challenges the tyrant by asking: "Don't you know that I come from the same father as those who have just died, that the same mother gave me birth, and that I was raised on the same teachings?" (10:2). The sixth brother similarly declares that he and his brothers "were born and raised to live by these principles, so we should die together on behalf of the same" (11:15). Both reminiscences appear to link the communication of Torah's teachings and principles primarily with parental nurture (though this would surely include, for example, attendance at the regular events of public worship and other regular community practices of Jewish life).

Only at one point does the author hint at another venue for what we might anachronistically call "religious education." In their response to Antiochus's invitation to acquiesce to his demands, the seven declare that, "if the old men among the Hebrews fulfilled their duty toward God by enduring tortures for the sake of piety, it would be even more fitting for us who are young to die in contempt of the same tortures that our aged teacher (ὁ παιδευτὴς ἡμῶν γέρων) overcame" (9:6). This may reflect the author's projection of a formal, pedagogical relationship between the priest and scribe Eleazar and the seven brothers, assuming a school setting in which educated Jews provided education in the cultural heritage of Judaism for the young. It may, however, simply reflect the "teaching" that Eleazar provided within the drama, choosing to die for the sake of piety rather than acquiesce (see especially 6:17–22). It may also be significant for this question that the author has nothing positive to say about Jason's *gymnasion*, speaking of it as negatively as did his source without any mitigating factors (2 Macc 4:12–15; 4 Macc 4:19–21), such as might have been the case had the author himself known a gymnasium that incorporated training in the Torah as part of its *enkyklios paideia* (that is, a specifically Jewish gymnasium run primarily to integrate the typical Greek disciplines with the parochial knowledge and practice of Judaism).

To the extent that the author projects his own experience onto that of his narrative, we might surmise that he experienced a formal, non-segregated Greek education in the "normal" venues within his city and received training in Jewish cultural knowledge and practice through private means, primarily through his parents and through the organs of Jewish community practice. If this is correct—and it remains quite conjectural given the nature of the "evidence"—then he represents a Jewish community that was quite fully integrated into the life of its city from a social standpoint, but that worked hard and intentionally to maintain its distinctive cultural identity and practice. The author's own experience of education alongside non-Jewish peers has not mitigated his commitment to (and zeal for *nurturing* commitment to) the distinctively Jewish heritage and way of life, nor tempered his convictions about its superiority to the Greek heritage and way of life.

Conclusion

If smoke can be relied upon consistently to signal the presence of fire, then the author of 4 Maccabees received Greek education consistent with what has been described as "secondary education," seen most clearly in his mastery of the exercises that comprised the *Progymnasmata* but also in his level of cultural literacy. There are also indications that he went on to pursue "tertiary education" to some degree, both in rhetoric and philosophy, though one must always leave open the possibility of his acquiring more advanced facility in the latter subject simply through personal study in the libraries of his city. The author's work reflects a person in whom Greek παιδεία and Jewish cultural literacy and practice join together seamlessly and without contradiction—though, of course, on every point using the former to promote valuing and pursuing the latter among his hearers.

2

Honor and Shame as Argumentative
Topoi in 4 Maccabees

The Fourth Book of Maccabees stands as a rather enigmatic piece of Diasporic Jewish literature. Scholars have long debated its form, audience, date, place, occasion and purpose. What, indeed, is the author's aim? What does the author hope to accomplish in regard to his audience, and how does he seek to attain this end? As a presentation of Jewish models of obedience to the Torah in Hellenistic philosophic garb, the book promises to reveal much about the relationship of Diasporic Jews to their Greco-Roman environments.

Analysis of the use of language related to honor and dishonor may provide an important key to 4 Maccabees. Considerations of honor—its preservation, its acquisition, and the proper demonstration of honor toward others—weighed heavily in the decision-making process of people in the Hellenistic world. Alongside the rhetorical genre of epideictic speech, which is devoted to the praise or censure of some particular person, collective body, or characteristic and so works by demonstrating or setting forth what is honorable and what is shameful, the rhetoricians also placed heavy emphasis on honor as a means of developing a deliberative speech. The author of the *Rhetorica ad Herennium*, for example, regards advantage (the aim of the deliberative speech) to be composed of two subheads—security and honor, the latter being composed of what accords with the cardinal virtues of wisdom, justice, courage, and temperance, as well as with what leads to an honorable remembrance (3.2.3–7). Quintilian goes further in holding up as the aim of all deliberation the discovery and pursuit of the honorable course of action (*Inst. Or.* 8.1). Seneca speaks of considerations of honor and its opposite as final (that is, determinative or decisive) topics: "the one firm conviction from which we move to the proof of other points is this:

that which is honorable is held dear for no other reason than because it is honorable" (*Ben.* 4.16.2).

Rhetorical handbooks from the Greco-Roman world also provide significant guidance for a text-centered method for investigating this realm of discourse, describing, as they do, the ways in which a communicator could successfully use considerations of honor to move the audience in the direction desired by the speaker. Aristotle's *Art of Rhetoric*, the *Rhetorica ad Herennium*, and Quintilian's *Institutio Oratoria* all discuss how the orator is to use honor and dishonor in deliberative and epideictic speeches in order to persuade the hearers. These theorists also provide a more precise idea of the place of honor among the values of Greco-Roman society, and what its component parts include. They also provide reliable guidance concerning how considerations of honor could be expected to provide the necessary motivation for an audience to respond as the orator urges (in deliberative rhetoric), as well as insights into how epideictic rhetoric might also be employed to persuade an audience to embrace a certain course of action over its alternatives.[1]

Rhetorical Genre and the Purpose of 4 Maccabees

Rhetorical genre and a document's situation and purpose are integrally related. Indications of genre, therefore, are extremely helpful in determining the goal that the author sought to achieve through his oration. Aristotle noted that no genre tends to be used exclusively in a speech, but rather the successful speech will utilize several genres in the service of the principle aim of the oration. For example, when the author desires to move his hearers to decide on a certain course of action, his primary genre will be the deliberative speech. Nevertheless, he may devote extensive sections to praise or blame (epideictic) or consideration of the just and the unjust (forensic) in the service of this aim.

4 Maccabees as Epideictic Oratory

Scholars would largely agree that 4 Maccabees belongs to the genre of epideictic, or demonstrative, oratory.[2] This category is the least well-defined,

---

1. See, further, deSilva, *Hope of Glory*, 1–33.

2. cf. Klauck, *4 Makkabäerbuch*, 659: "Diese allgemeine Gattungsbezeichnun »epideiktische Rede« ist zugleich die sicherste."

and, indeed, became a sort of catch-all category for speeches that were not clearly deliberative or forensic.[3] The language used by the author himself, nevertheless, points to this category. First, he uses the language of demonstration (ἐπιδείκνυσθαι, 1:1; ἀπόδειξιν, 3:19; ἀπέδειξα, 16:2). His concern to demonstrate a philosophical proposition, stated conspicuously at the outset, has led certain scholars to view the work as an example of diatribe.[4] Several scholars have questioned the adequacy of this description, based particularly on the author's own admission that his work includes an ἔπαινος (1:2), "praise," of virtue and seeks to praise (ἐπαινεῖν, 1:10) the Maccabean martyrs as exemplars of virtue.[5]

These two aspects of demonstrative oratory have led scholars to posit a number of plausible aims that the author sought to achieve through his writing. First, one may take the author at his word and understand his aim to be the demonstration of his thesis that "devout reason is sovereign over the emotions" (αὐτοδέσποτός ἐστιν τῶν παθῶν ὁ εὐσεβὴς λογισμός, 1:1).[6] Those who possess an εὐσεβὴς λογισμός, the author seeks to demonstrate, will achieve the highest honor. The faculty itself leads one to restrain the impulses that hinder justice, temperance, and courage (1:3–4), which are three of the four cardinal virtues seen as essential components of honor (e.g., Rhet. ad Her. 3.2.3). Furthermore, those who have displayed the sovereignty of this faculty are held up as exemplars of virtue (ἀρετή, 1:8) and, as such, are praiseworthy (1:10), the other component of honor according to the author of the ad Herennium (3.3.7). The author presents the cultivation of εὐσεβὴς λογισμός as a means of attaining true honor, which he sets in direct opposition to other forms of claiming and pursuing honor, which he calls "the malevolent tendency" (ἡ κακοήθης διάθεσις, 1:25) of the soul. Apart from "devout reason," all attempts

3. Kennedy, New Testament Interpretation, 73.

4. Schürer, History, 588; Hadas, Maccabees, 101; Anderson, "4 Maccabees," 531; Lebram, "Literarische Form," 81.

5. Schürer (History, 588) felt this tension of form when, having labelled 4 Maccabees a diatribe, he continued by saying that "at times it also verges into panegyric." Hadas (Maccabees, 102) also noted the possibility of arguing that "our book is rather a panegyric or encomium than a diatribe." Lebram ("Literarische Form," 83) favors this description: "Durch den Terminus technicus ἔπαινος ist die Gattung unserer Rede schon genauer bestimmt. Sie gehört zum γένος ἐπιδεικτικόν, zur Gattung der Prunk- und Lehrreden, wie z.B. der Panegyrikos von Isocrates und die Lobreden auf Städte von Dion von Prusa." Based on internal indications of oral delivery at a specific occasion and the suggestion of an epitaph for the martyrs in 17:8, he further classifies it as akin to the funeral oration: "Dieser Rede hat der Autor eine Form gegeben, die starken Einfluss des athenischen Epitaphios verrät" ("Literarische Form," 96). Cf. also Gilbert, "4 Maccabees," 317.

6. Translations of 4 Maccabees in this chapter are taken from the NRSV unless otherwise noted.

to satisfy the "thirst for honor" are but "empty reputation," "arrogance," and "boastfulness" (1:26; 2:15).

The epithet given to "reason" in the phrase εὐσεβὴς λογισμός points more precisely to the focus of the author's demonstration.[7] The emphasis is not on the Stoic ethical proposition that "reason is sovereign over the emotions,"[8] but rather on the nature of the reason that is able to achieve and maintain such sovereignty.[9] Lebram captures the essence of this shift in focus: "treuer Gehorsam gegen das jüdische Gesetz gleichbedeutend mit der Überwindung der πάθη ist. Dieser Gehorsam ist aber nichts anderes als die fromme Vernunft, der εὐσεβὴς λογισμός."[10] 4 Macc 1:15–17 brings the reader from more or less vague Hellenistic concepts squarely into the heart of Jewish particularity:

> Reason is the mind that with sound logic prefers the life of wisdom. Wisdom, next, is the knowledge of divine and human matters and the causes of these. This, in turn, is education in the law, by which we learn divine matters reverently and human affairs to our advantage.

Reason of the sort that leads to the life of virtue and praiseworthy remembrance realizes its goal by choosing the life that accords with wisdom. Wisdom is here further defined in the exact terms of Stoic philosophy (cf. Cicero, *Tusc. Dis.* 4.25.57: *rerum divinarum et humanarum scientiam cognitionemque quae cuiusque rei causa sit*). The manner of wisdom's acquisition, however, is "education in the Law" (ἡ τοῦ νόμου παιδεία, 1:17). The author clearly has in mind not the Stoic law of nature, at least not as presented by Antiochus in 5:8–9, but rather the Jewish Torah, as indicated by the

---

7. Lauer ("*Eusebes Logismos*," 170) considers the expression paradoxical or oxymoronic. Hadas (*Maccabees*, 144) rightly objects, however, that the use of "devout" as a qualifier of reason "is a logical solecism only if we equate 'reason' with 'rationalism'. In the Stoic view it is nearer tautology, for all reason is God-directed."

8. Schürer, *History*, 589.

9. Redditt ("Concept of *Nomos*," 249) is correct in saying that "the dominance of reason over emotion is, however, only the formal and not the crucial focus of 4 Maccabees," but only insofar as the author is concerned rather to demonstrate the nature of the reason which is so dominant, and in so doing advance his program for the promotion of obedience to Torah among Diasporic Jews who are constantly attracted to the advantages of some measure of assimilation to Hellenistic society.

10. Lebram, "Literarische Form," 81 ("faithful obedience to the Jewish Law is synonymous with overcoming the passions. This obedience is, however, nothing other than 'pious reason'."). Cf. also Schürer, *History*, 589–90: "Even the basic idea is a Jewish one recast, for the reason to which he ascribes command over the passions is not reason in the sense used by the Greek philosophers but religious reason, εὐσεβὴς λογισμός, i.e., reason that follows the norm of the divine law."

examples of particular commands from the Torah cited in 1:30–3:18. The Jewish Law teaches wisdom—the knowledge of things human and divine— and the one who adheres to this teaching will act reverently towards God and gain advantage in human interactions. In short, the Torah educates the reasoning faculty and leads to its mastery of emotions and thence to the individual's ability to live consistently in line with the virtues that stand at the core of personal honor and honorable remembrance.[11]

The examples of reason's mastery over feelings that the author chooses to present also point strongly in this direction. While the author declares that he can furnish proof of his thesis from any number of examples, he claims that the best illustrations of the principle at work are to be found in the history of the Maccabean martyrs, who "died for the sake of virtue" (1:7–8). It is precisely in Eleazar, the seven brothers, and their mother that one may see the mastery of devout reason over feelings—hence the re-occurring reference to the thesis after their deaths (6:31–33; 7:10; 13:1, 5; 16:1–2). Their suffering and deaths on behalf of "virtue" (1:8) or "piety" (6:22; 7:16; 9:6, 7, 30; 11:20; 16:17; 17:7) or "reverence for God" (7:22) were clearly also deaths on account of fidelity to Torah. That is, the matter at issue in the trials and tortures each faced was whether to transgress the Jewish Law (5:19–21, 29; 9:1–2, 4; 13:15). The author's examples of the sort of reason that conquers emotions, therefore, are examples of unwavering fidelity to the Torah. The author seems therefore quite intent on demon-strating that obedience to the Torah is what makes virtue (honor) and honorable remembrance possible.[12] The phrase εὐσεβὴς λογισμός becomes a sort of *leitmotif* for firm obedience to Torah.[13]

The true nature of the thesis that the author seeks to demonstrate be-comes even clearer when seen against the claims the author makes through-out his discussion concerning the attainment of the reason that masters feelings and leads to a virtuous and honorable life. Victory over the emotions

---

11. Cf. Eleazar's reply to Antiochus in 5:23–24: "It teaches us self-control, so that we master all pleasures and desires, and it also trains us in courage, so that we endure any suffering willingly; it instructs us in justice, so that in all our dealings we act impartially, and it teaches us piety, so that with proper reverence we worship the only living God." The appearance of piety here in place of wisdom is more an apparent than a real substi-tution. Wisdom consists, after all, of the knowledge of and proper response to human and divine matters, and so embraces justice and piety (cf. Plato, *Gorg*, 507: "In relation to other men [the temperate man] will do what is just; and in his relation to the gods he will do what is holy").

12. Cf. Anderson, "Maccabees, Books of," 452.

13. Cf. Collins, *Between Athens and Jerusalem*, 189: "'reason' in 4 Maccabees is virtually equated with obedience to the law," specifically, "the Jewish law in all its particularity."

that hinder the practice of justice comes "as soon as one adopts a way of life in accordance with the law" (2:8). Similarly, in unfolding God's provisions in the creation of humanity for a life of virtue, the author states that "to the mind he gave the Law; and one who lives subject to this will rule a kingdom that is temperate, just, good, and courageous (2:23)."[14] As the demonstration progresses and the audience is caught up more and more by the noble examples of fidelity to the Torah, the author becomes increasingly exclusive in his claims: "As many as attend to religion with a whole heart, these *alone* are able to control the passions of the flesh" (7:18, emphasis mine). Lest the reader think that the author speaks of religion in general terms, he adds an explanation for his claim that roots it in Jewish religion: "since they believe that they, like our patriarchs Abraham and Isaac and Jacob, do not die to God but live to God" (7:19). Finally, the author places upon the lips of the eldest brother the thesis that their deaths seek to demonstrate: "I will convince you that children of the Hebrews *alone* are invincible where virtue is concerned" (9:18, emphasis mine). They prove this through their unwavering fidelity to the Torah even in the face of the cruelest tortures.

Since the author seeks to promote obedience to the Torah as the exclusive means to attain and practice virtue, the work takes on a more protreptic nature than one would expect from an intellectual, philosophical demonstration. George Kennedy, a pioneer in adapting ancient rhetorical theory for use as a tool in New Testament interpretation, explains that this is not unusual for epideictic rhetoric:

> Aristotle sought to make a basic distinction between situations in which the audience are judges and those in which they are only spectators or observers . . . As Aristotle subsequently admits (2.18.1391b), the audience in [epideictic] cases becomes a judge, but a judge of the eloquence of the speaker rather than of his cause. Yet funeral orations and panegyrics were intended to be persuasive and often imply some need for actions, though in a more general way than does deliberative oratory. Greek orators regularly sought to give significance to their words by holding up the past as worthy of imitation in the future, and in the Roman empire epideictic orations celebrating the virtues of a ruler, Pliny's panegyric of Trajan, for example, often came to praise not the virtues he actually had, but virtues the orator

---

14. Hadas (*Maccabees*, 157) notes that the Stoic ideal of the wise person as king here is attained through the agency of Torah. One may also compare with this the Platonic ideal of the temperate person, who rules over his or her pleasures and passions (*Gorg.* 491).

thought he should cultivate. They thus take on a more or less subtle deliberative purpose.[15]

He mentions also in this context the chief purpose that modern rhetoricians attribute to epideictic rhetoric, namely "the strengthening of audience adherence to some value as the basis for a general policy of action." It is this subtly deliberative function of epideictic that leads scholars to see the demonstration of a thesis as merely the "formal function" of 4 Maccabees and not its crucial function. The author appears rather to seek "to inculcate and preserve national and religious loyalty" and "to advocate fidelity to the Law."[16] That such a program lies behind 4 Maccabees becomes even more evident as its ancillary rhetorical genre is examined more closely.

4 Maccabees as Deliberative Rhetoric

While the epideictic elements of 4 Maccabees are prominently placed on the surface of the text and have been noted by most scholars of the book, its deliberative elements have largely gone overlooked. These elements ought not to detract from the description of the primary genre as epideictic or demonstrative, but rather serve to heighten the protreptic purpose of the whole work, and clue in modern readers to the nature of the impact that the author hopes to make on his audience.

First, one should note the direct exhortations addressed to the audience. In 1:1, as a form of *captatio benevolentiae*, the author advises his hearers to pay earnest attention to philosophy, particularly the philosophy expressed by his theme, because of the fruits of the mastery of reason over the emotions, namely the unhindered practice of praiseworthy virtues. As we have already seen, however, this "philosophy" concerns obedience to Torah as the surest means of cultivating these virtues. Because of this, the initial encouragement to pay attention to philosophy can be transformed into the concluding exhortation of 18:1–2: "O Israelite children, offspring of the seed of Abraham, obey this law and exercise piety in every way, knowing that devout reason is master of all emotions, not only of sufferings from within, but also of those from without." From these exhortations, it is clear that the author seeks to move his audience to keep the Torah, and to secure their absolute loyalty to Torah as their "policy" upon which all other actions are based.

15. Kennedy, *New Testament Interpretation*, 73–74.
16. Hadas, *Maccabees*, 93; Anderson, "Fourth Maccabees," 532.

The author's expansion of the stories of the martyrs narrated more concisely in his source (2 Maccabees 6:18—7:40) allows him to create a sort of deliberative world within his epideictic discourse. This is evident from the explicit presence of two "counselors" in the martyrs' arena. That the two are opposed in their advice is clear from their juxtaposition in 9:2–3: "We are obviously putting our forebears to shame unless we should practice ready obedience to the Law and to Moses our counselor (συμβούλῳ Μωυσεῖ). Tyrant and counselor of lawlessness (σύμβουλε τύραννε παρανομίας), in your hatred for us do not pity us more than we pity ourselves."[17] Antiochus also presents himself as an advisor who presents considerations for the martyrs' deliberations: "I would advise you (συμβουλεύσαιμ᾽ ἄν) to save yourself by eating pork" (5:6); "Not only do I advise you not to display the same madness as that of the old man . . . but I also exhort you to yield to me and enjoy my friendship (συμβουλεύω . . . παρακαλῶ)" (8:5). In both cases, Antiochus offers several considerations that aim at moving the martyrs to choose a particular course of action (capitulation) over another (persistence in obedience to Torah).

As a deliberative speaker and counselor, Antiochus is given the opportunity to make a case for the course he urges. This results in the appearance of what Klauck fittingly called *Rededuelle*,[18] "speech-duels" in which Antiochus offers his counsel (5.5–13; 8:5–11; 12:3–5) and the martyrs present their reasons for rejecting his counsel (5:16–38; 9:1–9; 12:11–18). These speeches are important not only as means of heightening the drama of the contest but also as a means of engaging the arguments that could be presented against the author's thesis that the Torah is the way to virtue and that uncompromising obedience to the Torah is the equivalent of the mastery of reason over the passions. The arguments considered by the author may very well reflect those that certain members of the audience might have heard (and *entertained*) advocating greater assimilation to the Hellenistic way of life as a path to advantage in a context that did not universally respect Judaism.[19]

17. Hadas (*Maccabees*, 193) points this out as an intentional contrast.

18. Klauck, 4 *Makkabäerbuch*, 652.

19. See, for example, the calumnies against Judaism recorded and refuted by Josephus in the *Contra Apionem*, as well as the anti-Semitic presentation of Jews in Tacitus' *Histories*, Book Five. Even Quintilian manages to give evidence of this attitude in the midst of his discussion of epideictic rhetoric (*Inst.* 7.21): "founders of cities are detested for concentrating a race which is a curse to others, as for example the founder of the Jewish superstition." *Superstitio* was itself a derogatory term for a foreign religion among Romans.

Antiochus' address to Eleazar raises several issues: Is following Judaism on a parity with pursuing the noble task of philosophy (5:7)? Does not
Jewish law conflict with the law of nature, to which the wise person must
conform himself or herself (5:8)? Is it not unjust to treat nature's gifts with
contempt (5:9)? Does adherence to the Jewish law not amount to holding
an empty opinion with regard to the truth (5:10)? Would it not be better to
adopt a more philosophical guide, such as reasoning according to the truth
of what is beneficial (5:11)? Finally, Antiochus bids Eleazar consider that no
divinity would blame him for transgressing under compulsion (5:13), an
argument that appears again when he addresses the seven brothers (8:14).
Eleazar, however, answers each of these objections and defends the course
of resistance as reasonable and honorable.[20]

The second *Rededuell*—the exchange between Antiochus and the
seven brothers—raises another set of issues. Here, Antiochus proposes
a new benefactor-client relationship between himself and the brothers,
promising them advancement and positions of honor in his kingdom
(8:5–6). He knows how to benefit those who obey him, he claims (8:6): the
only requirement is that they conform to the Hellenistic way of life (which
is presented rather as a life of enjoyment): "Enjoy your youth by adopting
the Greek way of life and by changing your manner of living" (8:8).[21] The
only alternative is to suffer an excruciating death. Such deliberations again
suggest that the author indirectly addresses the peculiar tension which
would be felt by Jews living in the centers of Greek civilization, who had
themselves accepted Greek as their language and many aspects of Greek
thought as their thought as well. Perhaps some felt, as did the innovators
mentioned in 1 Macc 1:11, that separation from the Gentiles only meant
disaster and decline, that one was indeed faced with a choice of becoming
Greek in ever deeper ways so as to strengthen one's place in the network of
patronage and clientage that held together the Greco-Roman world or to
be subject to the tensions, deprivations, and marginalization of an ethnic
and religious minority group. The importance of these considerations for

---

20. Redditt ("Concept of *Nomos*," 250) rightly notes this apologetic aspect of 4
Maccabees: "the author attempts to show that the dictates of a rational, divine *nomos*
do not contradict the world order. Rather, *nomos* is the genuine criterion by which to
judge truth or philosophy." Similarly, he stresses how the author, in the voice of Eleazar,
is at pains to demonstrate that the Torah is in fact in deepest accord with the law of
nature, since both Torah and nature have their origin in the one God ("Concept of
Nomos," 257).

21. Significantly, this exhortation recalls the negative example of Jason, who
"changed the nation's way of life and altered its form of government in complete violation of the law" (4:19).

the author's audience is emphasized by the repetition of the offer and alternatives by Antiochus to the last surviving brother in 12:3–5.

The deliberative atmosphere of 4 Maccabees is heightened further by the author's creation of alternate or hypothetical responses by the seven brothers and the mother at 8:16–26 and 16:5–11. In these speeches, the author presents a line of reasoning which the martyrs *might* have adopted but *did* not. In their hypothetical speech, the brothers are depicted as capitulating to Antiochus' arguments that the necessities of their situation will excuse transgression (8:22, 24) and that Jewish particularism is indeed a "vain opinion" (8:19). These reasonings lead them to choose the king's friendship (which means a place of political honor and power) over "a disobedience that brings death" (8:18). The author, however, identifies this response as "cowardly and unmanly" (8:16), and sweeps it aside with the bold declaration of fidelity to the law which marks the martyrs' true attitude (9:1–9).

As a final deliberative element, one should not overlook the exhortations which the martyrs address to one another, but which, because of the fact that the whole speech is addressed to the audience and that the audience has been led at every point to identify with the martyrs, are also indirectly addressed to the audience. When Eleazar declares his refusal even to pretend to eat the food offered to idols, he closes with the exhortation: "therefore, O children of Abraham, die nobly for your religion!" (6:22). Similarly, the eldest brother expires with the exhortation on his lips: "Imitate me, brothers! Do not leave your post in my struggle or renounce our courageous family ties. Fight the sacred and noble battle for religion" (9:23–24). After the deaths of all seven brothers, the author reflects on how they exhorted one another to steadfastness to the Law, recounting these at length (13:9–18). Finally, he recounts the mother's stirring exhortation: "My sons, noble is the contest to which you are called to bear witness for the nation. Fight zealously for our ancestral law . . . Remember that it is through God that you have had a share in the world and have enjoyed life, and therefore you ought to endure any suffering for the sake of God" (16:16–19).[22] The

22. Seeley (*Noble Death*, 93–94) has argued that it is in fact the mimetic process which led to the martyrs' victory over Antiochus: "the martyrs become the 'cause of the downfall of tyranny' precisely because 'all people' marvel at their 'courage and endurance'. By inspiring others to re-enact their resistance they create an implacable barrier to Antiochus's efforts, sending him finally on his way . . . 1.11 and 18.5 make clear that the critical factor is the mimetic process by which others follow the martyrs' example." Furthermore, the author intends for his audience to be affected by the narrative so as to find the heart to imitate the martyrs as well: "It is clear that the vicarious effect of the martyrs' deaths can be appropriated mimetically even without having to re-enact literally their grisly end . . . Through describing the details, [the author] seeks to inspire obedience in his audience the way (he says) the martyrs' deaths inspired

auditors of such exhortations would no doubt have at least had to consider the applicability of such advice to their own situations.

While 4 Maccabees consists largely of epideictic oratory, then, it also contains a number of elements of deliberative oratory, including series of speeches which present various considerations and arguments as to which of two courses—capitulation or fidelity to Torah—is the better course. The auditors of the work are thereby called to consider the various issues raised within the framework of the martyr narrative, but are also provided a guide for evaluating these considerations by the author himself. Here we enter upon an examination of how the epideictic frame relates to these embedded deliberations.

Relation of Epideictic to Deliberative Rhetoric in 4 Maccabees

By setting the considerations of which of two courses to take within the framework of demonstrative oratory, the author is able to persuade the audience to take one course over the other not only by the arguments themselves (the responses in the *Rededuelle*) but also by means of his own commendation and censure of the various counselors, persons, choices, and actions. That is, the epideictic frame allows the author to show which choices and responses are approved as honorable and praiseworthy; to label as honorable or virtuous certain choices, reasonings, and their representatives; and to label as dishonorable, vicious, or deficient other choices, reasonings, and so forth.[23] It enables the author to set the conflict in a certain perspective in which the choice he recommends and in which he desires his audience to be confirmed may be presented as already positively evaluated.

In the ancient Mediterranean world, praise was closely linked with emulation. In Aristotle's words, emulation is

---

their contemporaries. This purpose accounts for the lingering, detailed description. By means of such mental re-enactment, the audience will benefit from the deaths. It will put itself in the martyrs' place, come to understand that it, too, could endure torment, and thus gain courage to live, or, if necessary, to die obediently (cf. 18.1, the first direct exhortation to the audience, which is told to 'obey this law')."

23. In this regard, the author of 4 Maccabees exemplifies the close relation of the two rhetorical genres spoken of by the rhetorical theorists. Aristotle (*Rhet.* 1.9.35–36), for example, writes that "praise and counsels have a common aspect; for what you might suggest in counselling becomes encomium by a change in the phrase . . . Accordingly, if you desire to praise, look what you would suggest; if you desire to suggest, look what you would praise." Similarly Quintilian (*Inst.* 7.28): "panegyric is akin to deliberative oratory inasmuch as the same things are usually praised in the former as are advised in the latter."

> a feeling of pain at the evident presence of highly valued goods,
> which are possible for us to attain, in the possession of those
> who naturally resemble us—pain not due to the fact that an-
> other possesses them, but to the fact that we ourselves do not.
> Emulation therefore is virtuous and characteristic of virtuous
> men, whereas envy is base and characteristic of base men; for
> the one, owing to emulation, fits himself to obtain such goods,
> while the object of the other, owing to envy, is to prevent his
> neighbour possessing them. (*Rhet.* 2.11.1)

In Thucydides' *History* (2.35), Pericles is given the honor of delivering a funeral oration which is somewhat self-reflective on the Greek practice of giving and hearing such a speech. Pericles approaches the task of praising the fallen soldiers with some caution:

> The man who knows the facts and loves the dead may well think
> that an oration tells less than what he knows and what he would
> like to hear: others who do not know so much may feel envy
> for the dead, and think the orator over-praises them, when he
> speaks of exploits that are beyond their own capacities. Praise
> of other people is tolerable only up to a certain point, the point
> where one still believes that one could do oneself some of the
> things one is hearing about. Once you get beyond this point, you
> will find people becoming jealous and incredulous.

Auditors of an epideictic speech that aims at praise apparently responded, if the speech was successfully constructed, with a feeling of emulation, affirming themselves inwardly as they heard the speech with assurances of "I could do that if I had to" and being drawn by the orator's praise into the conviction that one could oneself also act in a similarly praiseworthy manner. If one began to distance oneself from the subject of praise and from the possibility of upholding the values for which he or she was praised, the auditors would become unfavorable hearers.

As one might expect from a good orator, Pericles seeks to foster the auditors' feeling of emulation, even by direct exhortation and application: "We who remain behind may hope to be spared their fate, but must resolve to keep the same daring spirit against the foe" (2.43); "It is for you to try to be like them. Make up your minds that happiness depends on being free, and freedom depends on being courageous" (2.44). Similarly, the author of 4 Maccabees aims at inspiring the feeling of emulation among his auditors and seeks to strengthen their own resolve to "keep the same daring spirit," drawing them in by the hope of honor and praiseworthy remembrance and by their own sense of honor.

The author evaluates the character of the martyrs as honorable. They are associated in various ways with the virtue of καλοκἀγαθία, a word used in the LXX only in this book. According to Danker, who traces the use of this word in inscriptions to benefactors,

> to describe a person as *kalokagathos* (a perfect gentleman) or *kalēkagathē* (a noble woman) was one of the highest terms of praise in the Greek vocabulary. In some inscriptions the term *kalokagathos* appears as an alternate expression for *anēr tēs aretēs* (man of arete) and other terms used to describe high achievers or benefactors.[24]

The martyrs died "on account of καλοκἀγαθία" (1:10), die "equipped with καλοκἀγαθία," their deaths attesting to their character (11:22; 15:9), and lived with "a common zeal for καλοκἀγαθία" (13:25). This same virtue and virtuous description, however, is also made available to those of "temperate mind," who give religious reason dominion over their passions, this is, who emulate the martyrs' choices (3:18). The martyrs act out of a commitment to ἀρετή, "excellence" or "virtue" as well as the reputation for being of such a character. The brothers endure torture and die "for the sake of ἀρετή" (1:8; 10:10; 11:2) which assures them also of receiving the "prize of ἀρετή" (9:8); once again the emulation of this devotion to "excellence" is held up to the auditors in the form of a rhetorical question: "What person who . . . knows that it is blessed to endure any suffering for the sake of ἀρετή, would not be able to overcome the emotions though godliness?" (7:21–22).

In particular, the martyrs are credited with the virtue of εὐσέβεια, "piety," and ἀνδρεία, "courage." The former is not properly one of the four cardinal virtues of Stoicism or Platonism, but often appears as a replacement for one of those virtues (cf. Philo, *De spec. leg.* 4.147; Xenophon, *Memor.* 4.6). It may also be regarded as a subtype of justice, "giving to each thing what it is entitled in proportion to its worth" (*Rhet. ad Her.* 3.2.3) where what is due Deity is considered.[25] Piety and dutifulness are closely related values, as one sees in the frequent use of the epithet *pius* to describe the hero of the *Aeneid*, who is dependable, faithful, and dutiful with regard to the requirements of family, country, and divinities. As such, it is a very important social virtue. The martyrs in 4 Maccabees highly value this virtue, in that they suffer

---

24. Danker, *Benefactor*, 319.

25. Cf. also Socrates' definition of the temperate person in Plato, *Gorg*, 507: "And will not the temperate man do what is proper, both in relation to the gods and to men; —for he would not be temperate if he did not? Certainly he will do what is proper. In his relation to other men he will do what is just; and in his relation to the gods he will do what is holy; and he who does what is just and holy must be just and holy? Very true."

and die "on account of εὐσέβεια," a fact of which the auditors are reminded throughout the oration (5:31; 7:16; 9:29; 15:12; 16:13, 17, 19). Their choices are determined by their refusal to violate their life of εὐσέβεια and their reputation for this virtue (9:6, 25; 13:8, 10; 15:1, 3). As such, their deaths become a demonstration of piety (13:10).

Similarly, the martyrs demonstrate the virtue of ἀνδρεία, "courage," through their endurance of the most extreme tortures to the point of death. They are shown to possess a virtue that was highly praised in Greek culture. The funeral oration given by Pericles noted above takes as its keynote the fallen soldiers' demonstration of "manliness and courage" (which are synonymous terms in Greek thought). By their demonstration of ἀνδρεία, the martyrs win the admiration of all, including that of their torturers (1:11). The brothers endured the tortures bravely (14:9) as did the mother with even "greater courage than any man" (15:23, 30). Eleazar likewise exemplifies the "wise and courageous" person (7:23). In all their endurance of hardship, they shunned the course of ἀνανδρεία ("cowardice") and were not branded as δειλόψυχοι ("fainthearted") as those who did not hold firm to piety towards God expressed through obedience to the Torah would be (8:8; 16:5). They become exemplars of "courage" even to those engaged in military exploits, the traditional arena for the demonstration of "manliness" (17:23–24).

The author may therefore rightly commend them as καλός and γενναῖος ("noble") frequently throughout the oration (6:10; 7:8; 8:3; 9:13; 10:3; 15:24, 30). This nobility, however, is manifested in their choice to remain steadfast to God and the Torah in their encounter with the demands of Gentile society (cf. 9:27, where the second brother's choice is simply referred to as τὴν εὐγενῆ γνώμην, "his noble judgment"). It is precisely when their virtue is put to the test that their lives are seen to be exemplary and praiseworthy, and the end of their lives color the whole as dedicated to piety, courage, and the other virtues. It is in the outcome of their lives that their honor is secured, even as Pericles looks to the soldiers' deaths as the seal of their virtue: "To me it seems that the consummation which has overtaken these men shows us the meaning of manliness in its first revelation and in its final proof" (Thucydides, Hist. 2.42). Eleazar knows that his reputation for piety demonstrated through a long life of devotion is on the line in the test posed before him by the intrusion of Gentile demands—he may become an "example of ἀσέβεια" in an instant if he does not remain firm (5:18, 6:19).

As the consummation of their piety and courage, therefore, the martyrs' suffering and dying is lauded as endured "nobly" or "blessedly" (καλῶς, μακαρίως: 6:30; 9:24; 10:1, 15; 11:12; 12:1, 14; 15:32; 16:16). They are credited with having purged their πατρίς ("homeland") of a great evil (1:11: cf. Pericles' praise of the soldiers for the preservation of their country's freedom) through having achieved a victory over the tyrant and his forces (1:11; 6:10; 7:4; 8:2, 15; 9:6, 30; 11:20, 24–27; 16:14; 17:2). The results and rewards of their firmness clearly include a honorable remembrance (amplified by the oration itself, with its *encomia* of the martyrs in 7:1–15; 13:6–14:10; 14:11–17:6). They endured εἰς δόξαν, "unto a glorious reputation" (7:9, translation mine), and enjoy the distinction of being honored by God (17:5), by the patriarchs (who still "live" as a court of public opinion able to ascribe honor, 13:17), and by their nation as its saviors (1:11; 17:20). They now stand in the presence of God, the ultimate reward for God's servants (9:8; 17:5, 17–19; 18:23).

The noble character, choices, actions, and rewards of the martyrs stand in stark contrast to those of their antagonists and other figures presented in the narrative as anti-exemplars. Antiochus IV is presented as ὑπερήφανος καὶ δεινός, "arrogant and fearsome" (4:15; cf. 9:15). He is a formidable adversary, but not an honorable one. He lacks respect for what is due God, and so is described as ἀσεβής, "impious" (cf. 9:32; 10:11; 12:11). Indeed, the author sets up intentional contrasts (underscored by the μέν . . . δέ antithesis) between the martyrs' virtue and Antiochus' vice (e.g., "We, on the one hand, O most abominable tyrant, suffer these things on account of the education and excellence of God, but you, on the other hand, will endure unending torments on account of your impiety and cruelty," 10:10–11). Antiochus is further vilified as a "hater of virtue" (μισάρετε, 11:4) and as "bloodthirsty, murderous, and utterly abominable" (αἱμοβόρος καὶ φονώδης καὶ παμμιαρώτατος, 10:17). His actions are negatively evaluated as impious (9:31), unjust (11:6), and shameless (12:11, 13). No alliance with such a person (or like persons) is possible for honorable people.

The author of 4 Maccabees presents, however, a number of persons who did seek such an alliance. The first is Simon, who for political reasons sought to slander the noble high priest Onias (4:1). Failing to achieve political honor in this arena, he turned to court the favor and seek the praise of the Gentile leaders (4:2–4). He is presented as a betrayer of his πατρίς and described as κατάρατος, "accursed" (4:5). The second is Jason, who contracted with Antiochus to purchase the honored office of High Priest and who, receiving this power, "changed the nation's way of life and altered its form of government in complete violation of the law" (4:19), setting aside the Torah as the basis for the Jerusalem polity in favor of a Greek constitution and structures. Such a course of action is precisely what Antiochus hopes the brothers will adopt, faced with the alternatives of enjoying his favor and promises of advancement and the suffering of tortures to the point of death (8:8). Seeking advancement in Gentile society at the cost of obedience to Torah and honoring God, however, provokes the wrath of God and brings judgement upon the nation (4:21) and eternal torment upon individuals (9:9, 31; 10:21; 11:23; 12:12, 14, 18; 13:15; 18:5, 22). Not only is such a course "unmanly" and "fainthearted" (8.6), it is opposed to the course of virtue (by which the Torah leads the subject mind to "rule a kingdom that is temperate, just, good, and courageous," 2:23) and dishonors the One who is able to bring down both temporal and eternal tribulation on the heads of the disobedient and disrespectful (4:21; 13:15).

The path of the martyrs, therefore, is presented as the path of virtue and honorable remembrance. Those who seek to answer the demands of pagan society through loosening their observance of the Torah act dishonorably and irreverently, gaining a shameful reputation, in the author's estimation of honor, and earning the wrath of the Deity whom they despised through disregard for God's Law. As honor is a socially granted value, the author depicts the martyrs as engaged in a public contest, which takes place before Antiochus, his Friends, his soldiers, and his herded victims (5:1–2, 15, 27–28; 12:8; 17:14).[26] The martyrs receive honor from God and the patriarchs (13:3, 17; 17:5); since this court of reputation delivers an eternal verdict its opinion is of the highest importance. The author suggests, however, that the only way to receive lasting honor from the Gentiles is through obedience to the Jewish Law. Eleazar suggests, for example, that, at a deeper level, Antiochus would really despise the same capitulation he would seem to praise (6:21) and that transgression of the Law would lead not to honorable assimilation into Gentile society but would rather be an occasion for mockery and derision (5:27–28). To reinforce this perception, the author states that the martyrs' endurance provoked the admiration of their torturers (1:11; 6:11; 9:26; 17:16) and that Antiochus himself proclaimed them as an example of courage and manliness (17:23). Collins

---

26. A number of scholars have seen the importance of the public nature of these trials, since this puts not only martyrs' reputation but also God's honor on the line. The martyrs' steadfastness demonstrates their respect for God, just as their capitulation would enact disregard for God. See, for example, the comment by Hadas (*Maccabees*, 119–20): "A great distinction in gravity is made between sins committed in private and in public . . . more especially if public issue is being made of the transgression . . . When an issue *is* made, then even a slight transgression involves *hillul ha-Shem*, 'profanation of the divine name,' avoidance of which is the highest obligation . . . Hence it is no mere point of personal pride when Eleazar objects that he will be laughed at for violating his principles, no bolstering of pride when he refers to his reputation, and no bravado when he expresses indignation at the proffered ruse by which he would only *appear* to be transgressing. At all points Eleazar is behaving precisely as later codification . . . demanded." Hadas is followed on this point by Anderson, "Fourth Maccabees," 538 and Redditt, "Concept of *Nomos*," 254. An interesting parallel also appears in Rom 2:24, where Paul attributes the Gentiles' slander of God's name to the disrespect shown the Law by disobedient Jews.

rightly calls this a blatant fiction,[27] and the comments in other places of the narrative reveal a truer picture of the pagan estimation of these martyrs. Antiochus counsels the brothers against raging with "the same madness as that of the old man who has just been tortured" (8:5), as the torturers counsel the fourth brother not to "act the madman with that same madness your brothers have shown" (10:13, translation mine). Speaking to the youngest brother, Antiochus states: "You see the result of your brothers' stupidity, for they died in torments because of their disobedience" (12:3). The pagan view of these martyrs is that they died on account of "madness" (μανία) and "foolishness" (ἀπόνοια) rather than the virtues of piety and courage. Their deaths were not a noble contest with sufferings, but rather the just (and therefore all the more shameful) punishment of the disobedient. Nevertheless, the author holds up the hope that such a course of action will be recognized as virtuous and honorable in the deepest sense by all humankind (1:11; 18:3) and that the alternative course of capitulation will be universally recognized as cowardly and impious.

By means of his skillful use of epideictic rhetoric, the author has set two possible courses within an evaluative framework. His praise of the one course aims at moving the auditors to emulation, to the desire to demonstrate in their own settings the same dedication to virtue and thus to achieve the rewards of an honorable remembrance in this world and an honorable reception in the next.[28] His censure of the alternative course seeks to distance them from the possibility of transgressing the Torah by presenting this as a course opposed to honor and virtue and as a course that violates God's honor and leads to the provocation of God's wrath.

Audience and Effect

To whom was the author addressing this piece of demonstrative oratory? While a full discussion of the date, destination, and situation would be both long and unnecessary,[29] a few remarks concerning the audience

27. Collins, *From Athens*, 190.

28. This is succinctly expressed in Townshend, "Fourth Book," 653: "Immortality is their reward in heaven, while they enjoy on earth the honour of being held the saviours of their country, which noble title [the author] would inscribe as their epitaph. His impassioned eulogy is intended to rouse the patriotic and religious feelings of his audience to the highest pitch and harden them to the point of following so glorious an example."

29. The arguments concerning the date of the piece cluster around two likely periods—the years before Caligula's self-deification and the calamities that entailed for Jews throughout the empire (cf. Hadas, *Maccabees*, 95–99; Townshend, "Fourth Book," 654; Bickermann, "Date of Fourth Maccabees") and the period between the Jewish Wars

may be permitted. Schürer seems to indicate that the author was writing to Gentiles,[30] and Bertram sees a mixed audience as the recipients of an apologetic work.[31] Collins appears to be correct, however, in noting that the work "might not persuade many gentiles,"[32] especially since it rests on the assumption that the Torah has its source in the Deity, an assumption not shared by many Gentiles (such as those who regarded Judaism as a *superstitio*). I would agree with Klauck that 4 Maccabees "ist nach innen gerichtete Apologetik,"[33] an "inner-directed apology" presented to Jews who have lost their certainty with regard to the Torah as the surest path to the exhibition and attainment of true honor. The situation of the audience—Diaspora Jews—may best be described as one of "profound tension."[34] Victor Tcherikover expresses this tension as a fluctuation

> between two mutually contradictory principles: between the ambition to assimilate arising from the Jew's desire to exist among strangers by his individual powers, and the adherence to tradition, induced in the struggle for existence by the need of support from the strong collective organization represented by the community.[35]

These Jews were faced with the tension between remaining faithful to the ancestral Law, which alienated them in many ways from Gentile society, and attaining a place of distinction, acceptance, and honor in Gentile society. For some, the stakes may have seemed nearly as high as for the Maccabean martyrs—not torture and death, to be sure, but palpable economic and social deprivation.

For the different needs of the individuals who make up such communities, 4 Maccabees promises to achieve different effects. For those Jews committed to Torah, the author presents material to reinforce that commitment and fuel the heart for the endurance of whatever form the tension with the larger society will take. For wavering or confused Jews, the author

---

under Trajan and Hadrian's persecution (cf. Breitenstein, *Beobachtungen*, 173–75). There is, however, no need to "posit a time of extreme crisis and threat for the Jews" as the life setting of this text (Anderson, "Maccabees, Books of," 453). It appears to be safer and more useful to eschew the attempts to locate the book and its intended effects too narrowly and seek rather to examine how the book might have effect a more generalized audience.

30. Schürer, *History*, 590.

31. Bertram, "Παιδεύω," 612.

32. Collins, *From Athens*, 190.

33. Klauck, *4 Makkabäerbuch*, 665.

34. Redditt, "Concept of *Nomos*," 264.

35. Tcherikover, *Hellenistic Civilization*, 346.

presents material to exhort them to take a stand for the Torah and Torah-centered piety, calling them back to commitment to Jewish particularism as the means of achieving highest honor and reputation.[36] For Jews feeling the threat and loss especially deeply, the author provides examples to fuel endurance and courage to face the contest. Claims such as that found in 2:23 ("one who lives subject to [the law] will rule over a kingdom that is temperate, just, good, and courageous") and many like it will be heard in different ways by different hearers: the author's choice of epideictic oratory as the means to achieve his end allows for this ambiguity, such that the same piece may encourage the committed and challenge the wavering.

Honor, Shame, and the Embedded Argument of 4 Maccabees

Fourth Maccabees appears to address people faced with real alternatives, namely whether to remain faithful to God by means of Torah-obedience whatever the consequences or to seek compromises with Greco-Roman society that will facilitate greater acceptance and advancement within the framework of Hellenistic society. Attention to the language of honor and shame in this document has already provided a picture of the author's aim and strategy. Further attention to the details of what is presented as honorable and dishonorable action, moreover, leads to a clearer picture of the issues at stake for the author and his addressees. Here the consideration of the two aspects of one's sense of honor—that is, one's desire to attain honor and one's sensitivity to honor others properly—comes to the fore.

The martyrs, we have seen, are exemplars of honor in that they exemplify the cardinal virtues (1:7–10; 5:23–24; 15:10) and, through their actions, have attained an honorable remembrance (7:9; 18:3).[37] These are depicted as choosing honor above advantage (without honor) and compulsion. The highest compulsion, their spokesperson Eleazar declares, is obedience to the law (5:16), which translates roughly into piety or reverence for God (cf. θεοσέβεια, 7:22). The martyrs are highly sensitive to God's honor, even as Apollonius and Jason were insensitive to God's honor and provoked God's wrath (4:7–12; 4:21). The concern for showing respect for God's law guides their choices (5:19–21, 27–28; 9:4; 13:13) and is superior to the concern

36. cf. Hadas, 4 Maccabees, 133: the author's goal is "to furnish guidance to readers perplexed by real alternatives."

37. One may recall the division of the Honorable into the "Right" and the "Praiseworthy" in the Rhetorica ad Herennium (3.2.3–3.4.7).

for honoring the demands of Antiochus where these hinder observance of God's law (4:24, 26; 5:10).

This obedience to God is linked with the martyrs' experience of God as Benefactor and their hope for the continued experience of God's benefits. The mother urges her sons on to death in obedience to God's law based on God's beneficence: "Remember that it is through God that you have had a share in the world and have enjoyed life, and therefore you ought to endure any suffering for the sake of God" (16:18–19; cf. 13:13). The martyrs hope thus to gain future benefits from their Benefactor, both for the nation in the form of deliverance from political oppression (6:27–28) and for themselves as individuals in the form of eternal life in the presence of God (7:19; 9:8; 15:2–3, 13; 16:25; 17:18–19). As honorable clients, therefore, they set their hope in this Benefactor (16:25; 17:4) and demonstrate πίστις with regard to God (7:19; 15:24; 16:21–22; 17:2, 3). This "faith" has been variously interpreted,[38] but seems to retain its sense of "firmness" (hence, "reliability") or "loyalty" in 4 Maccabees. Faith, then, expresses the proper stance of a client toward a benefactor, the proper return for benefits conferred.

This gives particular moment to Antiochus' offers in 8:5–7, promising the brothers a place of honor in Hellenic society: "I encourage you, after yielding to me, to enjoy my friendship (παρακαλῶ συνείξαντάς μοι τῆς ἐμῆς ἀπολαύειν φιλίας)" (8:5), the king's "friend" being an influential position. He proposes to replace God, in effect, as their patron: "I can be a benefactor to those who obey me (δυναίμην . . . εὐεργετεῖν τοὺς εὐπειθοῦντάς μοι)" (8:6). Finally, he promises to raise them to positions of authority (ἀρχαί, 8:7). In 12:5 he repeats the promise of secular honors to the last surviving brother. The brothers refuse the offered relationship, holding to their relationship with God. Antiochus' promise (benefaction) can only effect temporary safety (15:3) and advancement; God's promise (benefaction) of eternal life is infinitely to be preferred (15:2). Their willingness to provoke Antiochus (who regards them thence forward as ingrates as well as disobedient, 9:10) is based on their proper evaluation of the danger of God's outraged virtue as the greater threat (13:14–15; cf. Matt 10:28). The ultimate tribunal is the

---

38. Cf. Townshend, "Fourth Book," 664: "The word 'faith' also occurs, in a distinctively religious sense . . . In this religious sense πίστις belongs not to Stoic, nor even to Greek thought, but to that devotional side of the Hebrew mind which was to be more fully expressed in Christianity. Here, however, as Maldwyn Hughes says, 'It is rather trust in an external Providence than an inner dependence arising from an inward relationship. Faith is not a renewing and life-giving power, but confidence in the providential order.'" Such a triumphalist understanding of "faith," however, obscures its true nature as a most admirable quality shown by both Jews and Christians towards God (cf. Hebrews 11).

court of God's judgement. This conviction enables them to disregard the verdicts of the lower court.

What, then, is shameful in 4 Maccabees? The author does not consider for a moment that the tortures and physical outrages to the martyr's bodies adversely affect their honor in any way. While such treatment is thought to include the destruction of a person's honor and place in society, for the martyrs it is a sign of honor. The author solves this problem philosophically: the tortures are a test of virtue (10:10; 11:2, 12, 20);[39] the treatment is undeserved and therefore not an insult or injury (9:15, 31; 10:10; 11:2; 12:11);[40] the despising of injuries is the sign of a wise and courageous person (1:9; 5:27; 6:9; 9:6; 13:1; 14:1, 11). Even if the body is stripped (exposed, shamed) or made to fall, the martyr remains clothed with virtue and his or her mind unconquered (6:2, 7).[41] The author also solves this problem metaphorically through the use of "contest" imagery, by which he turns ignominious death into a victory over a foreign invader (5:10; 7:3; 9:30; 11:20; 12:14; 15:29; 16:16; 17:11–16).[42]

Neither shameful treatment at the hands of Gentiles nor the failure to attain honor in Gentile society counts as shameful for the author, but rather the violation of piety and proper reverence for God. To those asking the question, "should we seek to acquire honor by extending our patron/client networks into the Gentile population at the expense of absolute obedience to the Torah?" the author holds up the negative examples of Simon and Jason and displays the martyrs' virtuous refusal to take such a course. In the voices of the martyrs, the author engages in a critique of the Greco-Roman society which does not make a place for Torah-observant Jews, but rather which lives itself contrary to the law of God and despises Jews for living by this law. Antiochus' punishment of the brothers shows his own ignorance of what is just and what is honorable: "For what act of ours are you destroying

39. Cf. Seneca, *Constant.*. 9.3: the wise person "counts even injury profitable, for through it he finds a means of putting himself to the proof and makes trial of his virtue."

40. cf. Seneca, *Constant.*16.3: "Both [Stoics and Epicureans] urge you to scorn injuries and, what I may call the shadows and suggestions of injuries, insults. And one does not need to be a wise man to despise these, but merely a man of sense—one who can say to himself: 'Do I, or do I not, deserve that these things befall me? If I do deserve them, there is no insult—it is justice; if I do not deserve them, he who does the injustice is the one to blush.'"

41. Cf. Plato, *Gorg*, 523–26. Socrates recounts the tale of the divinely appointed judgement of people at their deaths. Judging them while alive and clothed led to bad judgements, so they are now judged after death and naked. The goodness of the soul, not how the body fared in life, is what is judged and what determines eternal destiny.

42. Cf. Pfitzner, *Paul and the Agon Motif*, 23–48, for the use of this imagery in Greco-Roman and Hellenistic Jewish literature.

us in this way? Is it because we revere the creator of all things and live according to his virtuous law? But these deeds deserve honors, not tortures" (11:4–6). From the perspective of the court of God, Antiochus himself may be evaluated as shameless, lacking the essential element of honor which regards the honor due God and other human beings:

> You profane tyrant, most impious of all the wicked, since you have received good things and also your kingdom from God, were you not ashamed (οὐκ ἠδέσθης) to murder his servants and torture on the wheel those who practice religion? . . . As a man, were you not ashamed (οὐκ ἠδέσθης), you most savage beast, to cut out the tongues of men who have feelings like yours and are made of the same elements as you, and to maltreat and torture them in this way? (12:11–13)

Antiochus is thus censured as a dishonorable client. He does not acknowledge God's benefits and even sets himself against God's faithful clients. He also lacks that important element of αἰδώς which regards the honor of other human beings within the context of reverent fear of God. He is thus possessed of a ὑπερήφανος λογισμός ("arrogant reason," 9:30) rather than a εὐσεβὴς λογισμός, and so remains alienated from the attainment of virtue and honor.[43]

Conclusion: The Purpose and Message of 4 Maccabees for Jews in the Diaspora

The author's demonstration seeks to show that the sort of reason that achieves the Greek ideal of virtue is "devout reason," which is reason choosing wisdom as taught in God's law, the Jewish Torah. Attainment of virtue (honor) and an honorable remembrance depends on setting one's mind on following the training gained through obedience to the Torah. 4 Maccabees is especially concerned to present a model of honorable and praiseworthy response to the demands and tensions of the encounter with the Greco-Roman world. The author holds up the Jewish martyrs as the supreme examples of honorable choices, commitments, and actions. This will challenge those listeners who are wavering in their commitment to Judaism as a result of the encounter with Greco-Roman society.

---

43. He is thus a foil to David, as presented in 3:15–16. David refuses to drink the water stolen from the enemy camp at the jeopardy of two human lives. To cross the line and satisfy one's own desires with such disregard for other human beings' worth would be to act arrogantly in God's sight. He therefore reverently offers it as a drink offering. See chapter 4 below.

Through his presentation of deliberative considerations within the evaluative framework of epideictic oratory, the author seeks to convince the auditors that honoring God and remaining firm in their commitment (showing faith) toward God is the only reasonable and honorable course. They would, in this way, continue to know and experience God as their Benefactor. Dishonoring God for the sake of acceptance by and assimilation into Greek culture and release from tension (whether the physical tension of the rack or the social tension of identification with a minority group and a suspect people) and becoming clients of the dominant culture leads to the experience of God as avenger of God's outraged honor and violated beneficence (cf. God's response to Jason, 4:21).

Furthermore, the need exists to educate the inhabitants of the Greco-Roman world in the matters of true honor and piety by remaining firm in witness to God and devotion to God's educative Law. Antiochus embodies the extremes of Gentile error. Non-Jews need to learn true respect for God as creator and benefactor (12:11)—that is, instruction in piety; they need to learn true respect for other human beings as God's clients (12:13, cf. 3:15–16); they need to learn about the honorable and the just from the true perspective of God's court of reputation and God's standards of virtue and the praiseworthy (11:6).

Like the martyrs, the audience, too, is involved in the noble contest (16:16), striving to exhibit virtue and fidelity to God, striving with the other cultures of the world to bear witness to them (thus relating with them salvifically), learning from them (as exhibited by the author's use of Greek ideals and modes of argument), but not being beaten by them through assimilation. While the exact situation of the audience remains a mystery, the message of 4 Maccabees remains constant: as epideictic rhetoric it takes on a more timeless quality that speaks in different ways to different situations (as the different situations of each member of the audience constitute distinctive rhetorical situations, inviting the same text to work in different ways). Its diagnosis of Gentile culture as standing in need of learning to enact respect for other human beings out of a reverent fear for God is a message no less relevant today than in the first century.

3

Fourth Maccabees as Acculturated
Resistance Literature

The past three decades have witnessed an explosion of studies in biblical criticism and criticism of the history of interpretation that are generally held together under the rubric of "postcolonial studies" or "postcolonial criticism." These have been written largely, though by no means exclusively, by biblical scholars who belong to a minority group within a Western culture or who live in a country not considered part of the dominant culture of the "Western world," such as Asia, Africa, or Latin America. That it is a "hermeneutic" rather than another exegetical "method" is clear from the ways in which some of its most noted practitioners describe the approach. Postcolonial interpretation is "a mental attitude rather than a method, more a subversive stance towards the dominant knowledge than a school of thought."[1] It is an "optic," a lens through which to take a new look at Scripture and the way it has been, and can be, interpreted and used in real-life political and social situations.[2]

This lens has most frequently been employed to examine the use of the Bible and its interpretation as a means of advancing Eurocentric agendas and legitimating the hegemony of Western Europe and its partners, both in situations of formal imperialism and in the lingering aftermath of "empire."[3] The "mental attitude" has also contributed significantly to the reversal of the devaluation of indigenous cultures that accompanies imperialism and to the construction of an "alternative hermeneutics" that

1. Sugirtharajah, "Postcolonial Exploration," 93.

2. Fernando Segovia, "Biblical Criticism," 52.

3. On the former, see, for example, Rasiah Sugirtharajah's exploration of the use of the Bible as a symbol of Europeans bringing culture, knowledge, and morality to the "savages" (Sugirtharajah, "Biblical Studies," 14–15); on the latter, see Segovia, "Biblical Criticism," 51 n.3.

honors the culture, experience, and reading and interpretative strategies of non-Western peoples.[4]

While many practitioners focus the postcolonial lens on the analysis of how Scripture has been read and interpreted in particular situations, and on the analysis of particular readers of Scripture, I do not want to lose sight of the first level of analysis which, according to Fernando Segovia, postcolonial interpretation invites, namely the analysis of imperialism or colonialism in the Jewish and Christian Scriptures (and related literature) themselves.[5] How does the author of the text depict "empire"? How does the author present the "colonized" peoples? Does the author speak from the *margins* or from the *center* of power? Does the author speak *on behalf of* empire, legitimating it or advancing its interests (e.g., in the Old Testament conquest and monarchical narratives), or does the author speak *against* empire, creating spaces for resistance and for the affirmation of alternative interests (e.g., in the Book of Revelation)?

This study holds 4 Maccabees beneath this lens and asks these questions of its author, who appears at first blush to be so fully accommodated to the dominant culture that he cannot think about his own heritage apart from the master's categories, but on closer inspection reveals himself to be an author of resistance literature, subjecting empire to trenchant critique, opposing the devaluing of the culture and way of life of the colonized *ethnos*, and promoting a model for effective resistance in his narration of the victory of the nine martyrs over the foreign king for widespread imitation among his audience.

In a Greek City of a Roman Empire: The Author in His Setting

The author and addressees share the experience of Roman imperialism in the midst of a region long exposed to Greek cultural imperialism. They are members of an *ethnos* that had been subjected to the control of one empire or another for almost seven centuries.[6] Even the period of so-called political independence enjoyed by the Hasmonean dynasty was an independence granted and maintained through negotiation with imperial

---

4. Sugirtharajah, "Biblical Studies," 16.

5. Segovia, "Biblical Criticism," 57–63.

6. For the purposes of this study, the exact determination of date is not essential: all positions currently advocated in scholarship fall within the period of the early Principate, between Augustus and Hadrian. See deSilva, *4 Maccabees: Introduction and Commentary*, xiv–xvii for a discussion of date.

powers, and marked by the ongoing experience of cultural imperialism as Hellenization continued throughout Judea and the Eastern Mediterranean as a whole.[7] The formal arrangements of Roman imperialism overlaid this older and thoroughly pervasive cultural imperialism throughout the region from which this text originates.[8]

The author presents himself as a person who is fully competent to speak in a Greek city under Roman domination—indeed, as we have seen in chapter 1 above, as a person who has been quite fully "Hellenized." He has been thoroughly schooled, but no co-opted. He does not go the way of a Tiberius Julius Alexander or a Dositheus (3 Macc 1:3). Rather, like Philo, he uses his literary skill, facility in Greek rhetoric, and familiarity with ethical philosophy to promote continued adherence to the distinctive way of life practiced by the Jews for centuries before the rise of Hellenism. The author's "philosophy" remains the way of life and the values taught by the Torah, and his point of reference is always the Jewish Scriptures. The language and rhetorical forms of the dominant culture are utilized to make a place at the table for the way of life of the subjugated culture, and to defend the value of the colonized culture's historic and distinctive way of life. The author has mastered the master's tools, and uses them expertly to claim the right to speak (he speaks on a par with the spokespersons of the dominant culture), to cast doubt upon the public image of "empire," and to empower his Jewish audience to reject the dominant culture's devaluation of their way of life, proclaiming it instead by word and example as a way of life on a par with, even superior to, the finest philosophies embraced by members of the dominant culture.

The Character of Empire in 4 Maccabees

Imperialism takes on flesh in 4 Maccabees in the person of Antiochus IV, whom the author presents from the very outset as a "tyrant" imposing

7. See Hengel, *Judaism and Hellenism*, on the degree to which Greek culture reshaped Judea during the period of Greek imperialism, and Hengel, *Jews, Greeks, and Barbarians*, for the ongoing experience of cultural imperialism during the early Roman period.

8. Once again, determining the precise location within the Roman Empire would not greatly enhance the analysis of the text from a postcolonial perspective. To date, van Henten ("Jewish Epitaph") has advanced the most cogent arguments for a provenance between Asia Minor and Syrian Antioch, confirming (and somewhat widening) the scholarly consensus that looks to this region (particularly Antioch) as the most likely provenance. See deSilva, *4 Maccabees: Introduction and Commentary*, xvii–xx for a survey of research on this question.

"tyranny" upon the Judean people (1:11). This is an appropriate announcement of a major constellation of topics by means of which the legitimacy of Seleucid imperialism—and, by extension, all Gentile imperialist intrusions into the life of the Jewish *ethnos*—would be weighed in the balance and found wanting. The author indulges in biting irony as he labels Antiochus "the tyrant of the Hellenes" (ὁ . . . Ἑλλήνων τύραννος, 18:20).[9] The Greeks had been the ones to pride themselves on nurturing a political environment in which freedom and openness of speech was valued. Now, however, they find themselves in the opposite role of the tyrant and bearer of tyranny rather than "democracy" into other lands.[10]

Bernard Heininger has demonstrated the ways in which the author paints Antiochus as the stereotypical tyrant.[11] The portrait drawn by Lucian of Samosata of the tyrant Megapenthes (*Tyr.* 26) could be applied with only the slightest modification to Antiochus in 4 Maccabees. Antiochus uses his position to fill his coffers, taking bribes from Jason (as his brother Seleucus had tried to enrich himself by raiding the Temple). He displays savagery in his invention of tortures (4 Macc 10:16; 11:23; 18:20), appearing throughout as the ringmaster in the arena where the martyrs are brutalized.[12] He indulges in the corruption of boys, here at least in the sense of trying to lure the seven away from piety and justice, renouncing their ancestral way of life (4 Macc 8:12–14), the way of life so carefully instilled in them by their parents (cf. 4 Macc 18:10–19).

Antiochus exudes pride and arrogance (4 Macc 4:15; 9:30; 12:11–14), and the author invites us to consider Antiochus as the embodiment of "the arrogant logic of tyranny" (9:30). Arrogance involves an inflated sense of one's worth and what is due oneself, enacted at the expense of the honor due others. The author suggests, by his choice of Antiochus as the manifestation of imperialism, that arrogance lies at the heart of imperialistic intrusions *tout court*.

9. Translations of 4 Maccabees throughout this chapter are my own unless otherwise noted.

10. Tyranny was, to be sure, far from unknown in classical Greece, but the fall of the Thirty Tyrants and the development of Athenian democracy was seen to usher in a far more enlightened constitutional government. Aristotle would discuss tyranny as a form of government, though always inferior to a legitimate kingship or a democracy (*Pol.* 5.11 1313a24–1315b10). The best he could hold out for the tyrant was to try to conduct himself more like a king and in ways that set limits and checks on his power so as to diminish the potential for evil (*Pol.* 5.11.1 1313a18–33). Antiochus will behave in many of the ways that Aristotle identifies as inferior in the tyrant.

11. Heininger, "Der böse Antiochus," 50–53. On tyranny in Greece, see Berve, *Die Tyrannis*.

12. For classical references to these traits of tyrants, see chapter 1 above (n. 25).

How the "arrogant logic of tyranny" works can first be seen in the author's reconstruction of the logical argument presented by Antiochus to Eleazar as a case for leaving behind the way of life of the subjugated culture and assimilating to the dominant culture. The arrogance here is particularly visible in the tyrant's failure to sufficiently exercise himself to understand the "reasonableness" of the way of life practiced by a subjugated culture, the author of 4 Maccabees having collected an impressive array of topics and models familiar to dominant cultural discourse by means of which Greeks and Romans *could* readily come to such an understanding. Rather, the arrogant voice of imperialism moves too quickly to the response of diminishing the value of the indigenous way of life, a response that makes it easier for the imperialist powers to impose changes upon that way of life, whether minimal or radical.

Thus Antiochus regards following "the religious observances of the Jews" to be contrary to "exercising philosophical reasoning" (φιλοσοφεῖν, 5:7); it is, instead, a "foolish philosophy" (τῆς φλυάρου φιλοσοφίας, 5:11) and "nonsense" (τὸν λῆρον, 5:11) that leads a person into "senseless" and "unjust" behaviors (ἀνόητον . . . καὶ ἄδικον, 5:9). Ultimately, he will define it as "stupidity" or "madness" as he advises the seven brothers "not to rave with the same madness" as had Eleazar (μὴ μανῆναι τὴν αὐτὴν . . . μανίαν, 8:5) and, later, advises the fourth brother not to cling to his elder siblings' folly (μὴ μανῆς . . . τὴν αὐτὴν μανίαν, 10:13). Finally, he will point out to the last surviving brother the result of his siblings' "foolishness" (ἀπονοίας, 12:3). Being socialized into the subjugated culture represents, for him, a mental sleep from which Antiochus intends to rouse the aged Eleazar ("will you not awaken?" οὐκ ἐξυπνώσεις; 5:11).

We are not told how old Antiochus is, but one would assume him to be considerably younger than Eleazar, to whose old age and gray hairs Antiochus points as a sign that Eleazar ought to know better, after so much life experience, than to live like a Jew (5:7), thus incidentally belying Antiochus's early claim that he, indeed, "had respect" for the age of this Jew. This image of the younger Antiochus presuming to stand in judgment over the wisdom of the older Eleazar and trying to teach him a "better way" here at the twilight of his life well exemplifies the "arrogant logic of tyranny," according to which the party with the greater military and political power acquires on that basis the right to pronounce judgment on the value of other ways of life—particularly when the adherents of those ways have had considerably longer to test and examine the meaningfulness of the same.

The foundational premise of the "arrogant logic of tyranny" (9:30) is the argument from inflicting pain. At the same time that Antiochus offers rational arguments in support of capitulation, he brings out his guards and the instruments of coercion to remind the seven brothers—as Antiochus explicitly intends (8:12–14)—that the ultimate expression of arrogance by imperialism is that it will make the subject people adopt a "better way of life" whether or not they wish. According to this "arrogant logic of tyranny" (as explicated by the partisans of empire in 6:12–15), the colonized bring upon themselves the pains and degradations inflicted by the dominant culture's organs of repression. "Why are you destroying yourself irrationally (ἀλογίστως)?" they ask Eleazar (6:14), as if the aged priest is the one responsible for the mistreatment and ruin of his body, and as if he has no good reason for the losses he is incurring. The colonizing power does not question its responsibility or its correctness in proceeding as it does. The tyrant's actions are shielded by an unquestionable and irresistible "necessity" (5:13; 8:14), an immunity to moral self-examination. This becomes an important role for the seven brothers in their witness, as they summon the tyrant to this self-examination by their indictments of him (see especially 9:15; 10:10; 11:4–6; 12:11–14).

Another facet of the author's critique of the arrogance of imperialism emerges in the author's depiction of the way Antiochus tries to act generously toward the colonized. To Antiochus, it seems "beneficial" indeed for the colonized to submit to the way of life being imposed upon them (5:11b–12). But in inviting Eleazar to "prostrate yourself before my philanthropic comfort" (5:13), he calls for subjugation in a way that is foreign to true generosity. He is ugly—κακός—even when trying to act like a patron! When Antiochus will attempt again in 8:7 to offer his personal patronage, his "generosity" has a specific price—the brothers' renunciation of their identity as members of a different culture whose way of life merited respect and ongoing maintenance on a par with the culture of the Greeks. Greco-Roman ethicists distinguished sharply between the noble benefactor, who gave on the basis of positive regard for the beneficiaries out of a desire to help them for their own sake and not for oneself, and the ignoble "benefactor" who used patronage to manipulate.[13] Antiochus embodies empire acting in the latter category, using the offer of patronage as a bargaining chip by means of which to get what he wants out of the brothers, namely a public renunciation of Judaism that will counteract Eleazar's devastating example (8:7–8).

The "arrogant logic of tyranny" was not a matter merely of historical interest for the author and his audience. Adherents of the Jewish way of life faced ongoing disdain from the representatives of the dominant culture

13. Aristotle, *Rhet.* 2.7.5; Seneca, *Ben.* 1.2.3; 3.15.4; 4.49.3; see deSilva, *Honor, Patronage*, 106–109.

throughout the Roman period.[14] The author's contemporaries could indeed have enjoyed considerably less trouble and distress in their existence as a minority culture in the Greco-Roman world if they had relaxed those observances that drew the charges of atheism and misanthropy, fueling anti-Jewish slander and suspicion.[15] Implicit in the author's challenge to the audience to embody the same devotion to the Torah embodied in the martyrs, and in the crafting of their noble example for imitation, is a depiction of the audience as embroiled also in a struggle to resist "the arrogant logic of tyranny." The spokespersons of the dominant culture, like Antiochus, do not take sufficient trouble to understand the inner logic and "reasonableness" of the way of life they so readily ridicule and marginalize. Members of the dominant culture similarly exert pressure on the minority culture's commitment to their ancestral laws and heritage, using promises of favor to lure and coercive measures (from steady shaming to the occasional anti-Jewish pogrom) to goad the colonized to renounce their way of life and to act against their own conscience, formed in line with the norms and values of the subjugated culture.[16]

The author's depiction of Antiochus and his soldiers—the most visible means by which empire imposes its will—calls into question the legitimacy of empire from another important angle, and that is empire's ability to live up to its own press. As missionaries of civilization among the barbarians and savages (8:8), one would expect the Greco-Syrian king and his party to embody the civility that the Greek dominant culture vaunted as its legitimate claim to rule over others. Greek ethical philosophers claimed that self-mastery was prerequisite to exercising just and virtuous rule over subjects. Plato wrote that a good king must be "temperate and master of himself, and ruler of his own pleasures and passions" (*Gorgias* 491D).[17] Centuries later, Dio Chrysostom would write that "if a person is not competent to govern a single man . . . and if, again, he cannot guide a single soul, and that his own, how could he be king . . . over unnumbered thousands scattered everywhere?" (*Or.* 62.1; see also Xenophon, *Oeconomicus* 21.12). The

14. See, for example, Tacitus, *Hist.* 5.4.3; Juvenal, *Sat.* 14.98–99; Josephus, *Ap.* 2.137; Plutarch, *Superst.* 8 (*Mor.* 169C) for near-contemporary witnesses to Greco-Roman disdain for the Jewish way of life.

15. Dio Cassius, *Roman History* 67.14.2; Diodorus Siculus, *Bib. Hist.* 34.1–4; 40.3.4; Tacitus, *Hist.* 5.5; Josephus, *Ap.* 2.121, 258; 3 Macc 3:3–7.

16. This is particularly prominent in Eleazar's contest (4 Macc 5:27, 38; note the use of τυραννικόν and τυραννήσεις in those verses). Aristotle (*Eth. Nic.* 3.1.4 1110a5–9) speaks of physical force as the means by which tyrants typically make people act against their conscience.

17. In this regard, Moses the lawgiver and ruler acquits himself admirably, controlling his anger rather than giving it license (2:16–18).

author consistently presents Antiochus as a ruler who cannot rule himself, and thus lodges a major criticism against the Greco-Syrian king's rule.[18] This emerges in several ways.

First, when condensing the material from his source (2 Maccabees 4:18–6:17), the author removes Antiochus's primary defense for his assault on Jerusalem and violent suppression of the population. Here he is no longer responding to armed rebellion, as in 2 Maccabees 5:5, 11, but merely reacting heatedly against the population's expression of joy at the rumor that the monarch had died in battle. Second, after the tyrant was publicly defeated by Eleazar (that is, after all of his coercive measures could not break a geriatric!), Antiochus moves forward "exceedingly full of passion" (σφόδρα περιπαθῶς, 8:2). The tyrant's raging emotions are once again the impetus for his acts of oppression and brutality against the indigenous population of Jerusalem. That the passions, particularly those of anger, drive Antiochus is underscored yet again in 9:10–11. While the extravagant tortures will give the subjugated people an opportunity to demonstrate their self-mastery, "the torture itself, characterized by excess, is occasioned by the inability of Antiochus to control his own passions, especially his rage."[19] Even though the Judeans cannot be compelled by all his tortures to act contrary to their consciences, their brave refusal to betray their native way of life *does* have the power to compel Antiochus: "if by disobedience you arouse my anger, you will compel me (ἀναγκάσετέ με) to destroy each and every one of you" (8:9). Antiochus's subordinates are also driven by their passions in 10:5, as their experience of being "enraged" spurs them on to more acts of brutality,[20] to the point that they lose their human(e)ness and are transformed into vicious animals by their own donning of, and employment of, the instruments of torture (e.g., becoming "leopard-like beasts" in 9:28, as they put on their clawed gauntlets).

According to the dominant culture's ideology, the barbarians—the colonized—constituted a class of people who were driven by their passions and therefore inferior.[21] In a striking reversal, the author shows the representatives of imperialism to be, in fact, the "barbarians," while the colonized prove themselves to be more "Greek" than the Greco-Syrian king, who earns the epithets ὠμόφρων ("crude-minded," "savage-minded," *"uncivilized,"* 9:15), ὠμότατε τύραννε ("most uncivilized tyrant," 9:30), and, ultimately, θηριωδέστατε ("most beast-like," 12:13). It is the tyrant's bodyguard who

18. Thus, rightly, Moore and Anderson, "Taking It Like a Man," 253–54.
19. Moore and Anderson, "Taking It Like a Man," 254.
20. Moore and Anderson, "Taking It Like a Man," 254.
21. Hall, *Inventing the Barbarian*, 80–84, 124–33.

embody barbarism, scalping the third brother like Scythians (ἀπεσκύθιζον, 10:7),[22] while the Judean enacts the Greek ideal of "frank speech" (τὴν παρρησίαν, 10:5) that so repels the "Greek" imperialists.

If "Hellenizing" means "becoming like the Greek imperialists" (8:8), the author surely makes the way of life that produces an Antiochus or the kind of lackeys that one finds around him unattractive indeed. The distance the author creates between the Greek ideals of free speech, self-mastery, and the like and the depiction of the representatives of Greek culture is an important feature of his ideological critique of empire, further enhancing his attempt to demonstrate that to remain true to the Torah is, in fact, *also* to "be Greek" in the best sense, that of the Greek philosophers and their lofty ideals of morality.

The "Benefits" of Empire in 4 Maccabees

The author of 4 Maccabees begins his "narrative demonstration" (τὴν ἀπόδειξιν τῆς ἱστορίας, 3:19) of the philosophical thesis with a story about the escalating intrusion of the Seleucid imperial presence in Judea. Most noteworthy in this regard is his picture of Jerusalem as a city that exhibited Greek civic virtues *before* the attempts to Hellenize arose from within (i.e., before its transformation into a Greek city). Under the high priest Onias, Jerusalem enjoyed profound "harmony" (ὁμόνοιαν, 3:21) as a result of the lawful conduct (εὐνομίαν, 3:20) of its citizens. ὁμόνοια and εὐνομία are highly prized civic virtues in classical and Hellenistic literature. Greek politicians aimed to nurture a harmonious state, governed by just laws,[23] which was the context for the enjoyment of peace (εἰρήνη, 3:20).[24] The transformation of Jerusalem into a Greek city, however, overthrows the noble state of peace, concord, and compliance with the rule of law in that city. Antiochus, in fact, acts most tyrannically in his attempts to destroy the εὐνομία of the Judeans (4:24), the εὐνομία that Eleazar embodies (7:9) and that the martyrs restored among the people by their resistance unto death (18:4).

The author thus creates a picture wherein the "barbarians" living in accordance with their "barbaric" Law are the ones who fulfill the political virtues lauded by the "civilized" dominant culture. On the other hand,

---

22. Herodotus, *Hist.* 4.64.3, documents the practice. On the proverbial barbarism of the Scythians, see 2 Macc 4:47; 3 Macc 7:5; van Henten, *Maccabean Martyrs*, 109.

23. van Henten, *Maccabean Martyrs*, 259, referring to Aristotle, *Nic. Eth.* 3.5 1112b; *Eud. Eth.* 1.5 1216b; see further Adkins, *Moral Values*, 46–57

24. See Josephus, *A.J.* 7.341; Philo, *Spec.* 3.131; cited in van Henten, *Martyrs*, 260–261.

the forces that push for assimilation to the dominant culture from within (Simon, then Jason) and without (Antiochus) embody the political vices despised by the "civilized" dominant culture, notably here political disturbance of "the general concord" by introducing "innovations" (3:21, looking ahead to Jason), factiousness (4:1, looking to Simon's personal rivalry against Onias; see Dio, *Or.* 48, denouncing the civic vice of factionalism), and, in the person of Antiochus, tyranny.

Those parties pushing for Hellenization and the erosion of commitment to indigenous customs and institutions would regard themselves as acting in the best interests of the colonized population.[25] The author's message, on the other hand, is one that would be echoed in many other colonized regions: "we were doing just fine before the advent of the empire; the intrusion of empire brought with it the deterioration of our civic life; the balance and harmony of our state was restored only after the expulsion of the imperial power, and that at great cost and loss."

What does empire bring, according to the author? The first extended picture of a Greco-Syrian ruler in 4 Maccabees is that of a temple robber, a sacrilegiously penetrating intrusion into the sacred spaces of the colonized (4:1–14). This is a particularly ugly act to which Seleucid monarchs are frequently driven by the machinations of imperialism (for example, the imposition of a heavy tribute upon the Seleucid Empire by the mightier Roman Empire, as well as the designs of the Seleucids upon their neighbors to the south, the Ptolemaic Empire) and which imperialism opens up for them all too easily (the raiding of the temple treasuries of peoples they have themselves subjugated).[26]

Imperialism introduces additional opportunities for instability and factionalism to disturb the peace of the *ethnos*. The accession of Antiochus IV affords Jason an opportunity to supplant his brother as high priest, forming an alliance with the new regime in order to advance the interests of his faction (4:15–18). Such collusion, especially as it adversely affects the stability and εὐνομία of the *ethnos*, is consistently held up for censure by this author. This leads, in turn, to the debasing of the institutions of the subjugated culture (here, the office of the high priesthood) for the sake of exploiting the resources of the colonized (here, increasing tribute). The high priestly office, formerly held "for life" (4:1), is now an office to be purchased (4:17–18).

It is probably no accident that at the center of the innovations stands the *gymnasium*, an institution for the (re-)education of the young. The

---

25. Hengel, *Jews, Greeks, and Barbarians*, 62–63.
26. See, further, deSilva, *4 Maccabees: Introduction and Commentary*, 114–119.

high priest Jason (who holds his power only by reason of collusion), with Antiochus's support, introduces the gymnasium (4:19–20) as a replacement for the kind of "home schooling" the brothers received from their parents (18:10–19). The gymnasium is the vehicle by means of which the young would be alienated from their ancestral heritage and socialized into the dominant culture. Rather than act like Simon, Jason, and other censurable, factious people who "introduce innovations against the general concord" (3:21) and use their authority to loosen and destroy commitment to Torah-observance, the author directs "administrators of the Law" to imitate Eleazar, reinforcing observance of the ancestral way of life with their own blood (7:8), working to ensure the community's commitment to the Torah through their own example.

The Author's Strategy for Effective Resistance

One of the final images of imperialism in 4 Maccabees is the image of defilement. Driving out the tyrant and his forces is equated with the "cleansing" or "purifying" of the homeland (17:21). Such an image crystallizes the author's interpretation of empire and understanding of the proper response to empire—resist its defilement and cleanse the land of its pollution. This cleansing moves from within as members of the subjugated culture resist empire's evaluations of their native way of life and the value of the colonized based on the degree of their assimilation or non-assimilation to the imperial culture, through resistance in the spoken word to resistance in action and example, lending credibility to the words of resistance that were spoken and actualizing the positive valuation of the native way of life in refusing to relinquish it, even at the cost of life itself.

Valuing as Resistance

In the narratives of the encounters between the representative of empire and the representative of the local culture, resistance begins as the colonized refuse to accept the dominant culture's marginalization and diminishment of the subjugated culture's way of life. Antiochus's first assault on Eleazar is not the physical assault on his body but the ideological assault on his honor insofar as he remains connected with an allegedly inferior way of life (5:6–13), as discussed in the previous section.

Eleazar, however, resists Antiochus's labeling of the Jewish way of life as "not in accordance with right reasoning" (οὐ μετὰ εὐλογιστίας, 5:22; Antiochus had used the word "senseless," ἀνόητον, 5:9). Indeed, he takes

Antiochus to task for his lack of insight: "You scoff at our philosophy as though living by it were irrational, but [or, better, "for," γάρ] it teaches us self-control, so that we master all pleasures and desires, and it also trains us in courage, . . . in justice, . . . and piety" (5:22–24, NRSV). It is often difficult to hear the tone of the written word, but if we give full weight to the γάρ in 5:23 as introducing a rationale for Antiochus's sneering at the Jewish philosophy, we cannot help but hear a mocking irony as Eleazar lists the "reasons" Antiochus might have for his disdain, as if saying, "Fine reasons you have for your prejudice against the Jewish way of life!"[27] The author joins Philo in focusing on the educative and ethically formative functions of Torah (see Philo, *Mos.* 2.215–16; *Prob.* 80), justifying the attention given to Torah in Jewish culture by the ethical fruits that it produces in the lives of Torah's devotees. Notably, these remain cardinal virtues lauded by the dominant culture itself (φρόνησις καὶ δικαιοσύνη καὶ ἀνδρεία καὶ σωφροσύνη, "prudence and justice and courage and moderation," 1:18; σωφροσύνην τε . . . καὶ ἀνδρείαν . . . καὶ δικαιοσύνην . . . καὶ εὐσέβειαν, "moderation . . . and courage . . . and justice . . . and piety," 5:23–24), though demonstrated never so well as by the faithful Jewish martyrs.

The author, on Eleazar's behalf, refuses to accept the status degradation implied in the treatment of his body by the dominant culture's representatives. The way bodies are treated signals the honor due, or not due, the person. Changes in status are thus marked by physical actions that signal the change, such as the crowning or anointing of a king or priest (signaling the elevation of dignity).[28] The tyrant's guards subject Eleazar's body to every manner of indignity precisely in order to eradicate Eleazar's honor, to press upon him and upon those who witness the spectacle the dominant culture's judgment that he is a person of no worth as long as he resists assimilation. The rough treatment as he is dragged off (6:1), the stripping of Eleazar's clothing (the garments both providing some indication of former status as well as hiding the shame of his nakedness; 6:2), and the beating down of his body into a prone position at the feet of his torturers and the kicking of the fallen Eleazar with the foot (6:7, 8) all serve this end.

The author, however, explicitly undermines these images of status degradation with an alternative interpretation that creates room for the maintenance of self-respect and affirmation of the honor of the representative of the indigenous culture. Honor is located not in the treatment of the body, but in the state of the inner person and his or her ability to maintain

27. Grimm, *Viertes Buch*, 322; Dupont-Sommer, *Quatrième Livre*, 108
28. See Malina and Neyrey, "Conflict in Luke-Acts."

the integrity of his or her life in the face of coercion.[29] Eleazar remained clothed with "the seemliness of piety" even after he was stripped (6:2) and he kept his reasoning faculty "erect and unbending" (ὀρθὸν εἶχεν καὶ ἀκλινῆ τὸν λογισμόν) even as his body fell to the ground under the blows (6:7).[30] Indeed, the collapse of his body becomes a testament to his inner integrity, the real location of self-respect and recognition of honor. Eleazar himself refuses to accept the judgment that his stubborn resistance, resulting in the ruin of his body and eventually loss of life, is an irrational course of action. Against the courtiers' ascription of irrational behavior to him (destroying himself ἀλογίστως, 6:14), he retorts that the truly irrational thing (ἀλόγιστον, 6:18) would be to betray himself and his lifelong convictions now at the tail end of life.

The author underscores this point in the hypothetical speeches crafted to display the reasoning in which the martyrs might have indulged but refused. The first of these prominently displays the seven brothers accepting and internalizing the dominant culture's assessment of their way of life. They accept that resistance is "senseless" (ἀνόητοι, 8:17; this is the same term applied by Antiochus to Eleazar's way of life and potential resistance in 5:9–10). They accept that their commitment to their ancestral way of life amounts indeed to "empty opinion" (τὴν κενοδοξίαν ταύτην, 8:19) and that their rationales for resistance constitute "empty reasonings" (βουλήμασιν κενοῖς, 8:18) and "thinking hollowly" (κενοδοξήσωμεν, 8:24; see Antiochus's use of κενοδοξῶν to describe the kind of reasoning that would lead Eleazar to cling to his native customs to his own hurt in 5:10). They accept the dominant culture's claim to cultural superiority as they denigrate any persistence in their own convictions as mere "arrogance" (ἀλαζονείαν, 8:19).[31] The author censures their (hypothetical) acceptance of the dominant culture's attempts to dismiss the indigenous culture's way of life as inferior and to label attempts to preserve that way of life as hollow arrogance as the coward's path. Allowing the dominant culture's negative assessments to infiltrate one's own valuing of one's native way of

29. The author's strategy is very much in line with Plato's *Gorg.* (523D–525A), where Socrates insists that God is concerned with the state of the soul rather than the state of the body, and in fact that the fine trappings of the latter often obscure the wretchedness of the former.

30. Once again the author recalls—this time even more directly—the language and ideals of Greco-Roman philosophical ethics. "To hold reason straight (correct, upright; τὸ ὀρθὸν ἔχειν τὸν λόγον)" is the goal of the true philosopher, according to Epictetus (*Diatr.* 4.8.12), even as it is for Eleazar.

31. The Roman governor Pliny—the representative of Roman imperialism—would similarly assess of the resistance of Bithynian Christians to his demand for offering sacrifice to the emperor and traditional gods as *contumacia* in *Ep.* 10.96.

life undermines resistance. It is the leaven that must be kept out lest it leaven the whole lump, the inner defilement that would eventually allow the defilement of imperialism to remain in the land.

In fact, however, the brothers' response is quite the opposite. The first brother will not internalize the ascription of dishonor—the label of "deviant criminal"—that the tyrant intends by the physical assaults. Like Seneca's sage, he examines himself, confirms that he has done nothing unjust, and declares his integrity (see Seneca, *Constant.* 16:3–4). With his protestations of innocence of any genuine crime, he makes his death a vocal witness to the injustice of Antiochus's imperialism. Similarly, the fifth brother confirms his own innocence of wrongdoing, affirming that his refusal of the king's tyrannical command to transgress the Torah attests rather to his virtue. He accuses Antiochus of failing to understand what is virtuous and what is truly vicious, thus miring himself in a life of injustice.[32] The fourth brother responds to the tyrant's assessment of his elder brothers' deaths as "madness" (μανίαν, 10:13) with an assertion that their passing was in fact "enviable" (μακάριον, 10:15), since they were privileged to have maintained their integrity to the end.

Within the narrative world created by the author, resistance to the dominant culture's ideological assaults leads, in the end, to forcing the imperialist powers to come to a new respect for the colonized, modifying their earlier assessments of the colonized as "senseless" (a process that begins subtly in 9:26). Rather, "Looking at their courage born of moral excellence and their endurance in the tortures, the tyrant Antiochus proclaimed the endurance of those people to his own soldiers for an example" (17:23), in awe of "their endurance" (αὐτῶν τὴν ὑπομονήν, 17:17).

Fourth Maccabees itself, of course, represents the author's own attempt to give his audience every reason to value their ancestral way of life and, therefore, to continue to resist the dominant culture's representatives' ongoing assaults on the value of the same.[33] Promoting the value of the Jewish way of life in terms of Greek value structures and patterning the Jewish heroes after Greek champions of freedom—even if this never makes an impact on the dominant culture—will effectively insulate the audience further against those ideological assaults as their native way of life is seen to nurture the

32. See Plato, *Gorg.* 472C; 477B; Dio Chrysostom, *Or.* 14.18; LXX Prov 17:15, 26. In this regard, the confrontation between the fifth brother and Antiochus resembles that between Haemon and Creon in Sophocles, *Ant.* 692–699.

33. Van Henten, "The Martyrs as Heroes," 317; van Henten, "Jewish Epitaph," 69; deSilva, *4 Maccabees: Introduction and Commentary*, 26–27; deSilva, *4 Maccabees*, 43–46, 74, 76–97, 105–11.

dominant culture's loftiest ideals. If the Greeks fail to recognize this, it is a judgment upon them, not the Jews.

Thus, training in Torah is to be valued as a most suitable παιδεία, productive of the virtues prized by the dominant culture (e.g., 1:17–18; 5:22–24; this is thematic throughout the text).[34] The specific regulations of Torah outline a form of ἄσκησις comparable to that which was practiced by the Spartans or prescribed by Epictetus and Galen for the mastery of particular vices or weaknesses of character (1:31–2:14).[35] Aristotle's characterization of the young (*Rh.* 2.12) provides a helpful background. The young are unable, by nature, to control their urges toward pleasure, especially sexual pleasure (*Rh.* 2.12.3). They are "carried away by impulse and inferior to their passion" (*Rh.* 2.12.5). For the Jewish youths, then, to display a mature and fully formed ethical character, such that they can master the passions, is an astounding achievement, and speaks to the superiority of the education, the παιδεία, that Torah provides.

The value of Torah is seen in its fruits, namely the exhibition of καλοκἀγαθία (1:10; 3:17–18; 11:22; 13:25; 15:9) and ἀρετή (1:8, 10; 7:21–22; 9:8, 18, 31; 10:10; 11:2; 12:14; 13:24, 27; 17:12, 25), terms that embody the Greek ideal of excellence in character formation and moral achievement, by those trained by Torah. Indeed, it is notably in their *resistance* to cultural imperialism that the heroes of 4 Maccabees display the highest Greek values (καλοκἀγαθία; see 15:9–10). The formative experiences of Torah's παιδεία give the observant Jew the potential to match the Greek philosophical ideal of the "sage" (see discussion of the author's deployment of these topics in chapter 1 above), in whom the ethical ideal of mastery of the passions is most securely imprinted (even more securely than among non-Jews; see 7:18–19).

The author has thus devoted considerable attention to helping his audience value their own heritage and continue to ground their self-respect in their living in line with that heritage rather than accepting the labels of the dominant culture. He inculcates resistance as he leads them away from

34. See, further, deSilva, *4 Maccabees*, 59–74, 80–85.

35. "I am inclined to pleasure; I will betake myself to the opposite side of the rolling ship, and that beyond measure, so as to train myself. I am inclined to avoid hard work; I will strain and exercise my sense-impressions to this end, so that my aversion from everything of this kind will cease. For who is the man in training? He is the man who . . . practices particularly in the things that are difficult to master . . . Practice, if you are arrogant, to submit when you are reviled, not to be disturbed when you are insulted . . . Next, train yourself to use wine with discretion . . ." (Epictetus, *Diatr.* 3.12.7–11). Galen also underscored the need to attend to constant practice of specific exercises targeting vices (in his "On the passions and errors of the soul," discussed in Renehan, "Philosophic Background," 235–36).

asking "how can I achieve honor in the eyes of the dominant culture," toward asking "how can I prove *myself* worthy of kinship with the 'offspring of Abraham'" (13:2; 18:1).

Speech as Resistance

A second prominent strategy of resistance exhibited throughout 4 Maccabees is speech—the speech of the colonized expressing the value of their way of life, challenging the aggressive acts (ideological, physical, and otherwise) of empire, and nurturing one another's commitment to the subjugated culture (against the summons of the voices of the dominant culture).

The martyrs exercise "frank speech" (παρρησία, 10:5), an ideal of Greek democracy. The exercise of παρρησία was especially important where democracy was threatened by, or replaced by, monarchy or tyranny.[36] In such situations, as is manifestly the case in 4 Maccabees, παρρησία denotes speech uttered at some degree of risk to oneself.[37] But in precisely those situations, the exercise of frank speech is central to the preservation of the integrity of the dominated. By speaking, Eleazar and the other martyrs remain true to themselves, rather than become a "living being who is false to himself."[38] Thus Eleazar uses speech to deflect the devaluation of his life lived in accordance with Torah and declare his intent to preserve the integrity of that long life (5:14–38; 6:17–21). The brothers use speech to declare their innocence and virtue in the face of the tyrant's attempts to impose the label of "deviant" upon them (9:15, 18, 31; 10:10; 11:4–6, 16, 22, 27; 12:14) and to remind one another of their identity and convictions, which are directly at stake but worth preserving (9:23; 10:2–3, 16; 11:14–15; 12:16; 13:13–18). Speaking truth to power, or at least commitment to one's convictions in the face of power, is an act of courage that gives consistency to thought, speech, and action, preferable to "the security of a life where the truth goes unspoken."[39]

The exercise of παρρησία also offers honest, potentially reformative criticism of those in power.[40] The seven brothers use speech to summon the imperial power to moral self-examination by witnessing to the injustices of its actions against the colonized (see especially 9:15; 10:10; 11:4–6; 12:11–14). The martyrs give Antiochus and his court opportunities to

36. Momigliano, "Freedom of Speech," 260; see also Dio Chrysostom, *Or.* 6.57; 32.26.

37. Foucault, *Fearless Speech*, 19–20.

38. Foucault, *Fearless Speech*, 17.

39. Foucault, *Fearless Speech*, 17.

40. Foucault, *Fearless Speech*, 19–20.

change their view of Judeans, to examine the justice of their own actions, and to question the political virtue of their practice of torture and coercion. By articulating their position clearly and bravely, they reject the dominant culture's position that the recalcitrant colonials are "destroying themselves irrationally (ἀλογίστως)" (6:14), forcing again and again the question that the representatives of the imperial power are the ones behaving irrationally and viciously, creating the opportunity for reform.

But in situations of imperialist intrusions into other cultures, there is another audience. In presenting Eleazar's request for an opportunity to "address the assembly" (δημηγορεῖν, 5:15) in response to Antiochus, the author invites the hearers to imagine Eleazar speaking not only for his own benefit nor only the benefit of Antiochus, but also—and even more so—for the benefit of the other Jewish captives who need to have their own commitment to their way of life shored up at this critical juncture. His deflection of Antiochus's critique insulates his fellow colonials from the same and provides a rationale for resistance (5:14–26). His declaration of the consequences of his own capitulation outlines for other Jews what is at stake in their own decisions to acquiesce or resist (5:28–38; 6:17, 20–21). Finally, he subtly includes his fellow Judeans in his stalwart resistance and preservation of integrity ("Never may *we* feign a role unbecoming to us," 6:17) and explicitly summons them to join him in resistance (6:22).

The author continues to drill home through the following episodes of martyrdom that speech, followed by action that puts one's body where one's convictions are, empowers resistance in a situation of domination. Thus the brothers' speech prominently features encouragement directed toward one another to remain faithful to their shared heritage rather than defect individually (9:23–24; 13:9–18; 14:1). The author, moreover, demonstrates the efficacy of such speech to empower and multiply resistance. The first brother's summons not to "renounce our courageous family ties" (9:23) is internalized and re-vocalized by the third, fourth, sixth, and seventh brothers (10:2–3, 15; 11:15, 22; 12:16). The utterance has a powerful impact and escalates commitment to defend the native way of life against the assaults of empire.

The mother is the undoubted hero of 4 Maccabees, enduring greater pains than each of the brothers (since she had to endure the pains of *all*) and undergirding each of her sons' ability to resist with her own strength. The author develops her contest at length (chiefly, it is admitted, to provide the clinching evidence for his argument concerning the unparalleled ability of Torah to instill commitment to virtue, when it can do so to such an extent "even" in a woman, 14:11)[41] and emphasizes her active role spurring her

41. The NRSV (1989) transposition of the "even" to "more diverse agonies" rather

sons on in their costly acts of resistance and giving them her strength as she maintains eye-contact with them throughout their pains (15:19 is quite a powerful image in this regard), showing that women can indeed exhibit greater courage than males (the mother is ἀνδρῶν . . . ἀνδρειοτέρα, 15:30) in this mode of resistance. Their participation in armed resistance (for example, the Maccabean Revolution) would be limited indeed,[42] but they are not thereby excluded—nor excused—from participating in effective and costly resistance of other kinds.[43]

The mother's speech—her principal instrument of resistance—is almost exclusively devoted to promoting resistance among her fellow Judeans, particularly her sons. Renouncing the self-pitying speech that looks only at the personal cost of resistance (16:6–11), she chooses instead to use her speech to spur her sons on to resistance unto death (16:13, 16–24). Aside from her own acquittal in regard to preserving her feminine virtue intact (18:6–9), her remaining speech also positions her sons for resistance, reminding them of the foundational convictions taught by their ancestral heritage that make resistance unto death bearable and, ultimately, assure them that resisting leads to the transcendence of their own deaths (18:10–19).[44] The author retains the specific detail that the mother speaks in Hebrew (16:15)—the language of the subjugated group—although he omits the rationale given in 2 Macc 7:27 (where it is a means by which to keep Antiochus from understanding her true intent).[45] Here, as she calls her boys to live in line with the examples drawn from their Jewish heritage, she gives consistency to speech and thought by using the language of the subjugated culture. In her situation of cultural and political hegemony, language represents group boundaries and ideology; using her indigenous language is itself a form of resistance, rejecting the language of the dominating, intruding culture.

The author himself participates in speech-as-resistance as he calls his own audience to "obey this law and exercise piety in every way" (18:1),

---

than leaving it behind "a woman's mind" represents wishful thinking on the part of the translators: the Greek ὅπου γε καὶ γυναικὸς νοῦς πολυτροπωτέρων ὑπερεφρόνησεν ἀλγηδόνων is unambiguously sexist at this point.

42. Plutarch's collection of tales about "The Bravery of Women" (De virtutibus mulierum) is rather the anthology of exceptions that prove the rule that women did not participate in armed resistance.

43. The military titles that the author applies to the mother ("shield-bearer of piety," 15:29; "soldier, elder, and woman," 16:14; "conqueror of a tyrant," 16:14; destroyer of "the violence of the tyrant," 17:2) affirm that effective resistance is in no way the province of males alone.

44. See deSilva, 4 Maccabees: Introduction and Commentary, 258–65.

45. Dupont-Sommer, Quatrième Livre, 131.

that is, to remain firmly committed to the distinctive way of life handed down by their ancestors rather than the way of life imposed by imperialism (whether by enticement or coercion). That the very Greek-sounding opening exhortation to "pay earnest attention to philosophy" (1:1) could be modulated to the very Jewish exhortation to the "children of Abraham" to follow Torah as closely as possible is another indication of the author's mastery of the master's tools and employment of the same to nurture resistance to being at home in the master's house.

Exemplary Action as Resistance

The design of the story inexorably drives the audience to consider a third layer of resistance, in which action must be added to valuing and speaking. The encounter between the tyrant and the martyr is a public one in which the dynamics of honor and shame are clearly at play,[46] in which the colonized are called upon to give a public defense of the value of their way of life by means of action. Effective action will spell defeat for the imperial powers and public vindication of the value of the indigenous way of life (as Eleazar defeated Antiochus περιφανῶς, 8:2); capitulation will give testimony to the ability of people to be reformed by the presence of empire if the right pressures are applied (to paraphrase Pliny the Younger's perspective on the success of his efforts to impose conformity to the demands of empire in *Ep.* 10.96).

Resistance-in-action is the bringing forward of "evidence on behalf of the nation" (διαμαρτυρίας, 16:16),[47] just as hardships provided Epictetus's Stoic an opportunity to make visible through action the truth of what his or her philosophy promises (*Diatr.* 1.29.44–49). In an extended athletic metaphor, the author places the "manner of life of people" alongside the "world" in the spectator stands, witnessing the bout between empire and subjugated people. The martyrs' contest, whether to give up their manner of living or die because any other manner of living was not to be accounted worth living, would publicly decide its value.

In such a setting resistance-in-action means "enduring"—publicly enduring the coercive measures of imperialism. "Endurance" (ὑπομονή) is a species of "courage," the virtue by means of which a person stays his or her course in the face of "fearful things for the sake of what is noble" (Aristotle, *Eth. Nic.* 3.7.2 1115b12; see also *Rhet. Her.* 3.3.5), sometimes

46. Moore and Anderson, "Taking It Like a Man," 264; see also chapter 2 above. For the martyrs' awareness of the possibility of putting themselves and their ancestors to shame by failure to resist in action, see 5:18, 27b, 28, 35; 9:1–2.

47. O'Hagan, "The Martyr," 95.

even submitting "to some disgrace or pain as the price of some great and noble object" (*Eth. Nic.* 3.1.7 1110a20–22). Aristotle, however, regarded the battlefield as the place where courage exhibited itself most plainly (*Eth. Nic.* 3.6.8 1115a33–34), not the torture chamber.

Where the body is acted upon, endurance could be seen quite negatively: "silence, passivity, submissiveness, openness, suffering—the shame of allowing oneself to be wounded, to be penetrated, and of simply enduring all that—were castigated as weak, womanish, slavish, and therefore morally bad."[48] The historical experience of aggressive Greek males finding themselves confronted by a superior power (e.g., a tyrant who defeats their city-state in a war), and of philosopher-sages being tested by tyrants, provided a context in which "manliness" could be enacted from a position of relative powerlessness through bold and committed—but passive—resistance.[49] Despite an etymology suggestive of "remaining under" another person or power, hence in a stereotypically feminine and inferior position (the converse of ἀνδρεία, "manliness"), ὑπομονή ("endurance") becomes the means by which those "on the bottom" in terms of political and physical power can come out "on top."[50]

In the particular setting of the martyrs, the object of the tyrant is to gain access to the will of the colonized by whatever means necessary. The location of resistance is within, with the result that endurance of torture without capitulation constitutes the effective and courageous action required. While being torn apart, the sixth brother can therefore rightly claim to have defeated the tyrant: "we six boys have paralyzed your tyranny. Since you have not been able to persuade us to change our mind or to force us to eat defiling food, is not this your downfall?" (11:24–25, NRSV).

48. Shaw, "Body/Power/Identity," 279.

49. Shaw, "Body/Power/Identity," 287. Military and athletic imagery played an important role in turning passive "endurance" into a form of "manliness" or "courage," especially in Greco-Roman philosophical literature (see Dio Chrysostom, *Or.* 8; Epictetus, *Diatr.* 1.18.21; 1.24.1–2; 3.20.9; 3.22.56; Seneca, *Prov.* 2.2–4; see, further, discussions in Pfitzner, *Paul and the Agon Motif*; Croy, *Endurance in Suffering*, 43–76; deSilva, *Perseverance in Gratitude*, 361–64; Moore and Anderson, "Taking It Like a Man," 259–61). The author of 4 Maccabees stands within a long tradition of painting the person who resists a more powerful person (like the martyr who resists a tyrant's attempts at coercion) as the pugilist or wrestler who wins by wearing out the opponent or absorbing more blows than the opponent can dish out (6:10; 9:12; see Seneca, *Constant.* 9.4; Philo, *Prob.* 26–27; *T. Job* 27.3–5), such that even the endurance of torture is ennobled if endured "bravely" (Seneca, *Ep.* 67.4, 6). He uses military imagery to interpret the resistance of the martyrs in 7:4–5; 9:23–24; 11:22. His use of athletic imagery is considerably more extensive (6:10; 9:23; 11:20; 12:11, 14; 13:13, 15; 16:16; 17:11–16).

50. Shaw, "Body/Power/Identity," 287–88.

Nevertheless, even in such situations of powerlessness, the author suggests that there are ways to seize back some degree of power, autonomy, initiative. The fifth brother rejects wearing the demeaning role of victim. Rather than wait to be escorted to the instruments by the guards, he comes forward "on his own" (11:1–3). The small space afforded him to seize back the initiative turns him into an empowered equal who engages the tyrant rather than a subaltern to be abused against his will. The seventh brother also makes full use of the narrow space given to him for freedom, using it to speak the truth and to seize control over his own body out of the tyrant's hands by means of his self-immolation (12:19). The same can be said of the mother, who similarly takes her own life by throwing herself into the fire (17:1).

But there is a second, even more important facet to the public nature of the encounter. Throughout his contest, Eleazar is supremely aware that he is being watched not only by the tyrant and his party, but also by other members of the subjugated culture. He is aware of the impact his actions now will have on the commitment of his fellow Judeans. He knows that, if he is seen to eat the pork, he will weaken the resolve of other Judeans by his own acquiescence to the demands of the dominant culture, his public testimony that their ancestral way of life is not worth dying for (6:12–19). He cannot preserve his private virtue, only pretending to eat the pork without *really* putting it in his mouth, without maintaining his public testimony to the value of unflagging commitment to live by the Torah.[51] In such a setting, speech must be confirmed by deeds, as Eleazar will in fact do: "by your deeds you made your words of divine philosophy credible" (7:7).

A distinctive feature of the way the author of 4 Maccabees tells the tale of Antiochus's invasion of Judea is that he never mentions Judas Maccabeus and his revolutionary forces, even obliquely.[52] The author focuses

---

51. Eleazar is thus made to resemble Socrates, the primary hero of Greek philosophy, who submitted to an unjust death so as to provide an example of courage in the face of death, liberating human beings from the fear of death that frequently undermines perseverance in virtue (see Seneca, *Ep.* 24.4; Epictetus, *Diatr.* 4.1.168–169).

52. This is a matter of some debate, with Townshend ("Fourth Book," 684) and Williams (*Jesus' Death as Saving Event*, 171) attempting to make room for the Hasmoneans in the author's narrative. The striking lack of any explicit mention of the revolutionaries, however, provides strong evidence for the view that the author does not wish to share the martyrs' achievement with anyone else (thus Dupont-Sommer, *Quatrième Livre*, 150; O'Hagan, "The Martyr," 111–12; deSilva, *4 Maccabees: Introduction and Commentary*, 82–83, 254–55; Seeley, *The Noble Death*, 93. Why not give place to the Maccabean Revolution in such a text? It is surely not because the author opposes their attempt, in principle, to throw off imperial domination, an end that he also celebrates (4 Macc 1:11; 17:20; 18:4–5). However, the author seeks to demonstrate that the essential lessons about effective resistance are already learned from the martyrs' acts, and that learning these lessons must precede (axiologically, if not temporally) the taking

instead entirely on the effectiveness of the martyrs' resistance, an efficacy that works chiefly through example and imitation. Eleazar calls upon the other "children of Abraham" to "die nobly for the sake of piety" (6:22), and his exemplary death inspires the seven brothers to stand firm. The author again confirms the impact of resistance-in-action by depicting the brothers explicitly recalling Eleazar's actions as setting the mark to which they, the young, must also measure up (9:5–6).

Each of the brothers, in turn, urges their surviving brothers to follow his example (9:23–24; 13:8) and keep his elder brothers' actions in view as their own guiding compass (12:16). Finally, their collective example of resistance through endurance, defeating the tyrant's attempts to destroy their commitment to their ancestral way of life, leads to the revival of obedience to the Torah throughout Judea, and thus the utter defeat of Antiochus's plans (18:4–5). Dying as an example of resistance and as a witness to the value of the indigenous culture becomes the first cause of the eventual expulsion of the imperialist intruders,[53] the enacting of a "mimetic process" that ultimately stops empire's incursion into Judea.[54] The author contemporizes the struggle as he affirms that Eleazar's death is having the same effect on himself and his own audience as he delivers the oration, strengthening their commitment to the divine Law (7:9), as he calls upon contemporary leaders in the Jewish community to embody resistance-in-action as did Eleazar as the proper work for "administrators of the law" (7:8), and as those who respond to his closing summons (18:1–2) become themselves examples of commitment to the Jewish way of life, and thus of resistance against assimilation.

Effective Resistance Requires Solidarity

Perhaps no quality more prominently characterized the seven brothers and their mother in 4 Maccabees than their harmonious agreement with one another in their commitment to their ancestral way of life (8:29b; 9:23; 10:2–3, 15; 11:14–15, 22; 12:16; 13:6–9, 11, 13, 18; 13:19–14:1, 3–8; 15:9–10, 12; 16:12–13; 17:2–3, 5).[55] They were "of one mind" (8:29), which

up of arms against an invader. More centrally, the political setting of Diaspora calls not for armed resistance (as the tragic Diaspora Rebellion under Trajan would prove) but fidelity to the Torah whether in the face of mild disdain or overt hostility. The martyrs demonstrate the efficacy of this form of resistance, even as models of non-violent resistance have continued to demonstrate in the modern period.

53. Thus, rightly, van Henten, "Tradition-Historical Background," 123.

54. Seeley, *The Noble Death*, 89–97.

55. See discussion in Klauck, "Brotherly Love," 152–55; deSilva, *4 Maccabees: Introduction and Commentary*, 204–17.

was held to be a characteristic of "good people" who remain constant and consistent because they all strive together for "what is just and what is advantageous" (Aristotle, *Eth. Nic.* 1167b3–9; see also Dio, *Or.* 48). Aristotle held such concord to be especially appropriate between friends (Aristotle, *Eth. Nic.* 1155a23) and, therefore, among siblings (the affection of siblings being a type of friendship).

This solidarity expresses itself in speech designed to keep one another heading toward the shared goal of virtue. The author frequently speaks of the brothers as a chorus (8:4), a group of people who spoke with, essentially, a single voice to those outside (see 8:29; 13:8; 14:7–8) and who speak to one another in ways that consistently mirror the value of their ancestral way of life and the advantage of ongoing commitment to it. The author, indeed, gives significant attention to the role each brother played in helping his remaining brothers remain steadfast (see, e.g., 9:23–24; 13:8–18; 14:1), a role reprised by the mother (12:7; 16:12–13). By means of such solidarity, the brothers together formed a fortified harbor supported by seven pillars, able on the basis of their combined strength to bear the onslaught of the waves of the ocean of passions, making a safe haven for their virtue (13:6–7; see also 17:3). The author thus consistently emphasizes throughout the second half of his work the importance of corporate harmony, solidarity, and mutual support for the ability of individual members of the subjugated culture to resist the onslaught of the dominant culture.

This kind of harmony—this unison testimony—invests the values of the subjugated culture with a greater degree of absoluteness, as all the members of the community unite "in conferring both censure and praise, bearing for both classes, the good and the bad, a testimony in which each can have confidence" (Dio, *Or.* 48.6). It is instructive that the possibility of weakness, portrayed in the hypothetical response to Antiochus (8:16–26), enters the situation through lack of unanimity, where "some of them" (τινες) begin to waver in their commitment and spread the seeds of uncertainty (8:16). For the members of the minority culture to speak with different voices would be to replicate the confusion within the individual, torn between what he or she believes about his or her native way of life and the evaluations of the same being imposed by the powerful voices of the dominant culture. Lack of solidarity in speech fails to provide the external, objectivizing support required for resistance. Such solidarity could easily become oppressive if the individual forgets that he or she does in fact have a choice, but it also becomes a principal source of empowerment insofar as it reminds the

individual facing the seemingly irresistible coercive measures of the dominant culture that he or she *has* a choice.[56]

Breaches of solidarity are singularly damaging to resistance. The tyrant's desperation to gain a victory over the last surviving brother, both
addressing him individually himself and bringing his mother forward to
"persuade" him to capitulate, is a signal here, as is the way in which Antiochus and his part "relish" the prospect of the seventh brother's declaration
of capitulation (12:9). If Antiochus can succeed here, he will wipe away the
effects of the seven conspicuous defeats he had already suffered (a cumulative defeat exacerbated by the sixth brother's explicit declaration of victory
in 11:24–25). Because of this, breaches of solidarity become heinous acts
of betrayal of one's own. Great damage is done by every single person who
capitulates to the imperial power, both in terms of feeding the latter's commitment to remain and in terms of weakening the witness of those who
resisted previously (and thus the wills of those who continue to resist).
The author therefore offers the depiction of the brothers, nobly united by
a common commitment to justice and piety, as the model for the extended
kinship group that forms his audience, promoting solidarity as an essential
resource for effective resistance.

Resistance Is not Futile

The author frankly acknowledges that resistance often costs dearly and hurts
tremendously, both in terms of physical pain and emotional pain and bereavement (6:7, 11, 27; 13:27—14:1, 10, 12–13; 15:7, 14–22; 16:3). Nevertheless, he
affirms that resistance, even against seemingly insurmountable pressures, is
both possible and effective. Without drawing a sword, without organizing a
guerilla force, without the material resources necessary for military action,
these martyrs "became the cause of the downfall of tyranny" and "conquered
the tyrant" (1:11; see also 8:15; 11:24–25). Because of *their* resistance, empire
could not stamp out the way of life of the colonized, and eventually could
not even continue to occupy their territory (17:20–21; 18:4–5). What might
have appeared like failure on the part of the colonized constituted, in fact,
the defeat of the tyrant's power and the *successful* resistance of his imposition
of a foreign way of life. It is a genuine victory because the tyrant is indeed
"powerless" to get what he wants out of them. Where military action or other
venues for coercive resistance (e.g., economic embargoes) are unavailable, the
battle against totalitarian regimes must often be fought and won in the bodies
of those who would resist. These martyrs become a precedent and a symbol

56. See, further, the discussion of alienation in Berger, *Sacred Canopy*, 81–101.

that resistance of this kind is no less effective for loosening and unraveling the cords of tyranny than the other kinds.

Resistance is not only possible and effective, but also necessary. What is truly "compelling" for Eleazar (5:16) is the preservation of his integrity in regard to his inviolable values (5:28–38).[57] Eleazar can only maintain his self-respect, and his only legitimate claim to honor, by resistance unto death.[58] To do otherwise would be to betray himself, to betray the reputation for virtue (piety) gained through a long life of living in accordance with the way of life valued by the subjugated culture (5:18, 29, 34–37; 6:17–19). It would be to take on an unmanly disposition, suggested by the neologism μαλακοψυχήσαντας (6:17). The adjective μαλακός served "to differentiate women, girls, boys, youths, effeminate males, catamites, and eunuchs from 'true men.'"[59] Eleazar must resist, or else morally de-sex himself, allowing Antiochus to "force" him and thus impose an inappropriate feminine posture upon him.

The path of resistance is not the path of self-negation; it is the actualization of valuing oneself rather than devaluing the self. Eleazar refuses to eat defiling food out of a regard for the value of his own body and his responsibility to it. As the author expresses it in his encomiastic reflections on Eleazar's steadfast resistance, "you neither defiled your sacred teeth nor profaned your stomach, which had room only for reverence and purity" (7:6). Eleazar cannot brutalize himself in this fashion, betraying his own body by ingesting unclean food. Epictetus had sought to empower resistance against coercion from without by regarding the body and its constituent parts as somehow not "him" (*Diatr.*. 1.1.23–24; 1.29.5–8; *Ench.* 18). The author of 4 Maccabees, on the other hand, interprets Eleazar's endurance of torture as a dimension of his respect for his own body, and not denigration of or alienation from the same.

Taking the long view is necessary for effective resistance. The mother's deliberations bring this out most forcefully, as she weighs the "temporary" well-being of her sons (σωτηρίας προσκαίρου, "temporary deliverance," 15:2; τὴν τῶν τέκνων πρόσκαιρον σωτηρίαν, "the temporary deliverance of her children," 15:8; τὴν σῴζουσαν . . . πρὸς ὀλίγον χρόνον σωτηρίαν, "the deliverance that preserves for a short time," 15:27) against their "eternal" well-being (εἰς αἰωνίαν ζωήν, "for age-long life," 15:3), but appears in the

---

57. The heroine Antigone in Sophocles's tragedy is a stunning embodiment of this, contrasted with Ismene, who finds external pressures to be more compelling (*Ant.* 58–68).

58. In so doing, he walks in line with the canons of nobility lauded by Greek culture (see, for example, Pseudo-Isocrates, *To Demonicus* 43; Epictetus, *Diatr.* 3.20.4–6).

59. Moore and Anderson, "Taking It Like a Man," 263.

brothers' deliberations as well (13:14–15). The martyrs consistently show the necessity of looking beyond their current circumstances to the larger cause that their resistance advances (5:18; 6:19–21, 28–29; 9:24; 10:21; 11:3; 12:17–18)[60] or to the forces beyond death that would vindicate their stance and compensate their pains (9:8–9, 32; 10:11, 15; 12:12, 14; 13:14–15, 17). The author certainly affirms the reality of the former (1:11; 17:10, 20–21; 18:4–5), though he believes the latter to be true as well (16:13, 25; 17:2–6, 17–18; 18:3, 23).

Conclusion

The title of one of Audre Lorde's most celebrated essays claims that "the master's tools will never dismantle the master's house." Fourth Maccabees at the very least demonstrates how many of those tools, in the use of which the author is highly and visibly skilled, could be employed to shore up the house of the subjugated culture colonized by the imperialist masters. But the author of this strange book may indeed go further, using those tools indeed to strike against the ideological foundations of the house of the cultural imperialism of the Hellenistic kingdoms. As the author challenges the projected image of Greeks as cultured, virtuous masters of themselves, he challenges their attempts to legitimate their empire and calls attention to the underside of empire's "gifts." As the author examines his own ancestral heritage, he summons his audience—the colonized who are now largely expatriate—to renew their commitment to live in their own house, to value that house, to talk bravely about the meaningfulness and desirability of inhabiting such a house, and to defend that house with exemplary action that solidifies and unites their fellow Jews in devotion to that house. Surely the master would have regretted teaching *that* colonial the use of his tools.

---

60. Even though several of these are couched in the language of anticipating divine intervention, the object of this divine intervention is a decisive change in the political affairs of their native land and in the situation of imperialism.

Part 2

The Rhetorical Contributions of Intertexture

4

The Strategic Retelling of Scripture in 4 Maccabees

David's Thirst (4 Macc 3:6–18)

The story of David's thirst, appearing in 2 Samuel, 1 Chronicles, Josephus's *Judean Antiquities*, and 4 Maccabees, offers an interesting case study in "rewritten Bible." Surprisingly, the story has received little scholarly attention in this regard. The strategic crafting of the story begins in the earliest written witnesses, seen in the ways in which an originally independent story about David's wish for water from Bethlehem's well has been set within an interpretive frame with a particular goal by the authors of 2 Samuel and 1 Chronicles. This story is later adapted by Josephus, on the one hand, for slightly changed purposes, which still fall, however, well within the interpretive guidelines set for the story in the scriptural narratives. It is, on the other hand, much more dramatically and creatively re-written by the author of 4 Maccabees for a purpose, and with a focus, quite outside the interpretive guidelines set for the story in the Jewish Scriptures.

In this essay, the story is examined in each of its iterations with particular attention to how the literary context sets up the interpretive guidelines for hearing the same story, and to how the story is adapted by two late first-century readers and authors to serve their ends for the story. In this way, this article seeks to contribute to an understanding of the ways in which alterations to the particular story of David's thirst—from the minor adjustments by Josephus to the fearless alteration of detail and addition of material in 4 Maccabees—contribute to the different rhetorical goals for the story within each text.

The Story in 2 Samuel and 1 Chronicles

The authors of both 2 Samuel and 1 Chronicles set the story of David's thirst in the context of recounting the heroic deeds of David's chief warriors. The story is preceded in 2 Sam 23:8–12 by episodes chosen to show the bravery of the three men who attained highest rank among David's band by means of their valor and military prowess: Jeshbaal, Eleazar, and Shammah.[1] The story in 1 Chronicles 11:10–14 sets out to do the same, but Shammah's name has been accidentally omitted and his exemplary deed of valor conflated with that of Eleazar. In both 2 Samuel and 1 Chronicles, the story of David's thirst is followed by further memorable deeds performed by Abishai and Benaiah, and then by a roster of David's mighty men (the roster explicitly of "the Thirty" in 2 Sam 23:24, though the author concludes the roster by setting the tally of these names at "thirty-seven"; the Chronicler makes no attempt to tally them, and in fact launches into another full chapter detailing further the names and numbers of David's army). This context is extremely important for determining how the hearer/reader experiences the story of David's thirst in these accounts, since the context leads him or her to focus on the "deeds of valor" of the soldiers in the story more than on David's motivations or actions, which provide the opportunity for, and response to, another in a series of displays of courage.[2]

The story is briefly narrated in both 2 Sam 23:13–17 and 1 Chr 11:15–19. The episode, as it stands in both texts, begins with "three of

---

1. In the discussion that follows, these names will be consistently employed for the sake of simplicity, without giving attention to the many variations in their names between 2 Samuel and 1 Chronicles, the MT and LXX, and Josephus. On this complexity, see, for example, the list of alternatives for Jeshbaal in Begg, "Exploits of David's Heroes," 153.

2. McCarter (*II Samuel*, 495) correctly observes that the episode comes from earlier in David's life than the placement in 2 Samuel 23 suggests—after the king has aged, is no longer permitted to go out into battle by his troops, and whose last words have even been recorded. Indeed, they must fall before the victories recounted in 2 Sam 5:17–25. The Chronicler has attempted to fit the episodes of valor better into the flow of the larger narrative by placing them after the episodes of David's public anointing as king and the capture of Jerusalem and prior to those victories over the Philistines. Even so, the series is still a little out of place there as well: the story appears in 1 Chr 11:15–19, but the Philistines are not otherwise active in the Valley of Rephaim until 1 Chr 14:8, 13. Given the emphasis on David's "mighty men" before and after the episode of David's thirst, and thus the likely place where the emphasis will fall within the story as well, it seems that the Chronicler is not as likely to have been motivated to move this story forward, as Brueggemann (*First and Second Samuel*, 349) suggests, so much "as a clue and key for what follows" in David's story as to have sought by this move to streamline the chronology of his presentation without sacrificing the integrity of the encomium on David's warriors.

the Thirty" going to join David at the cave of Adullam. Second Samuel 23:13 adds the detail that it was "the beginning of harvest time,"[3] a season in which rain is not plentiful or regular, perhaps as an attempt to explain David's thirst and the need to make a raid on a water source to secure the needed supplies.[4] This explanation, if accurate, is absent for the reader of 1 Chronicles. The Philistines appear at first to be encamped in the Valley of Rephaim,[5] a valley that begins some distance south of Jerusalem (20 stadia, according to Josephus, *Ant.* 7. 12. 4) and extends as far as Bethlehem (2 Sam 23:13//1 Chr 11:15). The following verse, however, shifts the focus to David "in the stronghold" and the Philistines "in Bethlehem" (2 Samuel 23:14//1 Chr 11:16).[6] David "experiences desire" and says, "Who will bring me a drink from the well of Bethlehem that is by the gate?" (2 Sam 23:15//1 Chr 11:17). In response, "the three warriors" (2 Sam 23:16) break through the enemy camp, draw water from the well, and bring it back to David. He refuses to drink it, however, and instead pours it out as a libation to God (2 Sam 23:16//1 Chr 11:18). He utters an imprecation against himself were he to drink it, and alludes to the reason for his response in the rhetorical question, "Is it the blood of the men who went" (2 Samuel) and "brought" (1 Chronicles) the water "at the risk of their lives?" (2 Sam 23:17//1 Chr 11:19).[7] Both accounts conclude: "The three warriors did these things" (2 Sam 23:17//1 Chr 11:19). Forming an inclusio with the appearance of "three" chief soldiers at the opening of the episode, this conclusion re-enforces the interpretive frame for the story: it is about a feat of valor that glorifies David's "mighty men."

Several questions have occupied scholars commenting on this passage. The first concerns the identity of the three bold heroes of the story. The authors both of 2 Samuel and 1 Chronicles identify them with the

---

3. The LXX reads "to Cason" rather than "at harvest," reading the Hebrew at this point as a place name and merely transliterating.

4. McCarter (*II Samuel*, 495) understands this to be the significance of this detail. Anderson (*2 Samuel*, 276), on the other hand, does not assume that David and his soldiers were short on water. There is considerable debate concerning whether David was longing for water from a well or a cistern in Bethlehem, a detail that need not detain us here.

5. Called "the Valley of the Giants" in the LXX, with the place name being properly translated.

6. This shift is even more evident in LXX 2 Samuel which redundantly adds "and the corps of the Philistines was then in Bethlehem" at the close of 23:15 as well as 23:14.

7. McCarter (*II Samuel*, 491) notes that LXX 2 Sam 23:17 has already amended this question with the addition of πίομαι, "shall I drink the blood of these men?" Anderson (*2 Samuel*, 273 n.17.a-a.) effectively emends the Hebrew text to include "shall I drink" in his translation of the MT.

Three—Jeshbaal, Eleazar, and Shammah—whose individual deeds of valor preceded this tale.[8] This is clear from the editorial comment that closes the episode in each account, attributing the joint deed to "the three warriors" (2 Sam 23:17//1 Chr 11:19), using the same words to specify the elite group of the Three to which Eleazar belongs (2 Sam 23:9//1 Chr 11:12), and thus, by extension, Jeshbaal and Shammah. In this way, both accounts bring closure *after* the episode of David's thirst to the tribute to the Three begun at 2 Sam 23:8//1 Chr 11:11.

It is, of course, quite possible that they were mistaken in this identification. As Smith has rightly pointed out, the terms with which the three soldiers are introduced within the episode do not suggest that they have previously been mentioned in the narrative.[9] They appear as some previously unspecified cadre of three soldiers (the lack of definiteness is telling in this regard) and not as *these same* three men whose stories have already occupied the narrative. The authors of 2 Samuel and 1 Chronicles have themselves made the identification of this unnamed threesome with *the* Three, and chosen to weave this episode into their narrative at this point in order to enhance the presentation and appreciation of the courageous spirit specifically of *the* Three by means of this story.

We cannot distance the anonymous three from *the* Three, however, on the basis of the claim, often made in the scholarly literature, that the "Three" were not part of the "Thirty,"[10] and therefore, since the three credited with the raid on Bethlehem's well came from among the Thirty (viz., "three out of the Thirty," 2 Sam 23:13//1 Chr 11:15), they cannot be *the* Three. The texts themselves appear to present contradictory evidence in regard to whether or not the Three are distinct from, or part of, the Thirty,[11] and even whether or not there are multiple groups of Threes (see especially LXX and MT 2 Sam 23:19//1 Chr 11:21; LXX 2 Sam 23:23). The problem is only exacerbated by text-critical issues surrounding the numbers "three" and "thirty" at several points.[12]

---

8. Braun (*1 Chronicles*, 161) finds this identification "most natural" as well.

9. Smith, *Books of Samuel*, 385. So also McCarter, *II Samuel*, 495.

10. As in Anderson, *2 Samuel*, 274; Knoppers, *I Chronicles 10–29*, 533. Myers (*I Chronicles*, 88), however, has no difficulty regarding Jeshbaal and Eleazar to be two of the thirty.

11. The notice that Abishai is "honored above the Thirty, and he became their commander. But he did not attain to the Three" (1 Chr 11:20–21), for example, could easily suggest, as it does to Knoppers (*1 Chronicles 10–29*, 533) that there are two separate groups—a "Thirty," to the top of which Abishai rose, and a "Three," into whose ranks Abishai never made it.

12. Japhet, *I & II Chronicles*, 244.

The difficulties disappear, however, if one allows for fluidity first in the roster of the Thirty, and then in the roster of the top three among the Thirty. The fact that the author of 2 Samuel could list thirty-seven names—and explicitly give the tally of these names as "thirty-seven"—as the roster of the "Thirty" strongly points in this direction. New soldiers would rise to take their place among the Thirty as former members of this elite became disabled or died.[13] Moreover, the first Three heroes set the precedent for there being an elite of "three" within the Thirty, but this elite was also fluid.[14] Thus Abishai and Benaiah could rise to be regarded as among the "three" soldiers of highest-ranking status at one time, though the authors are careful to point out that no one ever matched the luster of the very first Three (namely Jeshbaal, Eleazar, and Shammah). In this way it could be said that Abishai, for example, "won a name among the 'Three'" (now comprised of Abishai, Benaiah, and another unnamed soldier), and that, "since he was the most highly regarded among the 'Three', he became their leader" (2 Sam 23:19), and at the same time that "he did not attain to *the* Three," that is, Jeshbaal, Eleazar, and Shammah, the soldiers *non pareil* who used to make up the "Three" earlier in David's time.

Another issue concerns the setting of the episode. A sizeable portion of the actual narrative is given to the setting (approximately one-third in both accounts) and, in this case, "less" would indeed have been "more," considering the problems it would have avoided. Indeed, the detail here is all the more surprising given the lack of details about the settings of the previously related three brave deeds (or two deeds, in Chronicles).

Commentators have found this setting problematic indeed. David appears to be at two different locations, with no rationale for how he gets from the "cave of Adullam" (2 Sam 23:13//1 Chr 11:15) to the "stronghold" (2 Sam 23:14//1 Chr 11:16).[15] The shift on the other side, with the Philis-

---

13. Thus Smith, *Books of Samuel*, 387: "That the names are more than thirty in number need cause no surprise, as we may suppose the corps to have been kept full after losses in war."

14. The translator of LXX 1 Chronicles seems to have this understanding when he places Benaiah among "the three mighty ones" (ἐν τοῖς τρισὶν τοῖς δυνατοῖς, LXX 1 Chr 11:24), using the same phrase applied to the first Three in 11:12, 19 (οἱ τρεῖς δυνατοί)— or, more precisely, to Jeshbaal, Eleazar, and Shammah (simply, τοὺς τρεῖς in LXX 1 Chr 11:25) while they occupied that top eschelon.

15. Wellhausen attempted to solve this problem by emending "cave of Adullam" to "stronghold of Adullam," a change requiring the alteration of the middle two letters of each word. While this proposal still finds supporters (as in McCarter, *II Samuel*, 491, 495), Knoppers rightly criticizes this as an artificial solution to the problem of David's whereabouts (*I Chronicles 10–29*, 538).

The town of Adullam is 16 miles southwest of Jerusalem (Anderson, 2 *Samuel*, 275), but the "stronghold" may be located at some distance from the town (perhaps closer to

tines occupying first the Valley of Rephaim (2 Sam 23:13//1 Chr 11:15) and, later, Bethlehem itself, raises similar questions (2 Sam 23:14//1 Chr 11:16). Neither the Chronicler nor the authors of 2 Samuel explain "the apparent discrepancies between the two locations of David and the two locations of the Philistines."[16] Sara Japhet concludes that the opening two verses of each account appear to come from two separate episodes, the first one preserving "the torso of an originally independent account, which was later combined with the story of the well at Bethlehem."[17]

If one were inclined to seek the simplest solution, it may well be that the authors of 1 and 2 Samuel use "cave of Adullam" and "stronghold" interchangeably, both here and at 1 Sam 22:1–5, where David's location similarly "shifts" from the "cave of Adullam" (1 Sam 22:1) to the "stronghold" (1 Sam 22:4–5) without explanation. Moreover, since the Valley of Rephaim extends as far as Bethlehem to the south, the Philistine occupation of Bethlehem is consistent with their encampment in the valley, and indeed would serve as a mark of the depth of their penetration into Judah. What is clear, at least, is that the editors of this material wanted to connect the episode explicitly to the early time of David's kingship, specifically to the movements of the Philistines in the Valley of Rephaim (2 Sam 5:17–25; 1 Chr 14:8–16), and to establish a setting in which David was alienated from his native town by the Philistine occupation force. This was sufficiently important to warrant giving thirty-three percent of the space occupied by the episode to setting the stage, and to risk the confusion documented by modern readers.

David's "desire" precipitates the action of the episode. It is significant that the biblical accounts say nothing about David being thirsty (although 2 Samuel might hint at this with the mention of the harvest season), just that he "experienced a longing." Mazar believes that lack of an adequate water supply motivates David;[18] McCarter finds "homesickness" and nostalgia to be the driving forces;[19] Smith suggests that it is, in fact, the quality of water that strikes David as desirable in that moment.[20] Such suggestions are all quite in line with the tenor of the NRSV and other English translations of David's expression of his longing, which tend to express it almost melodramatically as a wish—"O that someone would give me water to drink!" But these translations

---

Bethlehem, as suggested in Mazar, "The Military Elite").

16. Knoppers, *I Chronicles 10–29*, 549.

17. Japhet, *I & II Chronicles*, 245.

18. Mazar, "Military Elite," 315.

19. McCarter, *II Samuel*, 495; Anderson, *2 Samuel*, 276.

20. Smith (*Books of Samuel*, 386) suggests that the well was fed by a spring, so that the water would be fresh and cool. Knoppers (*I Chronicles 10–29*, 550) finds no grounds for this surmise.

blunt the force of David's expression of his longing, which is not a wish, but a challenge—"*Who* will give me water to drink?" It is a gauntlet thrown down into the midst of the soldiers gathered around David.[21]

Here the apparent acrobatics the authors went through to locate the event in Bethlehem and to put David in a situation where he could not go to Bethlehem suggest that the water may not be David's primary objective. David wants to enjoy access to the water of his own hometown in Bethlehem, a city currently occupied by those who have no claim before God to that land or its goods. Beneath David's expression of desire to drink from the waters of Bethlehem is his desire to retake what is properly his, his desire to be deprived of the proper state of affairs by the intrusion of the Philistines no longer, with Judeans free to enter Bethlehem and traverse the Valley of Rephaim again. "Who will bring me a drink of the water from the well of Bethlehem?" may be but the concrete and poetic expression of his deeper longing, a summons to his men: "Who will brave the Philistine army and restore my access to Bethlehem? Who is ready for this fight?"

The three soldiers show their readiness to get behind David's desire to expel the Gentile pest by fulfilling literally David's expression of that desire. "Lord, we are able!" On the one hand, the three express their utter devotion to David by bringing him the water, which is, in turn, a tribute to David and his charisma.[22] On the other hand, it remains first and foremost an expression of courage and readiness to engage the enemy, to brave whatever dangers must be braved to restore access to Bethlehem so that the King of Jerusalem can simply stop by his well in his territory and dip in his own ladle. The authors have carefully set the stage for this story so that it would be heard as the prequel to David's double expulsion of the Philistines from the Valley of Rephaim, pushing them back to Gazara.

The conclusion of the episode—and one can only wonder if it came as a welcome one to the three warriors who went through such trouble to bring the water—continues to suggest the symbolic nature of the water throughout the story. Here, it has become the symbolic equivalent of "blood," since the three men risked their lives to bring it. Putting their lives on the line for David, they have, in essence, presented him with their own blood, ready to

---

21. Knoppers (*I Chronicles 10–29*, 550) is, I believe, correct to suggest that, rather than thirst being the issue, "David is goading his troops." He may not, however, be "idly wishing for water from his hometown" (Knoppers, *I Chronicles 10–29*, 550, quoting and approving McCarter, *II Samuel*, 496, on this point).

22. Anderson (*2 Samuel*, 274) and McCarter (*II Samuel*, 495) regard it as a "foolhardy act of devotion" performed by "too loyal soldiers" who "act recklessly"; Anderson (*2 Samuel*, 278) later offers a somewhat more sympathetic reading as he observes that "to have the devotion of such men is also an indirect tribute to David himself."

be poured out at his command. David therefore treats it as blood, pouring it out to God according to the mandates of Lev 17:10–13; Deut 12:23–24.[23] Whatever may be said of David's initial motivations in calling for the drink, the conclusion shows that David is not interesting in putting his brave soldiers' lives on the line "to indulge his whims."[24] David showed that he is was devoted to them as they were to him, and that he "prized solidarity more than his own satisfaction."[25]

David's act of refusing the drink has an interesting parallel in Plutarch's *Alexander* 42.3–6. There, Alexander and his soldiers face the hardships of a long march in pursuit of Darius in the midst of a drought. Some Macedonians had fetched water for their children but, seeing Alexander parched, offered a helmet-full to him, saying that they placed a greater value on him than on their children's lives. Alexander was about to drink but forbore for the sake of the soldiers that were with him, putting camaraderie with them ahead of himself. Interestingly, the response of the soldiers was to re-invest themselves in the march and despise their own hardships, which the intended sequel to David's story would suggest also to have been the case there.

The purpose of the story of David's thirst in 2 Samuel and 1 Chronicles is clear: it serves above all to glorify three soldiers, whose glory is, in effect, coopted by both authors for the sake of their encomium on the top Three of David's mighty men, Jeshbaal, Eleazar, and Shammah. The story is ultimately not about thirst, but about a proof of courage/spirit ("eine Mutprobe") manifested in a reckless deed.[26] Indeed, the story would far better be called "the story of the raid on Bethlehem's well" than "the story of David's thirst," as these authors tell it. The setting, for all its problems, is vital, not only connecting the episode to the larger narrative of David's campaigns against the Philistines, but creating a context in which both the king's challenge and the soldiers' act could be interpreted as symbolic for the needs of the situation and the army's readiness to respond to those greater challenges.

The Story in Josephus's *Antiquities* 7.12.4 §§311–314

Thoroughly in line with the authors of 2 Samuel and 1 Chronicles, Josephus is primarily interested in the heroism of the Israelite soldiers displayed by this story and its neighboring material.[27] His many embellishments of the

23. McCarter, *II Samuel*, 496; Knoppers, *I Chronicles 10–29*, 550.

24. McCarter, *II Samuel*, 496.

25. Brueggemann, *First and Second Samuel*, 348–49.

26. Hertzberg, *Die Samuelbücher*, 334.

27. Josephus primarily follows the order of material in LXX 2 Sam 23:13–17, as

biblical accounts serve as a whole to enhance the reader's appreciation of the prowess and valor of the whole company of David's mighty men, substantiating his claim that they were ἀνδρεῖοι. Whereas the authors of 2 Samuel and 1 Chronicles appear to be more interested in capturing the renowned deeds of the principals among the thirty (the "Three," Abishai, and Benaiah), and are even concerned to maintain the "pecking order" among these five (see the authors' acrobatics as they affirm the status of Abishai and Benaiah at the top of the group, yet still below the first "Three," in 2 Sam 23:18–19; 1 Chr 11:20–21), Josephus explicitly offers the deeds of these five as evidence of the valor of all the members of the larger group of thirty-eight (*sic*) warriors.[28] Thus he opens his catalog by offering the particular stories of five members of the group "to make clear the heroic virtues *of the rest*" (7.307). Similarly, he closes this section with the like affirmation that "the rest of these men were of equal valor" (7.317). It is significant in this regard that Josephus omits the Scriptural authors' clarification of Abishai's status "below" the Three (2 Sam 23:18–19; 1 Chr 11:20–21),[29] since his goal is not to elevate the Three above the rest, but to elevate the host of David's heroes by the exploits of these five examples. His goal is not to reinscribe the ranking so carefully preserved in 2 Samuel and 1 Chronicles—an issue more pertinent to inner-group conversations about valor. Rather, he seeks to adapt this series of episodes to serve the larger apologetic goals of his *Judean Antiquities*, countering "current anti-Semitic claims that the Jews had failed to produce men of (military) caliber comparable to those with which Greco-Roman history is replete."[30]

A brief survey of Josephus's embellishments in treating the individual deeds of the Three, Abishai, and Benaiah, the episodes that provide the literary context for the joint exploit of the Three, attests to Josephus's primary rhetorical goal of arousing admiration for this band that surrounded David.

Jeshbaal engages the enemy more energetically in Josephus, where he "sprang repeatedly" against the enemy's ranks,[31] an enhancement of the

---

his treatment of the individual deeds of the Three makes clear (i.e., not conflating the deeds of Eleazar and Shammah and omitting the latter's name, as in 1 Chr 11:12–14), though he makes use of details from LXX 1 Chronicles as well (on this point, see Begg, "Exploits," 166–67).

28. Josephus departs from 2 Sam 23:39, which enumerates them as 37, though how even that tally was calculated remains unclear. The Chronicler does not attempt to give a total.

29. Begg, *Judean Antiquities*, 291 n.1162; Begg, "Exploits," 162, 167.

30. Begg, "Exploits," 169.

31. Thackeray and Marcus, *Josephus*, 525; Begg, *Judean Antiquities*, 289: "many times dashing."

picture in both 2 Sam 23:8 and 1 Chr 11:11, where he merely "drew his sword" against a great host on one occasion. Josephus also agrees with the Lucianic recension in setting the number of those defeated at 900,[32] versus 800 in 2 Samuel and 300 in 1 Chronicles 11 (in both the MT and LXX). The higher the death toll, of course, the more impressive the combatant.[33]

Eleazar's courageous spirit is indirectly enhanced as Josephus heightens the desperation of the Israelites' military position by adding that they were "dismayed" before noting, with LXX 1 Chr 11:13, that they "fled" (7.308).[34] Eleazar's hand no longer clings to his sword from muscle fatigue (as in 2 Sam 23:10), but from the stickiness of the Philistine blood that covers the hilt. So bent is Josephus on emphasizing the valor of the warriors that he takes the credit for the "wonderful and celebrated victory" that follows away from God (as explicitly in 2 Sam 23:10) and assigns it to the returning army with Eleazar at its head (7.309).

Against both the LXX text of 2 Sam 23:11 (which placed the glorious deed of Shammah at a non-existent site called "Theria") and LXX 1 Chr 11:13–14 (which overlooks Shammah completely), but in line with the Lucianic text of 2 Sam 23:11,[35] Josephus restores the location of the third episode, featuring Shammah, to Lehi, the site where Samson killed a thousand Philistines with the jawbone of a donkey. This setting invests Shammah with the added luster of his predecessor as he repeats Samson's heroism against the Philistines and routs their army, holding firm while his compatriots faltered. Josephus embellishes the account by likening Shammah to being "an army and a battle line in himself" (7.310), and again omits giving credit to God for the victory (as in 2 Sam 23:12), which would distract from the human achievement of the day, which is his main concern.[36]

32. Thackeray and Marcus, *Josephus*, 525 n.d; Begg, *Judean Antiquities*, 289 n.1140.

33. Similarly, in Josephus Abishai kills 600 (as in the Lucianic version of 2 Sam 23:18; Begg, *Judean Antiquities*, 291 n.1161) rather than 300, as in the MT and LXX.

34. Josephus uses a form of φεύγω with LXX 1 Chron 11:13; MT reads a little more softly by employing a verb that can signify "they went up" as well as "they withdrew"; LXX 2 Sam 23:9 represents this with a form of the more neutral verb ἀναβαίνω, suggesting a military retreat (corresponding to the technical use of καταβαίνω as the military term for "going down to engage" the enemy; Thackeray and Marcus, *Josephus*, 525 n.g) rather than a running for one's life. Josephus follows the LXX accounts which emphasize Eleazar's holding his ground alone (against MT 1 Chr 11:14) but preserves David's dignity by subtly disconnecting the episode he narrates in 7.309 from the episode where David and Eleazar are together "at Erasam." David is clearly present in MT and LXX 2 Sam 23:9 and 1 Chr 11:13; MT 1 Chr 11:14 had shown an interest in preserving David from appearing a coward, having him take his stand alongside Eleazar as the two of them successfully opposed the Philistines rather than fleeing with the rest of the army.

35. Begg, *Judean Antiquities*, 290 n.1148; Marcus and Thackeray, *Josephus*, 526 n.c.

36. He also omits reference to Shammah's apparent concern to hold a plot of ground

Finally, in regard to Benaiah, Josephus follows 1 Chr 11:23 in describing his Egyptian opponent as exceptionally tall rather than "handsome," as in 2 Sam 23:21, the former being more conducive to help readers appreciate Benaiah's victory. Contrary to the biblical accounts, where Benaiah at least has a staff to match the Egyptian's spear (2 Sam 23:21; 1 Chr 11:23), Josephus presents Benaiah as unarmed (γυμνός) in stark contrast to his "armed opponent" (ὡπλισμένον), which makes it all the more impressive that he could kill the Egyptian with his opponent's own spear (7.315). Josephus also gives greater space to Benaiah's killing of a lion trapped in a pit and makes it the climactic deed in Benaiah's "memorial" rather than the second of the three deeds narrated about this solider (as in 2 Sam 23:20–21 and 1 Chr 11:22–23). By emphasizing that the lion would have soon perished anyway, and, being trapped, no threat to anyone, he makes Benaiah's action appear all the more gratuitous an act of sheer spirit and courage (7.316–317).

When Josephus tells the story of David's thirst, then, we should expect to find similar embellishments of the narrative geared toward heightening the readers' appreciation of the valor of David's mighty men—expectations that Josephus the propagandist will not disappoint. However, we also find Josephus the historian emerging as he opens this narrative, for he changes David's location from the cave of Adullam to the citadel of Jerusalem itself. Thackeray and Marcus suggest that he is motivated by the concern to circumvent geographical difficulties in the biblical narrative, here particularly the alleged difficulty of understanding how the Philistines in the Valley of Rephaim could be an obstacle to getting water from Bethlehem when one is in the stronghold of Adullam, south of Rephaim and west of Bethlehem.[37]

It is more likely, however, that Josephus is motivated more by a desire to locate the episode more securely in the main story line of David's dealings with the Philistines. Josephus explicitly connects this episode with one previously narrated: "David went up to the citadel, *of which we spoke previously*, inquiring of God concerning the war" (7.311). Josephus transports the reader back to a specific point in the narrative, when David consults God regarding the timing for attack (1 Chr 14:10, 14–15; 2 Sam 5:19, 23; *Ant.* 7.72, 76) while the Philistine army occupies the Valley of Rephaim (1

---

full of lentils, perhaps as being too mundane a concern or earthy a detail.

37. Thackeray and Marcus, *Josephus*, 527 n.d. The same perceived difficulty in the biblical story—indeed the greater problem of David and the Philistines both appearing to be in two locations at the same time at the outset of the episode—has been noted by Knoppers (*I Chronicles 10–29*, 549) and explained by Japhet (*I & II Chronicles*, 245) as the result of the conflation of the opening of a lost episode, now used to link the present episode with the Three, with the episode of David's thirst.

Chr 14:9, 13; 2 Sam 5:18, 22; *Ant.* 7.71).[38] Moreover, while it is clear that David consults God while at the stronghold in 2 Samuel 5, Josephus seems to think consultation of God to be more natural at the central shrine in Jerusalem, where he assumes these two inquiries actually occurred. Thus Josephus's location of David at Jerusalem rather than Adullam is an attempt to weave this story more closely into the history of his campaigns against the Philistines.[39] It also has the benefit of removing any possible confusion regarding the (potential) dual locations of David and the Philistines in 2 Sam 23:13–14//1 Chr 11:15–16.[40]

Josephus makes it clear that David wishes for a drink of the water from his native Bethlehem, but curiously omits the explicit mention that he "longed" or "desired" prior to uttering his wish (against both the MT and LXX), replacing this experience of craving with David making an observation, giving his assessment of the superior quality of the water in the cistern in Bethlehem. This makes the utterance even more of a challenge to his troops than, as it might be interpreted by some readers of the biblical text, a wish born of weakness, a challenge that is "immediately" (παραχρῆμα) taken up by the Three "as soon as they heard" the king express the pleasure he would have from a drink of that water.

Josephus clearly identifies the three who dared to fetch water from Bethlehem with "the Three." At the outset of this section, he had promised to tell of "the deeds of only five" (ὧν πέντε μόνων διηγήσομαι τὰ ἔργα) of David's thirty-eight heroes (7.307), recounting the material found in 2 Sam 23 and 1 Chr 11 on Jeshbaal, Eleazar, Shammah, Abishai, and Benaiah. He places the incident of the raid on Bethlehem's cistern between the individual deeds of Shammah and Abishai, and speaks explicitly of "*these* three men" (οἱ τρεῖς ἄνδρες οὗτοι) performing the raid on the cistern by Bethlehem's gate, referring thus to the aforementioned Jeshbaal, Eleazar, and Shammah (7.313).[41] Even without the demonstrative, however, Josephus's tally of "five" would necessitate this identification.

---

38. Begg, *Judean Antiquities*, 290 n.1153 requires an ever so slight correction: this episode should not "remind readers of the king's *previous* inquiries of God in the face of Philistine assaults" (italics mine), as if it is a new instalment in the series, since it is to be identified with one of those inquiries.

39. The Chronicler had attempted to attend to the same by moving the entire block of stories from its location in 2 Samuel as part of a miscellany near the end of his treatment of David's career to the early period of David's career as king, just after David's capture of the citadel of Jerusalem.

40. Begg, "Exploits," 158.

41. Marcus and Thackeray (*Josephus*, 529) miss the οὗτοι in their translation of this passage, which Begg (*Judean Antiquities*, 291), however, correctly captures.

In keeping with his principal goal for these narratives and his *modus operandi* throughout this section, Josephus embellishes his account of the manner in which the Three "broke through the camp of the Philistines" (as it was simply put in 2 Sam 23:16; 1 Chr 11:18). Now they "ran out and dashed through the midst of the enemy's camp" and, after securing some water, "came back again through the enemy's camp to the king" (7.313). Because Josephus has re-located David to Jerusalem, moreover, the three now have to march through *miles* of enemy territory to get the trophy they seek, not merely skirt along the south of the camp and break through near Bethlehem.

Josephus strategically adds mention of the Philistine soldiers' reaction—"strategically" because their reaction becomes a model and vehicle for the readers' own response, as they find themselves also spectators of this audacious act: "the Philistines were so struck (καταπλαγέντας)[42] by their boldness and spirit (αὐτῶν τὸ θράσος καὶ τὴν εὐψυχίαν) that they remained still and dared nothing against them" (7.313). Since their numbers presented no threat ("they despised their fewness," though this was perhaps a mistake given what each of the Three could do to Philistines individually!), they could allow themselves a moment of quiet admiration for the bravery of their adversaries as the latter stride through the length of the camp as if the Philistines and their might were of no account.

The episode concludes much the same as in the biblical account, with Josephus making the king's rationale for not drinking the water himself more explicit, and adding a word about David's giving thanks to God for his soldiers' safety in connection with the libation (7.314).[43] These heroes are the real treasure for David, not the water nor anything else such men might bring him. In sum, then, Josephus tells the story with much the same goal as the authors of 2 Sam and 1 Chr, namely to preserve the honorable remembrance of David's mighty men and to evoke admiration for them. Josephus's embellishments and alterations largely serve the purpose of augmenting this admiration both for the individual heroes whose deeds are recounted in detail *and* for the remaining thirty-three, whose valor was equal to that displayed by these five men. In this he departs from the biblical account, where the ranking of each man's status was foregrounded, but still with essential agreement concerning the reasons to tell and revisit such stories.

---

42. Begg ("Exploits," 160 n.141) insightfully notes that this act of bravery on the part of the Three effectively answers the Philistines' counfouding (καταπλαγέντων) the Israelites with their numbers in 7.309.

43. Begg, *Judean Antiquities*, 291 n.1159.

The Story in 4 Maccabees

If the episode would be better entitled "the story of the raid on Bethlehem's well" in 2 Samuel, 1 Chronicles, and Josephus, in 4 Maccabees it truly becomes "the story of David's thirst" (4 Macc 3:6), the only other extant retelling of this episode from Jewish late antiquity. The author crafts the story so as to outline in detail the circumstances giving rise to David's experience of thirst, draws repeated attention to that experience, and develops the "irrational" feature of his desire. In the absence of the framing narrative found in 2 Samuel and 1 Chronicles (and the mention of "three soldiers" at both the outset and conclusion), the focus is taken off the deed of valor and placed squarely on the experience of an excessive craving and the example that David set by not, in the end, indulging that craving.

The author of 4 Maccabees writes within four or five decades of Josephus, from a province somewhere in what is now southern Turkey.[44] He writes in the form of a demonstration of the philosophical thesis that "pious reason is absolute master of the passions" (1:1), a familiar topic in Jewish and Greco-Roman ethical texts.[45] The "passions" include the experiences of physical sensations, emotions, and desires, and are viewed here, as in Greek ethical philosophy in general, as potential hindrances to one's commitment to walk in line with virtue (pain and fear, for example, being strong deterrents to persevere in the course demanded by courage, or greed and lust being forces that threaten to undermine one's commitment to temperance, prudence, or justice). His qualification of "reason" as "pious" hints at his deeper purpose, which is to assert the respectability, even superiority, of the Jewish way of life by demonstrating that those who follow the prescriptions of Torah and learn from the examples preserved in the sacred story of the Judeans (that is, those who enact "piety") achieve self-mastery in regard to the passions to a degree beyond that observed among the Greeks and others who hold self-mastery and a life in accordance with virtue as an ethical

---

44. The date of 4 Maccabees is generally set between 19 and 135 CE. The earlier part of this period was championed in Bickermann, "Date of Fourth Maccabees"; the latter part is favored by Dupont-Sommer (*Quatrième Livre*, 75–86) and Breitenstein (*Beobachtungen*, 13–29, 177–78). DeSilva (*4 Maccabees*, 14–18; *4 Maccabees: Introduction and Commentary*, xiv–xvii) favors a mid-first century date, while van Henten (*Maccabean Martyrs*, 73–78) tends to favor a date of 100 CE or shortly after. Regarding provenance, the most impressive evidence to date has been offered in van Henten, "Jewish Epitaph"; see discussion of this issue in deSilva, *4 Maccabees*, 18–21; deSilva, *4 Maccabees: Introduction and Commentary*, xvii–xix.

45. The thesis, or some variation, appears for example in *Ep. Aristeas* 221–22; Plutarch, *Virt. Mor.* 1 (*Mor.* 440D); Plato, *Phaedo* 93–94. The ideal of "self-mastery" is a sort of shorthand for this concept, as in Cicero, *Tusc. Disp.* 2.22.53; Plato, *Resp.* 431A; *Gorg.* 491.

ideal.[46] He therefore hopes to encourage Jews to remain committed to their distinctive, ancestral way of life, despite the disadvantages this might bring living in a Gentile-dominated world, by ennobling that way of life using the very concepts, ideals, and honorific terms employed by the Greek culture to affirm its own highest standards.[47]

The author accomplishes this goal first through examination of pre-scriptions of Torah, showing how the Jewish dietary laws provided op-portunity for the exercise of self-control (4 Macc 1:31–35) and how Torah's economic prescriptions curbed the power of greed by "forcing" the greedy to act contrary to nature and thus "learn a better way" (2:7–9). He com-bines this with a series of examples from the narrative portions of Scrip-ture that further demonstrate the benefits of the Torah-observant life for mastery of the passions and perfection of virtue. Thus Joseph shows how mindfulness of God's command that one should not covet one's neighbor's wife enables even those whose time of life renders the power of such lust the strongest to overcome the passions for virtue's sake (2:1–6), and Moses and Jacob each in his own way demonstrates the possibility of controlling anger (2:16–20). The author shifts more fully into the mode of "narrative demonstration" of the thesis at 3:19, giving the remainder of the oration over to the noble example of the nine martyrs who accepted torture unto death rather than violate the Torah.

The story of David's thirst (3:6–18) fits within the first, and far shorter, of these two sections. In particular, the author uses this story as the principle demonstration of the position he affirms within an inner-philosophical de-bate on the topic of the passions (see 3:2–5; the need for clarification on this point was announced earlier in the exordium, at 1:6b). With Poseidonius, the Peripatetics, and Plutarch, the author argues that the virtuous person should strive for *mastery* of the passions, not *extirpation* of the passions, the position that came to be associated with Stoics in the Roman imperial period.[48] The author holds to the first position because of his theology of creation, according to which it is God who "planted in [human beings] pas-sions and inclinations" with the intent that "the mind" that God "enthroned among the senses" should rule over them, even as the mind ordered itself and the whole person in subjection to the law of Moses (4 Macc 2:21–23; cf. 1:28–30). Since God made the passions to be part of the human being's constitution, the goal cannot be to destroy what God has created but rather

46. See, for example, the exclusive claims made in 4 Macc 7:18; 9:18.

47. On the rhetorical situation and strategy of 4 Maccabees, see chapter 2 above.

48. See Renehan, "Greek Philosophic Background." Cicero (*Tusc. Disp.* 3.22; 4.57) and Seneca (*Ep.* 116.1) were both ardent advocates for the uprooting of the passions.

to regulate it according to God's intended ordering of the person's interior faculties. The author uses the story of David's thirst as a proof from historical example that reason controls and surmounts the passions without extirpating them. At the end of the day, David still experiences thirst—but he has not allowed it to drive him to an act of injustice.[49]

Two words of LXX 2 Samuel 23:15—ἐπεθύμησεν Δαυιδ—provide the link between the story and the author's primary thesis, reason's mastery of desire, focusing here on ἐπιθυμία as one face of τὰ πάθη.[50] The fact that "David desired" or "craved" becomes the focal lens for the author's creative reflection upon the story as a whole in a way that is absent from the original texts and not exploited by Josephus.[51] The author thrusts this to the fore as the interpretive framework for the story by explicitly naming the episode "the story of David's thirst" (4 Macc 3:6), calling the hearers'/readers' attention to the experience of thirst as the story's central theme, and then reshaping

49. Dupont-Sommer, *Quatrième Livre*, 97.

50. Dupont-Sommer, *Quatrième Livre*, 98.

51. One other text that gives the story focused, if brief, attention is *Midrash Rabbah* on Ruth, 5.1. David's thirst is here also a primary focal point of reflection on the episode. "*And David longed, and said: Oh that one would give me water to drink of the well of Bethlehem.* R. Hiyya said: He was in need of a legal decision. *And the three mighty men broke through.* Why three? Because a law cannot be decided except by three." In this opening interpretive sortie, David's thirst is here not for water, but for clear guidance concerning the application of Torah, and the three mighty men have become three sages. The drawing of the water and David's refusal are similarly interpreted allegorically for the making of a legal ruling on the part of the three sages and David's establishment of the principle that "a king may make a breach in order to make a highway, and none may object." The thirst is similarly interpreted by R. Hunya, who said "in the name of R. Joseph: He had need of [information on] the laws concerning a captive maiden." R. Hunya recalls Deut 21:10–14, which discusses the licit procedure for slaking a decidedly different thirst. Finally, "R. Simeon b. Rabbi said: He sought to build the Temple." This climactic statement recalls David's greatest longing, which would go unsatisfied in his own lifetime. None of these rabbis have taken David's thirst, and the desire behind it, at face value, whereas the author of 4 Maccabees is interested in the story precisely as a case study in how to grapple with a very specific, mundane, human craving.

Thus far, the passage in *Midrash Rabbah* offers no expansions or alterations of the story, just symbolic interpretations of it. Embedded in this paragraph, however, is one interpretation that also involves giving the story a decidedly different setting and David different motives: "Bar Kappara said: It was the Festival of Tabernacles, and it was the time of the water oblation, and it was during the time that the High Places were permitted. *And the three mighty men broke through.* Why three? One to slay the enemy, one to remove the slain, and the third to bring the jug in purity." Bar Kappara interprets the action of requesting water, fetching water, and pouring the water out upon the ground literally, but transforms it into a regular drink offering in the context of the Feast of Tabernacles before the centralization of the cult at Jerusalem. In the process, he disregards David's motive—to satisfy his own desire by *drinking* the water. (The translation is that of Rabinowitz, *Midrash Rabbah: Ruth*.)

the story in line with the centrality of this theme.[52] Assisting this new focus is the complete disappearance of the narrative frame of 2 Samuel 23 (//1 Chronicles 11) that presented this story as one in a series of feats of valor testifying to the courage of David's soldiers. The focus is now squarely on David and how he deals with the sensation of thirst and the irrational desire that arises alongside it. The author further ensures that the original context of the encomium on the Three will not impose itself upon his re-telling of the story by eliminating the mention of the Three warriors, replacing them here with two anonymous, junior soldiers (4 Macc 3:12). This is no minor modification, given that the whole purpose of the story in the Scriptural accounts is to glorify David's top soldiers (whether or not they are mistaken to identify these three with *the* Three). Josephus clearly understood this to be the point of the scriptural episode, and he embellished it—and its surrounding episodes—in line with this purpose.

The author of 4 Maccabees sets the stage quite differently from the authors of 2 Samuel and 1 Chronicles, eliminating the references to the place names that occupied two verses in each biblical account and creating an opening scenario that differs markedly from that in the Jewish Scriptures:[53] "For since David was attacking the Philistines the whole day long, he, with many of the soldiers of the nation, killed many of them. Then when evening came, he pressed on, perspiring heavily, and came, exceedingly wearied, into the royal tent, around which the whole army of our forebears had encamped."[54]

Neither 2 Samuel nor 1 Chronicles suggests that David had spent the day in battle, though the author might have derived inspiration for his portrayal of a battle-weary David by reading the narrative in 1 Chr 11:12–19 (in 1 Chr 11:12–14, David and Eleazar are fighting together against the Philistines to defend a plot of ground) as two immediately successive episodes.[55] A David returning from a battle in which he was personally engaged the

52. Many of the distinctive features of the presentation in 4 Maccabees are often noted, as in Townshend, "Fourth Book," 670; Dupont-Sommer, *Quatrième Livre*, 98; Hadas, *Maccabees*, 158–159 (which throughout the annotations largely represents merely a translation and adaptation of Dupont-Sommer); Klauck, *4 Makkabäerbuch*, 701–2. The present discussion seeks to add to the conversation by analyzing the rhetorical significance of these changes.

53. So, rightly, Klauck, *4 Makkabäerbuch*, 701.

54. The details of the royal tent and the encampment of the army might also represent attempts to distance the re-telling of the story from being influenced by overtones of the original setting, which places the king in a cave and the Philistines in Bethlehem.

55. 2 Sam 23:17 would have been less conducive to such a reading, since there is a significant introduction of a new temporal setting, "in harvest time"—a detail that the author may also have chosen to omit on other grounds (see below).

full day, now dehydrated from the strenuous exercise, his water reserves having been expended in sweat, would certainly be seen to have a legitimate and pressing need for the refreshment of water, and that in abundance. This colorful, detailed scenario will help the audience imagine an experience of thirst that is compelling and legitimate, illustrating the author's subpoint (3:2–5) that such an experience of the passions—here, a physical sensation—was unavoidable. Such thirst cannot fail to be felt, as the Stoic mission of the extirpation of the passions would suggest, and the only concern for the ethical person would be how to respond naturally and moderately to the legitimate needs of the body.

The author introduces a detail concerning the setting not present in 2 Samuel or 1 Chronicles, namely that there were "plentiful springs" in the place where David was encamped, but that no amount of that water could satisfy his thirst (4 Macc 3:10). This may, in fact, run counter to the implications of the detail in 2 Sam 23:13 that the episode occurred at the beginning of harvest time, a dry season. However, it provides the necessary conditions that would render David's desire "irrational," rather than a reasonable need to provide for the necessities of the body. His thirst *ought*, by all rational standards, to have been satisfied after drinking from the springs that were close at hand. His desire became "irrational" when it set as its object other water that was beyond appropriate reach. The added detail concerning the presence of flowing springs near David's camp illumines the excess in his desire, and thus the excess in desire in general—craving something outside of one's lawful or reasonable grasp, something that lies beyond what is necessary. The author of *Letter of Aristeas* 222 captures the same principle: "In all things moderation is a good principle. What God gives take and hold; do not long for what is out of reach."

The author also suppresses the detail that David was longing for water from his own hometown of Bethlehem while it is occupied by the Philistine enemy (4 Macc 3:11). As we have seen, there is a certain appropriateness to David's desiring the waters of Bethlehem, since it represents a desire to have access to, and possibly retake, what is properly his own. Having erased any mention of David being at the cave of Adullam (which would have been appropriate in 4 Macc 3:8b), the author merely remarks that the water David craved was "in the enemy's territory," with no indication that David had any claim to this territory. In this way, David's desire becomes simply an expression of "I want what *they* have," an excessive and irrational desire when what David has at hand ought to suffice. In particular, it is an expression of "wanting what the ἀλλόφυλοι have," the author using the customary LXX term for Philistines (3:7).

In the author's rhetorical situation, addressing Diaspora Jews who are continually challenged by the sight of what the Gentiles around them enjoy, and what they could more easily enjoy were they to adopt a less strict posture in regard to the Torah, this is surely significant. David's thirst is thus presented in such a way as to align with the audience's social setting, connecting with their more general experience of wrestling with desires to have what lies beyond rightful reach and with their specific experience of wavering between finding satisfaction in what being Torah-observant Jews affords them and desiring more of what the Greek dominant culture would offer them if they eased their commitment to the particulars of dietary laws, Sabbath observance, and the like. That David would conquer his irrational longing in the end would, of course, give them assurance that persisting in the virtuous course was in fact possible. The author brings David's experience of craving to the fore in 3:11b as he speaks about David experiencing the "constricting" and "loosening" of the craving, borrowing Stoic language for how desires work upon the mind.[56] This inward focus, entirely absent from the biblical accounts, heightens appreciation for the force of the craving's assaults upon his reason, as well as brings his discussion of Jewish traditions into the orbit of Greco-Roman ethical philosophy.

In 2 Samuel, 1 Chronicles, and Josephus, the three soldiers could not wait, it seems, to answer the king's challenge. A very different picture emerges in 4 Maccabees: "Therefore, since his armor-bearers were complaining bitterly about the desire of the king, two young, sturdy soldiers, feeling shame (καταιδεσθέντες) with regard to the king's desire, armed themselves in full array and, taking a pitcher, assailed the barricades of the enemy" (3:12). The participle καταιδεσθέντες could be taken two ways. In the translation above, it suggests that the junior soldiers were embarrassed for the king, whose possession by an irrational craving was lowering his estimation in the eyes of his guards, and so they acted decisively to bring an end to this sorry display of weakness. The participle could, quite to the contrary, mark the respect that these two soldiers had for David even while their comrades balked at the idea of risking their lives for the king's whim. Given the lack of any indicators of contrast that might distance the junior soldiers' response from their peers' complaints, however, the former sense seems more likely. The author has thus introduced a very uncomfortable dynamic into the story—David's loss of repute in the eyes of his guards and soldiers—for the sake of advancing his rhetorical goal of displaying the consequences for one's honor (here, displayed by David's repute) of allowing the

---

56. Dupont-Sommer, *Quatrième Livre*, 98.

passions to gain the upper hand, preventing one from responding rationally and naturally to the needs of the senses.

The embellishments continue as the author tells how the water was acquired. First, the mention of the army being at dinner (4 Macc 3:9) places the actions that follow at nighttime, probably under cover of dusk or darkness. From the mention that the two junior soldiers "elude the notice of the guards at the gates," the reader gets the sense of a stealthy operation—a detail entirely absent from the biblical accounts, and quite different from the picture in Josephus, where the Three *parade* through the enemy camp in plain sight. Here, the soldiers are keenly aware of their peril as they undertake their mission. As the author draws out their time exposed to the enemy, moving "through the army of the enemy, searching everything out" to find the water source,[57] the hearer's appreciation of their prolonged peril increases. This will, in turn, augment the hearer's appreciation of the "danger to David's soul" posed by drinking the water, brought at such great risk.

The story ends as expected with David pouring out the water as a libation (the same conclusion as one finds in 2 Sam 23:16–17; 1 Chron 11:18–19),[58] but the author develops more fully the internal sensations and rational processes occurring within the protagonist. The author makes explicit David's inner consideration that drinking the water would pose "a fearful danger to his soul" (3:15). David's explicit declaration that the water was the equivalent of the blood of the soldiers who fetched it is given here as an indirect and artful abbreviation (David feared to drink "what was of equal potency as blood"),[59] leaving the rationale for this equation (the fact that it was brought at grave risk to human life) to be inferred.

Why would drinking this water, however, pose such a threat? The water was not literally blood, such that the proscriptions of Lev 17:11–14 applied. Moreover, the water is poured out as a libation—a drink offering—not a sacrifice of atonement, which is the proper ritual use for blood according to Lev 17:11–14. Aechylus's *Agamemnon* provides an informative comparative text. Clytemnestra entices the returning hero Agamemnon to enter his house treading upon a scarlet runner, an entrance fit for such a victor. Agamemnon's response shows the sensitivity to *nemesis* that must also have motivated David: "Draw not down envy upon my path by strewing it with tapestries. 'Tis the gods we must honor thus; but for a mortal to tread upon broidered fineries is, to my judgement, not without

---

57. A detail made possible by the author's dissociation of the episode from Bethlehem, where the soldiers would know exactly where to go to get the water ("the well by the gate," 2 Sam 23:15).

58. DeSilva errs on this point in *4 Maccabees: Introduction and Commentary*, 108.

59. Klauck, *4 Makkabäerbuch*, 702.

ground for dread. I bid thee revere me not as a god, but as a man" (*Agam.* 920–925). Submitting at last to Clytemnestra's request, Agamemnon recognizes the "fearsome danger to his soul" of arrogating such honors and prays that the gods overlook this act of his (*Agam.* 943–947), which, of course, they don't. David's response suggests that he, too, is mindful of the dangers of ὕβρις, of provoking God's anger by claiming for himself more than was his due as a mortal. Since spending something so costly as that water on a mortal person's desire would be to take more than is one's due, David gives the drink to the only One who would merit such a gift, becoming thereby a further example of "justice," a virtue the discussion of which was initiated in 4 Macc 2:6b.

Fourth Maccabees 3:15–16 contain two further details, unique to this version of the story, that directly advance the author's goals for the episode as an "argument from example." First, he reminds the hearers that, even as David pours out the libation, he is still "burning with thirst" (3:15a), a remarkable detail insofar as the biblical narrative never tells us that David was thirsty, but which has become the major focal point of this retelling (3:6, 8, 10–12). He cannot eradicate his experience of this sensation, which offers proof against the notion that extirpation of the passions is the necessary goal, rather than mastery of the same. David does succeed in achieving mastery, however, for even in the midst of suffering thirst he does not allow it to lead him to commit injustice. Second, the author interjects the description of the "means" that enabled David's libation—"setting reason against desire" (3:16), recognizing and distinguishing what was proper for a mortal from what was proper for God alone and acting on this knowledge, contrary to the impulses that were assailing him. This is, of course, most salient to the author's principle thesis that reason instructed by the God-given Law masters the passions.

The author has shaped this episode to serve as an effective foil for another episode[60] in David's life when a desire for sexual intercourse with a woman under another man's roof led him to arrange for the death of one of his most loyal officers (notably, an ἀλλόφυλος, a foreigner). David could have slaked that thirst with any number of the many women under his own roof, but instead he craved what was in another's territory and, rather than releasing her as a metaphorical offering to the God who had given him his kingdom, drank deeply from that illicit draught and brought God's justice upon his head. The present episode becomes the ethical triumph that the other fails to attain. Here, the author can present a David whose

---

60. I mistakenly call this an "earlier" episode in deSilva, *4 Maccabees: Introduction and Commentary*, 109.

piety is displayed as he puts virtue (in particular, giving God God's due) ahead of his own passions—an example that the author hopes his audience will continue to seek to embody.

Conclusion

The "story of David's wish for water" (perhaps the most neutral way to put it) appears in three basic forms in Jewish literature. In 2 Samuel and 1 Chronicles, it has been adapted largely through the immediate literary frame ("three of the thirty chiefs went down . . . The three warriors did these things," 2 Sam 23:13, 17//1 Chr 11:15, 19) and the neighboring literary context (the recounting of the heroic deeds of David's warriors, 2 Sam 23:8–12, 20–23//1 Chr 11:10–14, 20–25) to add to the luster of Jeshbaal, Eleazar, and Shammah (who may well not have been the original three warriors intended by the story), the first and famous "Three" among David's mighty men. In this context, it becomes the "story of the raid on Bethlehem's well."

This title would also work well for the version of the story in *Judean Antiquities*. Josephus has largely followed the interpretive guidelines for the story provided by the authors of 2 Samuel and 1 Chronicles (and their identification of the soldiers as *the* Three), embellishing the warriors' display of courage by emphasizing their boldness and fearlessness as they stride through the enemy camp in plain sight, and by displaying the reaction of the Philistines to their courage. These embellishments are quite in keeping with his retelling of the individual feats of Jeshbaal, Eleazar, Shammah, Abishai, and Benaiah. He departs from his source material, however, in eliminating any indications of the "pecking order" among the thirty, using the acts of valor of these five men rather as typical tokens of the bravery exhibited by the whole company of the thirty.

The author of 4 Maccabees, however, departs dramatically from the interpretive guidelines provided for the episode in the Jewish Scriptures, and indeed thoroughly rewrites the story to illustrate and support his very different rhetorical goals. Here it truly becomes the "story of David's thirst" (4 Macc 3:6). Stripped of the interpretive frame of the "deeds of valor" of David's warriors—and of the historical context of the Philistine occupation of the Valley of Rephaim and Bethlehem—the story now focuses on David's experience of thirst (which is absent from the Scriptural story), the irrational desire that drives him to crave the water that the non-Jews have in their territory, when plentiful springs are to be found close by (another detail absent from the original story), and the means by which he finds the strength to do what is just rather than wrongfully self-indulgent. The story is so crafted as to become a narrative demonstration that, though one cannot *eradicate* certain "passions," one can *master* them so as to discern and choose the virtuous course of action.

Josephus and 4 Maccabees continue to bear witness to the fixedness and fluidity of the biblical stories, and to the range of liberties authors felt free to take when re-presenting the biblical story to achieve their own particular goals for their new texts. Both exhibit a great deal of freedom and creativity as they attempt to enter into the world of the story from their particular vantage point and through the lens of their particular interests, "invent" or "discover" new angles on the story, and return to present—in the case of 4 Maccabees, at least—a very different story that purports, however, to represent the same episode. The minute analysis of a particular "midrash" on a historiographical account from Scripture may continue to assist interpreters negotiate and interpret the differences in other "synoptic" retellings of the same episode, as the omissions, embellishments, and occasionally conflicting details provide points of entry into the authors' uses of the story for "proclamation."

5

Engagement with Greco-Roman Intertexture

Conversations about Maternal Affections

The author of 4 Maccabees drank deeply from the Greco-Roman environment that surrounded him. Dismissals of him as a philosophical dilettante have been overturned by careful examinations both of the complexity of Middle Stoicism and the complexity of the author's interaction with that common topic of philosophical ethics, the "mastery of the passions."[1] Hans-Josef Klauck meticulously examined the treatment of "fraternal/sororal affection" in Plutarch and 4 Maccabees, showing both their close affinities and 4 Maccabees's distinctive development of that constellation of topics.[2] Jan Willem van Henten carefully explored the connections between 4 Maccabees and Greco-Roman traditions about a life given in exchange for others.[3] This study continues the investigation of the author of 4 Maccabees's formative interaction with the philosophical and literary topics of his Greek environment and to analyze his strategic use of these topics to advance his overarching goal (namely, promoting continued observance of the Jewish way of life as the path to attain the highest Greek ideals),[4] by giving similar attention to the characterization of the mother and her relationship with her seven sons. In particular, this study pursues a comparative analysis of the author's treatment of the topic of parental affection (4 Macc 14:13–19; 15:4–10), the passion that the mother particularly must master, and his invention of a fictive lament such as the mother might have uttered after such bereavement as she suffered (4 Macc 16:6–11) with extant works by non-Jewish Greek authors.

1. Renehan, "Greek Philosophic Background"; deSilva, *4 Maccabees*, 51–75.
2. Klauck, "Brotherly Love."
3. Van Henten, *Maccabean Martyrs*.
4. This is a broad point of consensus (see deSilva, *4 Maccabees*, 43–46).

The present study focuses on comparative texts that bear a strong re-semblance to these passages in 4 Maccabees in genre, purpose, and content. The *digressio* in 4 Macc 14:13–19 (supplemented by material in 15:4–10) presents a miniature discourse concerning affection for offspring, resem-bling Plutarch's larger-scaled discourse and, secondarily, Aristotle's briefer comments about parental affection in the *Nicomachian Ethics*. All three texts present philosophical reflection on the sources and natural manifesta-tions of this particular emotion. Fourth Maccabees 16:6–11 introduces a dramatic lament, a "set piece" *not* uttered by the bereaved mother, similar again in form, purpose, and content to the laments placed on the lips of bereaved women in Euripidean tragedy.[5]

After a brief introduction locating the author's treatment of the moth-er within the overall framework of his philosophical argument, this study examines points of contact between the treatment of parental affection in 4 Macc 14:13–19; 15:4–10 and the comparative material in Plutarch and Aris-totle, followed by an analysis of how the author has employed these topics as he advanced his philosophical argument promoting Torah-nurtured piety as the infallible path to mastery of the passions. The study then turns to the author's invention of a tragic lament drawing on vocabulary and topics familiar from Euripides's *Trojan Women* and *Hecuba* and to an analysis of why, according to the author, the mother of the seven refuses to give voice to such a lament as one would naturally expect from loving mothers bereft of their children, and thus how parental love indeed reaches its consummation in her urging her children on to martyrdom.

---

5. These comparative texts do not, by any means, exhaust the list of Greco-Roman treatments of virtuous mothers, the ethical demands of parenting and of placing a high-er premium on virtuous action than on reacting to the pain or suffering of a child, and the like. The larger genre of 4 Macc 14:11—17:6 is a laudatory encomium on the moral achievement of the mother, whose "manliness" surpassed that of males (4 Macc 15:30), with which it has been profitable to compare Plutarch's "On the Bravery of Women," a collection of stories narrating the surprising achievements of women (including the mother, Megisto), frequently in regard to their superior embodiment of "male" virtues (see deSilva, *4 Maccabees*, 83–84). Seneca's *Consolationes*, particularly his *Ad Marciam*, would be appropriately compared with 4 Maccabees again on the basis of likeness of form (addressing a bereaved mother; see the apostrophe in 4 Macc 17:4), purpose (au-thors attempting to help a mother come to terms with the experience of bereavement) and content (the use of similar topics, such as the blessed state of the deceased or the possibility of displaying bravery in the face of hardship). Because these comparative texts are not written with the development of the topic of parental affection or the dramatic expression of maternal bereavement in mind, they will not be prominently featured in this study except as they stray into the focal points of this study.

The Role of the Mother's Achievement within the Philosophical Argument

Fourth Maccabees presents itself as a philosophical demonstration (ἐπιδείκνυσθαι, 1:1; τὴν ἀπόδειξιν, 3:19; ἀπέδειξα, 16:2) that places particularly heavy emphasis on proof by example (1:7–9). This emphasis on virtuous exemplars leads quite naturally to the amplification of encomiastic elements throughout the text, which the exordium alerts hearers to expect (ἔπαινον, 1:2; ἐπαινεῖν, 1:10). Attempts, therefore, to divorce the two parts of 4 Maccabees (i.e., 1:1–3:18 and 3:19–18:24) as originally separate units ("philosophical discourse" and "encomium") or to view them as functioning essentially independently ignore the author's own claims concerning how the discursive and narrative sections work together in concert (1:12).[6]

The examples of the martyrs, then, contribute both proofs of the philosophical demonstration and praiseworthy models for behavior that support, in turn, the hearers' commitment to embody the way of life embedded in the philosophical proposition that *"pious* reason"—the decision-making faculty that has been trained by the Jewish Law (1:15–18)—"masters the passions" (1:1).[7] The author proceeds to advance the more exclusive claim that *only* this kind of training results in a decision-making faculty that is fully equipped to master any passion, consistently choosing virtue and nobility (one hears the steady crescendo through 2:23; 7:18–19; 9:17–18). We want to attend, therefore, both to how the author's heroine matches the highest achievements and ideals expressed by Greek authors, and to how she surpasses the achievements of their models.[8]

The mother's example (14:11–17:6) is, both implicitly by placement (as the final proof) and explicitly by way of introduction (14:11–12), the ultimate example of the author's thesis. Jason of Cyrene (or his epitomator) also gave special attention to the mother's moral achievement in the face

---

6. These positions were advanced, respectively, in Lebram, "Literarische Form," 82–83; and Breitenstein, *Beobachtungen*, 132–33; see also Dupont-Sommer, *Quatrième Livre*, 19. Among the unpersuaded are Redditt, "Concept of *Nomos*," 262–63; Klauck, *4 Makkabäerbuch*, 648; van Henten, *Maccabean Martyrs*, 69; deSilva, *4 Maccabees*, 25–28, 46–49; Stowers, "4 Maccabees," 844–45.

7. A similar combination appears in Seneca's *De constantia sapientis*, which introduces familiar examples of philosophy at work, delivering what it promises in the persons of Cato the Younger and Stilbo of Megara, praising the achievements of these "complete persons" so as to render the Stoic philosophy both credible and desirable.

8. In so doing, this study also seeks to advance the important conversation about the characterization of this mother *qua mulier* in 4 Maccabees, such as been helpfully begun in Young, "Woman with the Soul of Abraham"; Moore and Anderson, "Taking It Like a Man."

of such horror (2 Macc 7:20–23). Fourth Maccabees expands the source's attention both to her firmness in faith and her role in spurring her sons on to virtue in the face of pain and death.[9] The ability of this mother, being bereft of seven sons, to remain steadfast in her commitment to God and to the pious course of action represents, for the author, the perfection of ἀνδρεία—"courage" as "manliness" (see 15:30).

Before we enthusiastically congratulate the author for giving the woman her due, we should consider that he makes the mother his climactic example precisely because it is so *unexpected* that she would perform so well under such pressures. The deeply rooted prejudice that women were more prone to be led by their passions and less naturally well-equipped for mastery of the passions (see Aristotle *Pol.* 1.13 1260a12–14; Philo *Leg. All.* 2.44–50; Seneca *Marc.* 7.2) served to legitimate their subordinate status within the household. The author of 4 Maccabees exploits this prejudice with an adverbial καί: the audience should not be astounded that reason exercised control over "these males" (τῶν ἀνδρῶν), since "*even* a woman's mind (καὶ γυναικὸς νοῦς) was able to master more diverse agonies" (14:11). The highest achievement of the Torah is nurturing such discipline that "even a woman's mind," shored up by the defenses of piety, can master the passions.

"On Affection for Offspring" in 4 Maccabees, Plutarch, and Aristotle

The passion that most occupies this woman *qua* mother is "love for off-spring" (introduced as early as 2:12), a generally positive emotion that must nevertheless never be allowed to get the upper hand when its drives conflict with the requirements of virtuous behavior. The author identifies this as, in fact, the most powerful of emotions, causing the mother to internalize the sufferings and the passions that rack each of her children, feeling them as deeply within as her children experience them in their own bodies (14:11b–13; 15:11, 16, 22; 16:3). His use of common topics related to affection for

9. Both authors thus depart from the Thucydidean tradition of avoiding public speech about women: "great is her glory of whom there is least talk among men whether in praise or in blame" (*Hist.* 2.45.2). They align rather with "the Roman custom" which, according to Plutarch (who also followed it himself), "publicly renders to women, as to men, a fitting commemoration after the end of their life" (*Mul. Virt.* Introduction [*Mor.* 242F]). The author of 4 Maccabees would concur with Plutarch in his view that studying virtue-in-action in both male and female subjects leads to a clearer perception of virtue itself (*Mor.* 243C) and with Seneca in his estimation that women are as capable of displaying virtue, and, in particular, enduring suffering and toil, as males (see *Marc.* 16.1–2).

offspring, such as can be observed in the writings of Plutarch and Aristotle, amplify the force of natural affection upon this particular mother, and thus amplify her achievement of self-mastery.

In *De amore prolis* (*Moralia* 493A–497E), Plutarch considers Epicurus's rebuke of human parents whose care for their children is an investment made with a view to the children returning the favor, as it were, in their care for their parents in their old age (*Am. prol.* 2 [*Mor.* 495A–B]). He examines the examples to be found in Nature, where the "special characteristics" of natural and proper behavior are "preserved pure and unmixed and simple," that is, free from the distortions introduced through human culture (*Am. prol.* 1 [*Mor.* 493C]).[10] Animals display pure motivations for procreation (neither the indulgence in the pleasure of sexual intercourse, nor the desire to qualify to inherit under the Roman *ius trium liberorum*) as well as tremendous "forethought, endurance, and self-control" in regard to the bearing and care of offspring (*Am. prol.* 2 [*Mor.* 494A]).

Plutarch dismisses the bee as an overused commonplace (*Am. prol.* 2 [*Mor.* 494A]), and so takes the reader to the king-fisher, the shark, the she-bear, the lion, an unspecified bird, a female dog, partridges, and hens. The king-fisher is remarkable for its preparation of a protective nest, and the shark for similarly exotic means of keeping its vulnerable young safe. The proverbial bird (Plutarch recites Homer, *Iliad* 9.324) provides a model of self-control and altruism, feeding her young "at the cost of her own hunger." The lion, she-dog, partridge, and hen all distinguish themselves in defense of their young, whose well-being they seek to safeguard at all costs without regard for the danger to themselves. Plutarch gives special attention to the partridge and the hen valiantly warding off the encroacher (*Am. prol.* 2 [*Mor.* 494E–F]).

The author of 4 Maccabees draws heavily on this cluster of topics in his initial characterization of parental love:

> Observe how intricate the affection of parental love is, drawing everything toward a sympathy coming from the inmost parts. Where indeed even the unreasoning animals have sympathy and affection of the same kind as found among human beings toward those born from them, for even among birds the tame ones defend their nestlings by building upon the rooftops,[11]

10. Aristotle also regards "the affection of parent for offspring and offspring for parent" to be "a natural instinct, not only in human beings but also in birds and most animals" (*Eth. nic.* 8.1.3).

11. My translation follows Dupont-Sommer (*Quatrième Livre*, 138), who accepted Adolf Deissmann's emendation ("Vierte Makkabäerbuch," 169) to ὀροφοκοιτοῦντα, "making a bed/nest of thatched reeds."

while others, making the peaks of mountains and sheer parts of ravines and the holes and highest parts of trees their nests, bear their young and hinder the one who would approach. But if they are even then unable to hinder [the encroacher], flying around them, pained with affection, calling out with their own voice, they[12] help their children as much as they can. And why is it necessary to demonstrate sympathy towards children through unreasoning animals, when indeed even bees, around the season for making honeycomb, defend themselves against the encroachers and, just as with an iron sting, strike those approaching their brood and defend them even to death? But sympathy for her children did not dislodge the mother of the young men, like-souled with Abraham as she was. (14:13–20)

Both Plutarch and the author of 4 Maccabees look to the examples of nature (birds and bees are prominent in both accounts), concluding that Nature has implanted in parents the strong drive to secure the well-being of their offspring through the provision of safe homes and through selfless, even frenzied, attempts to rescue their young when threatened with harm.[13]

The powerful emotion of maternal love (in particular) comes from deep within the person of a mother, involving her entire body in their agonies (14:13). The Greek ethical tradition identified a number of factors involved in this attachment. Aristotle treats parental love as a kind of friendship, finding that "parents love their children as themselves (one's offspring being as it were another self—other because separate)" (*Eth. nic.* 8.12.3). Aristotle's definition of a friend as "another self" is well-known, as is his identification of "likeness" as the basis for friendly feelings (*Eth. nic.* 8.8.5). Aristotle understands the affection of parents to exceed that of their children because of the longer period of time in which parents "love" the child: "parents love their children as soon as they are born, children their parents only when time has elapsed and they have acquired understanding, or at least perception" (*Eth. nic.* 8.12.3). Plutarch shares the conviction that parental love begins at the earliest moment of the child's life (*Am. prol.* 3 [*Mor.* 495C]). But this factor also explains for Aristotle why mothers experience love for offspring more deeply than fathers, for mothers have nine additional months during which to nurture the feeling of emotional connection with the life growing within them (*Eth. nic.*

---

12. The singular verbs are still governed by the neuter plural nouns of vv. 15–16.

13. Seneca will also seek out Nature's proper, intended limits for grieving in the behavior of birds, arguing that prolonged grief is contrary to Nature (*Marc.* 7.2).

8.12.3).[14] The time of the child in the womb is understood to be a time for special bonding between mother and child.

Plutarch draws further attention to the biological arrangements that assume and point to a deeply implanted love for offspring, particularly in mothers. The re-routing of the flow of the mother's blood from monthly evacuation to the nurturing of the fetus, thence to the production of milk after the child's birth, shows Nature's forethought and argues, as from effect to cause, for the affection for offspring that Nature implants in the mother (in particular), without which the apparatus would be useless (*Am. prol.* 3 [*Mor.* 495E-496B]). Plutarch also understands nature to have arranged the mother's body to promote intimate interaction that feeds love for off-spring. Breast-feeding is a prime example of this for, "while other animals have their dugs hanging loose beneath the belly, in women they grow above, upon the breast, where mothers can kiss and embrace and fondle the infant, the inference being that the end and aim of bearing a child is not utility, but affection" (*Am. prol.* 3 [*Mor.* 496C]).[15]

Fourth Maccabees resonates deeply with these conversations about the connection of parent (in particular, mother) and child.

> O, how can I describe the children-loving emotions of parents? We impress a wondrous similarity of both soul and form into the miniature stamp of a child. And mothers especially, because mothers become more sympathetic than fathers from their sufferings for those born from them. For the weaker[16] mothers are, and the more children they bear, the more they love their children. And the mother of the seven children, who was given strong affection by means of seven pregnancies, loved her children more than all mothers, and on account of the many pangs suffered for each of them was compelled to have sympathy for them. But on account of reverence toward God she disregarded the temporary deliverance of the children. Not only so, but on

14. Euripides (*Frag.* 1015) also bears witness to this truism: "The mother, however, always loves the children more than the father."

15. Psuedo-Plutarch similarly promotes breast-feeding by the natural mother (as opposed to a wet-nurse) on the grounds that, by so doing, "mothers would come to be more kindly disposed towards their children, and more inclined to show them affection" (*Lib. ed.* 5 [*Mor.* 3D]).

16. Rahlfs reads ἀσθενόψυχοι, "weak-souled," with Alexandrinus, but Sinaiticus reads ἀσθενέστεραν (changed by a corrector to ἀσθενέστεραι). The discussion below is based on the reading in Sinaiticus, which, if original, shows the author presenting a strictly physiological assessment of the mother's constitution. Alexandrinus could be construed as a statement about mothers' psychological or moral capacity, which runs against the tendency of this author to promote childbearing as a source of fortitude.

account of the nobility and goodness of the sons and their ready obedience to the law she had even greater affection for them. For they were so just and self-controlled and courageous and magnanimous and loving towards their brothers and towards their mother that they obeyed her, guarding what was lawful even unto death. (15:4–10)

In this second passage on "affection for offspring," the author introduces the topic of "likeness" as a factor contributing to the "emotions of parents who love their children" (15:4).[17] The attention given to the moral character of these children (15:9–10) may support viewing moral likeness as a bond between mother and children, since the author attributes their noble character as endearing them further to their mother and their steadfastness to the point of death as a reflection of her moral formation of her children.[18] The author also develops the biological basis for the deep feelings experienced (uniquely) by the mother. With the implanting of the seed and its growth in the mother's womb, a deep-seated emotional attachment to the child was also implanted (15:6). The birth pangs that racked the mother's abdomen and genitalia further augmented this attachment (15:6–7). The topic of breast-feeding (which emerges explicitly in 16:7–8) is no doubt intended as a component of "nurture, feeding" (τροφεία) in 15:13, though the author has not developed it explicitly as a natural process that fed the mother's affection.[19]

The author introduces new material on the topic of maternal love in 15:5. He asserts that a mother's love does not diminish for each of her children the more numerous those children become, as if she possessed only a limited amount of love to parcel out among a growing number, but actually grows with the number of children. The author conjoins "weakness" with repeated

17. In this, the author recalls not only Aristotle, but also the more detailed observations made by Stoic authors that this likeness manifests itself not only in physical features, but also in moral and psychological properties. For example, Cleanthes declares that "we become like our parents not only according to the body but also according to the soul, in the passions, in the habits, and in the dispositions" (Arnim, *Stoicorum*, 1.518, translation mine), and Pseudo-Plutarch observes that Stoics, in general, "maintain that seed derives from the entire body and from the soul and that likeness in form and character is molded from the same origins, appearing to the beholder like an image painted with the same colors" (*Plac. Philos.* 5.11.3, as translated in Hadas, *Maccabees*, 220; also Arnim, *Stoicorum*, 2.749).

18. The author uses their nobility as a topic augmenting parental affection, but it could also provide a topic of consolation, as in Euripides, *Hec.* 591–92: "but the report of your nobility [in the face of death] has taken away the excess of my grief."

19. He also does not call attention specifically to maternal embraces here (see Euripides, *Tro.* 757, where Andromache exclaims, "O child that my arms have held [ὑπαγκάλισμα], so dear to your mother!"), though he uses the topic in connection with the fostering of fraternal affection (ἐναγκαλισμάτων, 13.21).

childbirths (καὶ . . . καί . . .) as linked causes for greater maternal devotion.[20] In pre-industrial societies, pregnancy and childbirth pose significant threats to the life of the mother. To the degree that mothers put themselves at risk and pour out their own strength and vitality for the sake of bringing children into the world, to that same degree their attachment to those in whom they have invested so much of themselves increases. Taken together with the more commonly adduced topics mentioned above, this may justify the author's claim that the mother-seven-times-over (ἡ ἑπταμήτωρ, 16:24) "loved her children more than any other mother" (15:6).

The first common denominator between Plutarch and 4 Maccabees is that "affection for offspring" drives parents to act to preserve the lives and well-being of their offspring, often in ways that put the parents themselves in jeopardy. Fourth Maccabees particularly highlights this face of φιλοτεκνία-in-action in 14:15–20, using examples of animal behavior very similar to those invoked by Plutarch.[21] The mother's natural inclinations are to protect her children from danger and rescue them from harm by any means necessary, which would here include capitulation to the tyrant's demands.[22]

Acting in line with these natural impulses, however, will not reliably lead parents to do what preserves the lives and well-being of their offspring for the long term. It responds to immediate threats and dangers but must be tempered by rational judgment with a view to preserving them from greater threats and dangers—even if that requires allowing children to suffer (dramatically) adverse circumstances in the immediate situation. Commitment

20. Dupont-Sommer (*Quatrième Livre*, 140) and Hadas (*Maccabees*, 221) find the placement of ἀσθενέστεραι difficult, transposing it conceptually to stand outside and prior to the ὅσῳ-clause, but this violates the author's clear syntactic signals.

21. See also the analogy of the care shown by a mother bird in Euripides' *Trojan Woman*, as Andromache embraces Astyanax who has run to her for help, "falling like some young bird into the embrace of my wings" (*Tro.* 751).

22. Redditt ("Concept of *Nomos*," 256) posits a distinction between the meanings of φύσις in discussions of fraternal and parental affection from the meaning of this term in 4 Maccabees 5 as a "structure in harmony with which men [sic] ought to live." I find, on the contrary, that the φύσις that implants φιλοστοργία and φιλαδελφία into people's hearts is one and the same as the φύσις that represents the harmony of the cosmic order and provides the guide to life for the philosopher. When the author (and this would be true of both the author of 4 Maccabees and Plutarch) looks to animals for clarity regarding "natural" love of offspring, he is still looking for the "harmony of the cosmic order" represented in the relationships between its constituent parts. In making this distinction, Redditt appears to me to miss the significance of the claim being made in 4 Maccabees that Nature itself (a potential rival to Torah as ultimate norm) is an insufficient guide to virtue. It would lead Eleazar to compromise virtue if adopted as the norm in chapter 5 just as surely as it threatened to do for the brothers and the mother as they struggled with the pains born of the parental and fraternal love which φύσις ("Nature") implants and for which it pleads.

to piety, to keeping God's covenant inviolate, has enabled the ἑπταμήτωρ to do this very thing. If she urged capitulation, she would only attain "temporary deliverance" (σωτηρίας προσκαίρου, 15:2; τὴν . . . πρόσκαιρον σωτηρίαν, 15:8), "deliverance lasting for a short time" (πρὸς ὀλίγον χρόνον σωτηρίαν, 15:27), for her children, but she would then leave them exposed to the far greater danger of God's anger against the ungrateful and the consequent loss of eternal well-being. By refusing to act in line with the promptings of natural love for children, she preserves them from that greater threat and secures for them "eternal life" (αἰωνίαν ζωήν, 15:3). What "love for offspring" could only wish it had the strength to achieve for its children (i.e., well-being *forever*), only love for offspring subordinated to "love of religion" can enable.

Fourth Maccabees expands the scope of the mother's maternity in ways that have only opened up for her because she allowed her love for God to determine the shape of her expression of love for offspring. She gives a second and far more enduring birth to her sons—"rebirth for immortality" (16:13). Like the first birthing experience, this one also involves sharp and all-consuming pains (15:17) but, like those earlier pains, these are also fruitful rather than empty. The resistance of these martyrs, moreover, had political consequences for the entire nation at a critical point in its existence (1:11; 17:20–22; 18:4). By helping her sons stay the course, she also gave rebirth to the nation (hence is hailed as "mother of the nation" in 15:29), her sufferings being the birth pangs of the restoration of Torah-observance and reconciliation with God that saved Israel from disaster. Her commitment to piety enabled her to bring benefit not only to her biological children, but also to the generations of her spiritual "descendants" in the nation of Israel, discharging her responsibility to them and becoming a symbolic maternal figure binding them together as a single family. By means of unwavering commitment to pious action before God she raises her potential as a life-giving mother to ever greater levels of efficacy. The actions of the mother thus embody not the neglect of love for offspring, nor its negation, but its perfection and fullest fruition.[23]

A second major point of correspondence between Plutarch and 4 Maccabees emerges in the focus on the natural processes of gestation, lactation, and nurture as all productive of affection for offspring (as well as predicated upon it). Fourth Maccabees employs these topics for amplification, in particular as the means by which to show how the mother's experience of the tortures could be as sensate and physical, in a sense, as that of the brothers,

---

23. The author holds this particular "passion" in high esteem. "Natural inclination and parental love and affection for offspring" is "sacred" or "holy" (15:13), in stark contrast with several other "passions" that he has treated (particularly in 1:1—3:18). But, like any passion, it cannot be the ultimate, determinative guide to behavior.

to whose bodies the instruments of torment were actually applied (14:11–12; 15:16, 22). The *ekphrasis*, or "vivid description," in 15:14–22 assaults the audience with a series of horrific images, bringing together the seven episodes narrated in 9:10–12:19 into a single, accumulated experience, replicating the mother's experience of the scenes that the reader has already encountered seriatim. Emphasizing the physical springs of maternal affection, located in the σπλάγχνα (15:23),[24] the author draws attention to the deeper locus for the mother's suffering than the eyes or the ears, as if she responded merely to the horror of the *spectacle* (i.e., as the reader/hearer experiences the scenes in the narrative).[25] In this way, he augments the audience's appreciation of the magnitude of the mother's contest with the passions, and thus the immensity of her victory and, ultimately, the power of the Torah-observant life to prepare the human being to walk consistently in line with virtue, unmoved by *any* disturbances of the soul (16:1–2).

Laments of Bereaved Mothers in 4 Maccabees and Euripides

The author uses the rhetorical technique of "speech in character" throughout the narrative demonstration but does so most conspicuously (since artificially) at two key points where he develops "the road not taken" by his heroic exemplars. The first appears after Antiochus has laid out the options for the seven brothers, presenting the response they might have made had they been "faint-spirited and unmanly" (δειλόψυχοί . . . καὶ ἄνανδροι, 8:16; the speech is found in 8:17–26). The second appears after the author's depiction of the ordeal being faced by the mother, presenting the response she might have made had *she* been faint-spirited (δειλόψυχος, 16:5).[26]

24. Traditionally the seat of the emotions (Klauck, *4 Makkabäerbuch*, 745), but most appropriate here as the place where maternal love originates.

25. The relationship between the mother's experience of the passions and her female reproductive apparatus gives particular poignancy to the author's comments concerning reason's imparting masculinity/courage to the mother (15:23, 28–30), as Moore and Anderson ("Taking It Like a Man," 265–67) skillfully explore.

26. Scholars have debated whether the author *expects* a mother typically to prove fainthearted. A close translation of 16:5 would read: "For, indeed, consider this: that if the woman [were] fainthearted, although being a mother (καίπερ μήτηρ οὖσα), she would have lamented over them." Both Dupont-Sommer (*Quatrième Livre*, 145) and Hadas (*Maccabees*, 227) argue against reading καίπερ in its most common, concessive sense here, preferring to see this clause introducing a rationale for the mother's potential faintheartedness ("being, as she was, a mother"). Previously, Deissmann ("Vierte Makkabäerbuch," 172) had insisted on taking the καίπερ in its natural sense. I concur with the latter. While mothers are particularly vulnerable where their offspring are

Ah, wretched me (ὦ μελέα) and many times thrice-unhappy, who, having borne seven children, have become a mother of not even one. Ah, seven empty (μάταιοι) pregnancies, and seven profitless (ἀνόνητοι) ten-month periods, and fruitless nursings, and miserable (ταλαίπωροι) breast-feedings! For nothing (μάτην), O children, I endured many pangs for you and the more burdensome concerns of rearing you. Ah, my unmarried children and my married ones without progeny (ἀνόνητοι)! I will not see (οὐκ ὄψομαι) your children nor be blessed with being called "grandmother." Ah, me, a woman with many and beautiful children (πολύπαις καὶ καλλίπαις), now a widow (χήρα) and alone, wailing bitterly! Nor will I have any of my sons to bury me when I die. (16:6–11)

The hearers would probably recognize this as something worthy of the stage, perhaps as a lament that might have come from the stage. The author begins with the standard (often self-referential) vocative ὦ μελέα so much at home in Greek tragedy,[27] expressing the speaker's sorrows with melodramatic multiplication ("many-times-thrice unhappy," πολλάκις τρισαθλία).[28] At the speech's beginning (16:6b) and ending (16:11) he draws attention to the tragic reversal of fortune that is the essence of the Greek stage, as the speaker goes from having seven children to "not even one," exchanging her "many children" (πολύπαις) for "much wailing" (πολύθρηνος).[29] The artful use of language to embellish the contrast, such as this last pair demonstrates, elevates this prose above ordinary speech.

The author uses topics and vocabulary familiar from lamentations placed by Euripides on the lips of mourning mothers, especially *Trojan*

---

concerned, the author, who chooses his conjunctions and inferential particles with considerable care, has chosen a word that signals a concessive relationship between the concepts of maternity and faintheartedness. Motherhood is itself a proof of a particular woman's fortitude and endurance (by reason of the rigors of labor and delivery), whereas those who have not yet carried and delivered a child remain "unproven" in this regard.

27. See, for example, Euripides, *Tro.* 144 (ὦ μελέαι); 165 (μελέαι); 601 (ὦ μελέα).

28. Seneca also speaks of such self-referential epithets among grieving mothers as almost proverbial in *Marc.* 5.5: "Do not, I pray you, covet that most perverse distinction—that of being considered the most unhappy of women!"

29. See also Euripides, *Tro.* 101, 474–499, 1203–1206; *Hec.* 55–58, 282–285, 956–960. Although the theme occurs in other plays in relation to the fates of many characters (Oedipus and Creon are noteworthy examples), Hecuba became a lasting symbol of the mutability of fortune, an association that survives in the Medieval Latin poem immortalized in Carl Orff's *Carmina Burana*: "*Fortuna rota volvitur . . . nam sub axe legitur 'Hecubam reginam'*" ("Fortune's wheel keeps on turning . . . We read beneath its axle, 'Queen Hecuba'").

Women and *Hecuba*.[30] This is appropriate since both Hecuba and the mother of 4 Maccabees are celebrated as having especially numerous offspring.[31] The author may have known these laments either from reading them or seeing them performed in his city. His knowledge of Greek language, Greek philosophical ethics, and Greek rhetoric make it quite plausible that he had equal interest in, and exposure to, Greek literature.

Hecuba laments the reversal from many children to none: "I gave birth to children of great excellence . . . These sons I beheld slain by the Greek spear" (*Tro.* 474–480). Common in these laments is the use of compounds of -παις, used by Hecuba in a dramatic contrast: "I was blessed with children (εὔπαις) once, but now I am both old and childless (ἄπαις)" (*Hec.* 810; compare 4 Macc 16:6, 10). Cassandra speaks of Achaean women also "dying in widowhood (χῆραι), while others died childless (ἄπαιδες) in their houses, having reared children all for nothing," (*Tro.* 380–381; compare 4 Macc 16:10). The "fruitlessness" and "purposelessness" of childrearing when the child dies prematurely is poignantly expressed by Andromache after the Greeks announce their decision to execute Astyanax, the little son of the Trojan hero Hector: "It was for nothing (διὰ κενῆς) that this breast of mine suckled you . . . and all in vain (μάτην) was my labor!" (*Tro.* 758–760; compare 4 Macc 16:8).[32] Similarly, Hecuba laments the death of Polydorus, "born to no purpose (ἀνόνητα)" (*Hec.* 766; compare 4 Macc 16:7, 9). The permanence of the separation is expressed by Hecuba in terms of no longer seeing the deceased: "No hope have I of being seen of them, no, nor of seeing them for evermore (ὀφθήσομαι . . . ὄψομαί ποτε)" (*Tro.* 487–488; compare 4 Macc 16:9).[33]

---

30. Many of these references have been listed before (see, e.g., Klauck, *4 Makkabäerbuch*, 747–48; deSilva, *4 Maccabees*, 73), but not closely explored.

31. Quotations are taken from Euripides, *Children of Heracles; Hippolytus; Andromache; Hecuba* (ed. David Kovacs; LCL; Cambridge: Harvard University Press, 1995) and Euripides, *Trojan Women, Iphigenia Among the Taurians, Ion* (ed. David Kovacs; LCL; Cambridge: Harvard University Press, 1999).

32. Seneca imagines a similar objection, based on a parent not enjoying the anticipated (and justly expected) return of benefits from her deceased son, being voiced by Marcia: "I shall have no one to protect me, no one to keep me from being despised" (*Marc.* 19.2). The emphasis on childlessness in these laments generally, and the absence of grandchildren in 4 Maccabees in particular, may work to intensify the experience of grief by denying a common topic of consolation, namely the common topic of considering the comfort to be had from remaining family members, especially surviving children and grandchildren (see Seneca, *Marc.* 16.6–8; *Polyb.* 12.1; *Helv.* 18.2, 4).

33. Seneca employs the topic of no longer "seeing" the loved one, and thus the loss of the enjoyment of face-to-face interaction with the loved one, in a fictive lament placed on the lips of his own mother (deprived of seeing her son on account of his exile).

Deprivation of help in old age and, in particular, funerary rites is perceived to be a tremendous loss. Hecuba laments that "Neither male child nor female, of all I have given birth to, can help the poor woman that is me" (*Tro.* 504–505), and that Astyanax will not make good on his promises to mourn at his grandmother's tomb, since she is burying him instead (*Tro.*1180–84). Many Greek mothers are similarly deprived: "There is no one who near their tombs will give the earth an offering of blood" (*Tro.* 382; compare 4 Macc 16:11).

The author sharply distances the mother of the seven from the feelings, convictions, character, and resultant actions exemplified by the fictive lament. It is not merely that the author wants to cast the Greek archetype of the mother in distress as less stalwart than the Jewish mother, for the author could not have been unaware of stories circulated in the Greek culture about woman who showed stalwart courage in the face of death, including the deaths of their children.[34] Nor does the author intend to impugn the Greek tragic heroines for their examples upon the stage. But he does wish to make clear that those who have been instructed by the Torah have come to a different view of death, one that naturally enables greater courage and hope in the face of death (and, therefore, greater resources to help them overcome the onslaught of the passions in life-threatening circumstances).

Caution is required when assessing the author's claim that the mother did not weep (15:19), nor shed tears (15:20), nor wail, lament, and "grieve as they were dying" (16:12). It would be easy to be led astray by such claims into thinking that the author has moved into contradiction, as exhibited by at least one fine scholar: "While the author of 4 Macc consistently emphasizes mastery rather than extirpation, the examples of Eleazar, the seven brothers and the mother clearly suggest the *apatheia* which was attained by the Cynic and Stoic sages . . . and the accompanying experience of *aponia* ('toil-lessness' or lack of pain)."[35] This same author finds the author "repeatedly emphasizing that these courageous martyrs experience no human suffering."[36]

34. Particularly noteworthy is the attitude of Lacaena, a Spartan mother, who responds to news about her son's death in battle. "To that end . . . had I borne him, to be a man who should not hesitate to meet death for his country" (Cicero, *Tusc.* 1.102; LCL). By dying in line with prized virtues, the child brought to full fruition his life and his mother's nurture. See also Plutarch, *Mulierum virtutes* (discussed in deSilva, *4 Maccabees*, 70, 80–84) and the literature discussed in Moore and Anderson, "Taking It Like a Man," 267–68.

35. Aune, "Mastery of the Passions," 136.

36. Aune, "Mastery of the Passions," 137. Against this position, see O'Hagan, "The Martyr," 101: the author "does not slip into the Stoic philosophic extreme of insensitivity and complete indifference: the technical terms ἀπαθεία and ἀναισθηρία never occur

On the contrary, the author of 4 Maccabees leaves room for the human experience of these emotions,[37] expecting "affection for offspring" to bring the mother into an experience of deep, abject suffering. He amplifies the mother's actual experience of her sons' misery and her own grief to promote his rhetorical goals. The more frenzied the experience of passion through which Torah-observance enables one to remain steady in one's moral purpose, the more fully he can laud the Jewish way of life as the superior ethical philosophy. The mother thus *feels* συμπάθειαν (the shared, inward experience of anguish) with her children in their "varied tortures" (15:11). Her mettle is tested by "sharper pains" (πικροτέρων . . . πόνων) than those very real pains of labor and delivery (15:16). She is "tortured with such diverse and many tortures" as were being inflicted upon the bodies of her sons (15:22). She was "overwhelmed from every side by the flood of the passions" (15:32) and felt her innate parental love raging more furiously than Daniel's lions and more intensely inflamed than the furnace that threatened the three young Judeans in Nebuchadnezzar's Babylon (16:3–4). In all these statements, we hear nothing of "toil-lessness" and everything of brave endurance in the face of the experience of horrific pains. Indeed, the whole point of the *ekphrasis* of 15:14–15, 18–22 is to amplify the audience's sense of the magnitude of the mother's sufferings (15:13, 16–17) and thus her achievement (15:11–12, 14, 23). It is not that she remains untouched by these sufferings, but that she remains unmoved in her moral purpose by them (15:11; 14). Her will remains fixed on pursuing piety and enabling piety in her sons to the end, no matter how much it hurts her and her dear boys.

Euripides's *Hecuba* illumines the significance of the mother's refusal to cry, wail, or grieve. Polyxena, one of Hecuba's last surviving daughters, has nobly decided to accept her fate and die at Achilles's grave rather than plead for her life, dying as a model of nobility for the whole Greek army, but her mother's quite natural expressions of grief have a strong effect on her. After Hecuba and Polyxena have fallen into a lament together, and Hecuba pitifully wails, "I am already dead before my death, killed by my misfortunes," Polyxena asks Odysseus to take her away, "for the heart within me, before

---

in 4 Maccabees, and the other two great Stoic words ἐγκράτεια (5:34) and ἀταραξία (8:26) only once each with greatly diminished impact."

37. In regard to the martyrdoms of the brothers, the narrator asserts that the fifth brother was "in anguish of body" (11:11), affirming that the brothers actually experienced the most intense kinds of sufferings (14:9–10)—in pointed contrast to the hearers' armchair experience of his report concerning those sufferings. The sixth brother's taunt that the tyrant's "fire is cold" and "catapults painless," therefore, must constitute a hyperbolic expression of the tyrant's impotence to compel them to act against their will (the fact that his "violence" is "powerless," 11:24–25). It is not a report about the martyr's lack of physical sensation.

my slaughter, has been made to melt with the lamentations of my mother, and I melt her heart with mine" (*Hec.* 431–434). The melting of the heart is a common image for the softening of resolve, something in which Polyxena can no longer indulge if she is to achieve the noble death she has set for herself. Hecuba, in fact, cries out after her as she departs, "Ah, ah! I am faint! My limbs are unstrung! Daughter, take hold of your mother, stretch out your hand, give it to me, do not leave me childless!" (*Hec.* 438–440). It is clear that Hecuba would turn Polyxena from her resolve, and turn back the tide of events, if she could.

The mother of the seven sons will not do as Hecuba did. She feels the pains as bitterly as could be felt, but she will not weaken in her resolve, nor do those things that would weaken her sons' resolve. Thus she refuses to cry, shed tears, and do those things generally that elicit pity and would add to her sons' burden. She had to master her own feelings (and their visible expression) so that she could be available to help her sons master theirs (15:12).[38] The relationship between the mother's visible expression of grief and the effects on the children is brought into sharper focus in 16:12: "But the holy and god-revering mother was bewailing none with this dirge, nor was she attempting to dissuade any of them so that they would not die."

Dissuasion would be the force of such a lament. With or without words, bringing her feelings to her face would cry out "pity me" and undermine her admonition to her sons to "keep faith with God" (16:22).[39] The lament that the author has crafted, largely from traditional literary motifs, presents a whole list of rationales on the basis of which the children could indeed elevate pity for their mother above keeping faith with God (pregnancies, the pangs of childbirths, nursing, nurturing, and the watchful care that mothers provide throughout the child's life, all with no return for her benevolence should they all perish).[40] On the contrary, this pious mother will urge her

38. Compare the explicit invocation of this topic in Seneca, *Polyb.* 5.4: "This is the way that great generals act in times of disaster—they purposely make pretense of cheerfulness, and conceal their misfortunes by feigning joy, lest the soldiers themselves should likewise grow faint-hearted if they saw the spirit of their leader broken." Seneca argues that it is Polybius's duty to provide a strong example for his surviving brothers, so that the latter will not lose heart in the midst of their own grief for the deceased.

39. The NRSV translates πίστιν πρὸς τὸν θεόν as "faith in God," but πίστις here denotes another facet of the faith-based relationship, namely faithfulness toward God (Pfitzner, *Paul and the Agon Motif*, 64–65; van Henten, *Maccabean Martyrs*, 131–32; deSilva, *4 Maccabees*, 120).

40. In Sinaiticus (favored as the original reading by Dupont-Sommer [*Quatrième Livre*, 131] and Klauck [*4 Makkabäerbuch*, 734]), 4 Macc 12:6 also makes explicit the connection between the experience of grief and the resultant action of dissuasion. Prior to the torture and death of the seventh and last son, Antiochus brings the mother forward "in order that, taking pity on herself as she was bereft of so many sons, she might

sons to keep faith with God and give their full attention to giving God a fair return for his gift of life and a share in this world (16:18–19), not placing her own desires and deserved recompenses above God's due.[41]

The mother also refuses to lament and to grieve because she does not share the dominant culture's estimation of what makes motherhood "profitable," having been taught by Torah (and by the development of personal eschatology in the Second Temple period) about lasting "profit." According to the latter view, the deaths of the seven sons meant not their loss but their preservation. For Hecuba and Andromache, the deaths of their children constituted their alienation from those whom they loved and the shipwreck of their maternal investment. For example, Andromache equates death (here, in relation to her sister Polyxena rather than her son Astyanax, whose sentence has not yet been made known) with non-being, the equivalent of not having been born (Euripides Tro. 635–642). The same principle applied to Astyanax would mean the erasure of her entire experience of motherhood.

For the ἑπταμήτωρ, however, the deaths of her sons meant their transference to the realm in which they would never again be separated from her, thus the "perfection" of her investment. It marked the completion and full fruition of her work as a mother who loved her children, whose task it was not simply to give birth and nurture for their lives in this world, but to give them "rebirth for immortality" by nurturing their unshakable rootedness in God and in covenant loyalty (as in 16:18–19).[42] Motherhood is *not* in vain if the children die as a result of their commitment to the virtues instilled by their parents, since for their steadfast commitment to God (16:18–19) they will live eternally with God (16:25). Rather than grieving,

---

urge the remaining one on toward the ready obedience bringing deliverance" (ὅπως [ε] αὐτὴν ἐλεήσασα τοσούτων υἱῶν στερηθεῖσαν παρορμήσειεν ἐπὶ τὴν σωτήριον εὐπείθειαν τὸν περιλειπόμενον). He expects the mother to "break" like Hecuba did at the prospect of losing Polyxena, and thus join him in trying to weaken the last son's resolve.

41. The author's reasoning superficially resembles Epictetus's injunction that children are to be given back to the Giver when demanded (*Diatr.* 4.1.107; *Ench.* 11). However, the author does not share Epictetus's objectification of children as external things (alongside property, offices, reputation, and one's physical well-being), and therefore things to be released, like any other external good, for the sake of maintaining unperturbedness (*Diatr.* 4.7.35). Rather, they are the active agents who render God the service that is *their* due by returning life for the gift of life. Moreover, by releasing her children for God's sake she preserves their family relationships for eternity rather than surrendering them upon death as something "not our own" (see Epictetus, *Diatr.* 3.3.15; 3.19.1; 4.1.67, 87, 100, 111; 4.7.35; *Frag.* 3; *Ench.* 18).

42. Epictetus (*Diatr.* 1.11.21–26) expresses broad agreement as he argues that natural affection demands rendering our children assistance even when it is painful for us to see them in distress (rather than trying to avoid the distressing sights or circumstances).

which would undermine the credibility of this conviction, the mother allows her conviction that she would enjoy her sons forever if they but hold fast now to temper her own response and give her, in fact, the "edge" she needs to master her passions.[43] The author provides in 17:5–6 a pictorial confirmation of her hope: the last image of this mother (within this particular section) is of her surrounded, once more, by her seven sons, now honored in the court of God forever, an image superseding the graphic depiction of them degraded in the court of Antiochus.[44]

Conclusion

The author's portrayal of the mother's deep feelings for her seven sons, the pains of seeing them suffer at the hands of Antiochus's guards, the response that she refused to indulge, and, indeed, the response she did make all continue to bear witness to his thoroughgoing interaction with—and valuing of—Greek philosophical thought and literary expression. He uses these not so much to build stark barriers between his Jewish audience and the Greek *culture* around them, as to assert that, as long as their commitment to Torah-observance remains unyielding (and the barriers strong in that regard), they will continue to embody the highest values embraced by their neighbors and even surpass the Greek philosophers' highest expectations.

By submitting even what is commendable in their nature to the demands of piety rather than taking Nature as the final norm, they both continue to embody a life in accordance with Nature and bring Nature's implanted drives to a higher level of fruitfulness. Because of their hope in God, they are empowered to face extreme hardship with a fortitude seen only rarely in the Greek world, replacing any sense of self-pity with hope for God's renewal of their fortunes in the life to come. Through his portrayal of the mother, the author thus demonstrates that the virtues and goods prized by all are most securely held by the pious Jew.

---

43. In 1 Thess 4:13, Paul similarly leaves room for the experience of pain at the loss of Christian sisters and brothers but draws attention to the resources of hope for life beyond death so that grief takes a distinctive form.

44. Fourth Maccabees most resembles a "consolation" here as the author addresses the mother in an apostrophe to urge her to "take heart" in the midst of the grisly scene of loss in Antiochus's court on the basis of the post-mortem reunion she would enjoy with her sons. Seneca twice utilizes the presumed blessedness of a post-mortem existence, specifically shedding the mortal coil with its "blemishes and stain" and reunion with the "saintly band," the heroes of old and family members who welcome the deceased, in his consolations (*Marc.* 25.1–2; *Polyb.* 9.3).

6

"Father Knew Best"

Intertextuality and Argumentation
in 4 Macc 18:6–19

The author of 4 Maccabees is skilled in many rhetorical and literary devices, not least of which is the device of *prosopopoiia*, or "speech in character." He excels at crafting speeches appropriate to people at different stages in life (from the aged Eleazar to each of the seven brothers in descending order of age), in different stations in life (from the arrogant tyrant Antiochus to a priest, a mother, and several youths from a people that, though subjugated, remain proud of their heritage), of different genders (the male tyrant, priest, and sons vis-à-vis the "manly" yet none the less female mother), and even in alternate and contradictory mindsets (the speeches that certain characters *could* have given, had they lacked courage and conviction, over against the speeches the same characters *actually* gave, since they possessed the requisite virtue). Here I focus on one such instance of *prosopopoiia*, the second speech attributed to the mother of the seven brothers, 4 Macc 18:6–19. What distinguishes this speech from all the others is the thickness of scriptural intertexture, and that not only at the level of allusion (which also characterizes the mother's first speech, 16:16–23, as well as the brothers' encouragements to one another, 13:9–12), but also at the level of recitation or explicit quotation. We are interested here primarily in what this speech tells us about its author's Bible, which is indeed a "Greek Bible," and how this "Greek Bible" is put to use within this speech and to what ends, both in regard to its fictive setting (a mother addressing her seven sons, all of whom face the prospect of death as a consequence of fidelity to their faith and covenant loyalty) and its actual setting (an orator addressing, or an author's work being read by, an audience).

(How) Does 4 Macc 18:6–19 Fit?

A major and preliminary issue in the interpretation of this passage is the question of its origin, whether it was composed by the author of 4 Maccabees and located precisely here as part of his original design, or whether it is somehow out of place in the discourse (whether as a dislocated speech or a later interpolation). The speech is admittedly poorly prepared for, dropped into the peroration rather than woven into the developing fabric in any natural way.[1] This stands in stark contrast with the mother's first speech (16:16–23), which is clearly located within the framework of the story (16:15), even if the author has given some mixed signals in this regard.[2] The abruptness of the transition to this section and the lack of clear integration into the flow of the narrative give strongest support to the view that the passage is a later interpolation.[3] Excise the speech, and what remains still makes for a perfectly adequate conclusion to the whole, perhaps even a better one.[4] It may have value as a "naive and charming" window into the ethos of the Jewish family,[5] but an impressive array of scholars deny that it has value as an integral part of the author's speech (and, therefore, rhetorical purpose).

Other arguments advanced in favor of regarding the paragraph as an interpolation carry less conviction. Freudenthal had pointed to (1) the alleged inferiority of its Greek, (2) its propensity to cite the Jewish Scriptures, and (3) the author's lack of interest elsewhere in domestic life as evidence against

1. So Klauck, 4 Makkabäerbuch, 657: the speech "sehr plötzlich und unmotiviert eingefügt wird" ("was inserted abruptly and without rationale").

2. In 4 Macc 12:6–7, the author, following his source (compare 2 Macc 7:25–29), invited his audience to envision the mother addressing her last surviving son, explaining that he was deferring the content of this speech until later ("as we shall tell a little later," 12:7, NRSV); when he gets back around to recounting this speech, however, he depicts the mother addressing her words to *all* her seven sons while Eleazar is being tortured (16:15).

3. See Freudenthal, *Die Flavius Josephus*, 155–56; Deissmann, "Das vierte Makkabäerbuch," 175; Dupont-Sommer, *Quatrième Livre*, 152–54; Rost, *Einleitung*, 81.

4. Dupont-Sommer, *Quatrième Livre*, 152.

5. Dupont-Sommer, *Quatrième Livre*, 154. Incidentally, here is just one of hundreds of examples of how Moses Hadas has cribbed observation after observation from André Dupont-Sommer without giving credit to his source. Compare Dupont-Sommer, *Quatrième Livre*, 154: "il reflète, en effet, d'une manière naïve et charmante, les sentiments de la famille juive au second siècle de notre ère: *l'idéal de stricte pudeur de la jeune fille, l'attachement de la femme à son mari* et à son foyer, *l'amour des enfants*, le rôle religieux du *père lisant* lui-même *la Sainte Écriture à son épouse et à ses fils et cultivant en eux la piété*"; with Hadas, *Maccabees*, 239: "it presents a charming picture of domestic piety: *the strict chastity of the maiden, the devotion of the wife to her husband, the love of children, the father reading Scripture to the family and instructing them in religion.*"

the speech having been a part of the author's original.[6] Deissmann, however, found the language not to be inferior, and, indeed, "a section comprised largely of brief Scriptural quotations and allusions does not lend itself to great artistry."[7] Moreover, there is a significant degree of overlap between the Scriptures to which 18:6–19 refers and those referred to in earlier speeches throughout the book (Isaac, 13:12; 16:20; Daniel, 16:21; the three men in the furnace, 13:9; 16:21), giving a certain thematic coherence to the whole. Scriptural references and allusions are characteristic of significant blocks of the speech (e.g., 1:30b–3:18), though there are no *strings* of recitations comparable to 18:14–19. The allegation that the author shows a general lack of interest in "domestic life" does not accord with the author's *intense* interest in the development of love for offspring and love for siblings precisely *through* the mechanisms of domestic life (see 13:19–25; 14:13–20; 15:4–8).[8]

Despite this tendency to divorce 18:6–19 from its context—and this despite the lack of any manuscript evidence for the omission or for its

---

6. *Die Flavius Josephus*, 155.

7. Deissmann, "Das vierte Makkabäerbuch," 175; Hiebert, "4 Maccabees 18,6–19," 448. Townshend ("Fourth Book," 655) shows appropriate caution and admirable humility as he writes: "For myself I am inclined to distrust those confident critics who on the evidence of style say dogmatically 'the author wrote this, the author did not write that.'"

8. Deissmann ("Das vierte Makkabäerbuch," 175) would prefer to solve the problem by regarding 18:6–19 as authentic but displaced from following directly the mother's earlier speech in 16:16–23. This would, however, introduce a significant problem in regard to redundancy, since both speeches refer to many of the same examples (see above). Dupont-Sommer (*Quatrième Livre*, 153) regards the passage as an interpolation, though he (surprisingly) agrees with Deissmann that it is better suited to follow 16:23 and that it was written by the same author as the remainder of the discourse. He posits that the author of this bonus material wrote this second speech on a separate sheet which did not remain in the same place in the codex when copied by another scribe and merged into the document. This is ranging far into the realm of speculation. Townshend ("Fourth Book," 655) rightly objects that to introduce this speech at any earlier point in the narrative would intrude artlessly upon the story: "Of course it is a digression even here, but if we look back to where he has the Mother in the front of the scene during the previous chapters there is no place where these verses would not have been ten times more out of keeping. He had far too much literary skill to spoil his effect by putting the passage in the wrong place, and he reserved this piece about her early days till he could use it as a relief to the tension of the tortures, and so lead up to the final roll-call of the heroes." Hiebert ("Original Text," 448) appears to approve Breitenstein's suggestion most fully: "It appears to me not impossible that the second speech of the mother was also composed by Pseudo-Josephus, perhaps as a variant, which however was not fully worked out but was left in a raw state, literarily speaking" ("So scheint es mir nicht unmöglich zu sein, dass auch die zweite Rede der Mutter von Ps-Ios verfasst worden ist, vielleicht als *Variante*, die aber (noch) nicht vollständig ausgearbeitet, also gleichsam im sprachlichen Rohzustand, vorliegt"; 1976:156). How the "variant" became part of the permanent text *at this point* remains unexplained.

transposition to another location[9]—it nevertheless fills an appropriate role in the peroration as it stands. While tending to view the passage as out of place and ill-fitted, Klauck nevertheless observes that, "through the introduction of the hitherto missing spouse and father in v. 9, an empty space in the whole is filled" (translation mine).[10] The father has been conspicuously absent to this point, even though the effects of his impact on his sons has been evident and, indeed, referred to obliquely throughout the narrative (see, e.g., 13:24: "for having been educated in the same law and exercised in the same virtues and nurtured in the same righteous way of life," νόμῳ γὰρ τῷ αὐτῷ παιδευθέντες καὶ τὰς αὐτὰς ἐξασκήσαντες ἀρετὰς καὶ τῷ δικαίῳ συντραφέντες βίῳ). Now that training in the Torah, and the ways in which it fortified their minds (their λογισμοί) with first principles that promoted piety and empowered them to persevere in embodying piety to the end, are brought out to the fore. This passage affords a glimpse into precisely the "formative education" or "discipline" (παιδεία) in the Torah that has been celebrated from the beginning (1:15–18). Reproducing a small segment of the seven brothers' catechesis at the feet of their father allows the author, moreover, to remind the audience of the lessons of their own heritage, which would provide further motivation for them to heed the exhortation on 18:1: "O Israelites, children descended from the seed of Abraham, obey this law and exercise piety in every way." The Old Testament examples and quotations cited have been selected and crafted in a manner particularly appropriate to the contest faced by the brothers and remain apt guidance for the audience as it struggles with remaining steadfast in a Greek world.

The attention that the mother gives to her own commitment to the female virtues of seclusion and chastity (18:6–9), though technically in the nature of a digression, are also far from out of place. One might look, by way of comparative material, to the outstanding exemplar of the Athenian commemorative address—Pericles's Funeral Oration (Thucydides, *Hist.* 2.35–46)—which also rather abruptly, and as something of an afterthought, concludes the praise of the fallen Athenian soldiers with a few words of exhortation to Athenian women. The advice given there, namely that a woman's greatest honor is to be least talked about among males (whether in praise or censure), coheres remarkably well with the model of secluded feminine virtue

---

9. See Hiebert, "Original Text," 441–46. While the Latin *Passio Sanctorum Machabaeorum* does omit the passage, this text is marked by "a process of deliberate and comprehensive abbreviation of the narrative that is an inner-Latin development. This curtailed tradition cannot be construed as evidence for the original state of the text of 4Macc" (Hiebert, "Original Text," 449).

10. *4 Makkabäerbuch*, 658.

upheld in 4 Macc 18:6–9.[11] Both factors mitigate the perception that 18:6–19 is intrusive or otherwise out of place where it stands.

A Model (Also) of Feminine Virtues

The mother's testimony about herself connects her suicide in 17:1 with a longer story of absolute commitment to modesty and chastity, keeping her body in every way from the touch of men other than her husband.[12] She who was "manlier than males" (15:30) and lauded for courage and endurance—and who thereby provided a goad to men and women alike to exhibit fortitude in the face of pressures (internal and external) to loosen covenant loyalty—also cannot be seen to have fallen short of properly "female" virtues in any way. In this regard, the portrayal of the mother recalls the tensions in the portrayal of Judith, who cannot sacrifice her feminine honor in the course of trying to win the more masculine honor of killing the enemy.[13]

The mother's second speech opens, then, by promoting the mother as a model also of the more traditional virtues of women, who for the sake of modesty and chastity remained within the private spaces appropriate for women ("I did not transgress the boundary of my father's house," 18:7). The classical ideal is articulated by Euripides's Andromache (*Trojan Women* 645–653), who sought all her fame "beneath Hector's roof,"

11. Townshend's response to the question ("Fourth Book," 655) merits a fulsome restatement here: "The main argument for the conjectural placing of the original conclusion at this point is that the Mother's account of her early life, which occupies fourteen verses immediately after it, is of the nature of a digression. So it is, but the reason is not far to seek. The author, through the main part of the book, has dealt chiefly with men and the manly virtues, courage in particular. He gives the heroine of his story, the Mother, due praise for this virtue, but he also desires to insert in his work a fit encomium on the domestic virtues which as a Jew he considers to be most important for the women of his race. Courage he has already praised; now he lays stress on the woman's more commonplace duty of stopping at home and attending to the house, of her father first and later of her husband. Above all, she must be very careful to run no risk of contamination by any deceiver, be he man or be he devil, inside or outside the house. So he makes the Mother say with pride in this last chapter, 'I kept guard over the rib that was builded into Eve'. Like Eve she was to be a helpmeet for man, but she was not, like Eve, to dally with the false beguiling serpent. Clearly the writer was determined to get in his point about female virtue, and he does it." On the Greco-Roman ideal of female behavior, see deSilva, *Honor, Patronage*, 183–85.

12. Young, "Woman with the Soul," 79.

13. See deSilva, *Introducing the Apocrypha*, 101. Moore and Anderson ("Taking It Like a Man," 270), Mary Rose D'Angelo ("*Eusebeia*," 155–57), and Robin Young ("Woman with the Soul," 79) are all probably correct to see 18:6–9a as an act of domesticating the mother, providing intentional balance to the depiction of the woman of *andreia* that dominated the narrative demonstration of the author's thesis.

avoiding the ill fame that comes "if [the woman] abide not in the home." Philo (*Spec. Leg.* 3.169) maintains this ideal among first-century Alexandrian Jews, stating explicitly that "women are best suited to the indoor life which never strays from the house, within which the middle door is taken by the maidens as their boundary, and the outer door by those who have reached full womanhood."[14]

In addition to remaining within the proper domestic spaces, the mother fulfills the two requirements of the Julian laws enacted by Augustus: she guards herself against adultery, and she remains with a man during the time of her fertility (incidentally fulfilling the ideal of the *univira* as well, 18:9a).[15] The mother's profession to have guarded "the rib that had been built up" (τὴν ᾠκοδομημένην πλευράν, 18:7) recontextualizes three words that take the reader unmistakably to LXX Gen 2:22: "And the LORD God built up (ᾠκοδόμησεν) the side (τὴν πλευράν) which he took from Adam into a woman/wife."[16] "The rib that had been built up" is, of course, the mother's own body, conceived here not as her own, to use (sexually) as she might please, but as belonging essentially to her future husband, something uniquely *his* to be restored to him, in effect, through marriage and guarded for him until then and thereafter. When these "two become one flesh," he will be complete again and God's design for the two, as for Adam and Eve, would be fulfilled.

As a corollary of cooperating in fulfilling her destiny as the wife made to be the helpmate particularly for her future husband, she heeded the cautions of the Torah concerning the seducer who might destroy her chastity. 4 Maccabees 18:8 recalls the case of the opportunity rapist recorded in Deut 22:25–27, recontextualizing the phrase ἐν πεδίῳ and describing rather clearly the same circumstances (being accosted and raped in a deserted place). By remaining in the private spaces of her father's house, she took all possible precautions against this eventuality. What follows is an interesting reading of the Fall of Eve and the activity of the serpent in the garden. The language of Eve's defense in Gen 3:13, "the serpent beguiled (ἠπάτησεν) me," reflects the language of seduction found in Exod 22:16 (ἀπατήσῃ), which describes a case similar to the one covered in Deut 22:25–27. The author of 4 Maccabees makes this same connection when he refers here to "the deceitful (ἀπάτης) serpent," suggesting that Satan is particularly interested in corrupting women through

14. Cited in Hadas, *Maccabees*, 239.

15. D'Angelo, "*Eusebeia*," 156.

16. Schaller, "Textzeuge," 329; D'Angelo, "*Eusebeia*," 152. The reading of the present tense participle οἰκοδομουμένην in Sinaiticus conveys more of a dynamic sense that, as the young woman was growing to maturity, she was "becoming" more and more that helpmate for which God first removed the rib from Adam's side.

the extramarital advances (consensual or otherwise) of males. Paul in 2 Cor 11:2–3 evokes the same suggestive overtones of Satan's activity as seduction (here, though, away from "fidelity" to Christ, the metaphorical bridegroom of the Church). The mother's vigilance against any assault incidentally contributes not only to her own honor, but also to the honor of the seven brothers, affirming the legitimacy of their birth.

The Mother's Construction of the Father's Instruction

The mother's brief testimony to her more typically female virtue quickly gives way to a summary of the relevant lessons the sons learned from their deceased father, who, by his early death, was spared the pains that the mother had to endure (18:9b).[17] D'Angelo reads with perhaps too sharp a hermeneutic of suspicion when she concludes that 18:9–19 "demotes the mother from teacher of her sons to student of her husband."[18] The mother is never explicitly depicted as learning her piety from her husband (as are the Roman women praised by Pliny and Plutarch in the texts that she cites), but rather recalls for her children the lessons he taught them, lessons that fall in line with her own exhortation in 16:16–23. In so doing, she adds his authority to her own and shows the essential harmony and concord of the training the children received in the household, both parents agreeing—with the *mother's* voice continuing to be the primary pedagogical influence when reinforcement mattered the most, also selecting here *what* mattered most at this moment. The text is vocal in regard to the father's tutelage of his sons, but silent in regard to his alleged tutelage of his wife, their mother.[19]

17. Euripides's *Suppliants* provides an emotionally charged example of how a father could grieve the loss of his children, matching the more common dirges of the mothers in his plays.

18. D'Angelo, "*Eusebeia*," 156.

19. In his careful study of the Alexandrinus text of 4 Maccabees, Marcus Adams ("Alexandrinus," 228) observes: "The reader of A finds the mother included in the circle of those instructed by the father (18.10, 11, 12, 15, 16) in a way not found in the text of R[ahlfs] (or the text of S[inaiticus] for that matter) because of the abundance of plural first person pronouns in A. Although the mother is never the object of the verb διδάσκω in these verses (e.g. 18.10, 12), she is included in the group of those to whom the father read (18.11), spoke (18.12), sang (18.15), and recounted (lit. 'made proverbial,' 18.16)." This observation is based on the tendency of A to substitute ἡμῖν for ὑμῖν throughout this passage, though significantly *not* ἡμᾶς for ὑμᾶς. The picture we get in A is that the mother was present for the father's instruction of their children ("he read to *us*," "he spoke to *us*," "he sang to *us*," "he recounted to *us*") without the accompanying claim that the father "taught *us*"—there the "*you*" is retained. These divergences from S and

The father of the seven sons fulfilled the injunctions of Deuteronomy (see Deut 4:9; 6:7; 11:19),[20] teaching his children the commandments of God, the paradigmatic models of faithfulness, and the significance of covenant-keeping.[21] Each paradigm and Scriptural lesson that the mother recalls for the sons has immediate relevance for their situation. The significance of each story is not explicated but can readily be discerned. It is also possible that one ought not to conclude too quickly, with Armin Lange, that these appear here "in a medley without apparent sequence,"[22] as argumentative connections and developments between paradigms and citations may be inferred. I am assuming an audience that has the requisite cultural knowledge to negotiate so terse and oblique a passage as we find in 18:10–18, hence an audience of Jews that have not been strangers to the synagogue nor to their own heritage.

That the mother's reconstruction of the father's curriculum is being crafted as a response to the specific situation of facing trial for the sake of preserving piety is evident from the beginning to the end of this passage, not least from the fact that the mother chooses, as her starting point, not creation, nor Adam and Eve, but the death of a righteous person at the hands of an impious person. Abel (see Gen 4:1–8, especially 4:7) is a model of piety, doing what is pleasing in God's sight; Cain models impiety, for which reason his sacrifices were not acceptable to God. The story becomes a paradigm, then, of the hostility experienced by those who please God at the hands of those who do not please God, especially the Gentiles whose sacrifices to idols are, like Cain's, in no way acceptable. The story would brace the pious Jew to expect hostility and also prepare him or her to understand that whatever they suffer is not a mark of their *own* unworthiness of divine favor or aid, but of the other party's alienation from God and virtue.

The paradigm of Isaac in the *Aqedah* (Gen 22:1–19, esp. 22:2, 13) figures prominently in 4 Maccabees (see also 13:12; 16:20; 18:11), providing a situationally appropriate model of being willing to die for the sake of fulfilling the demands of piety if God should require it (here, fulfilling the explicit, if unexpected and uncharacteristic, command of God to Abraham to perform a particular sacrifice as a proof of obedience). The author appears to rely on later developments of the story that emphasize Isaac's informed consent (e.g., Pseudo-Philo, *LAB* 32.2–3), which would

the critical text would not seem to me to necessitate the reader's viewing the mother as relegated to the circle of *learners* and even retains second person plural pronouns in key places to steer the reader *away* from such a conclusion.

20. Hadas, *Maccabees*, 240.

21. O'Hagan, "The Martyr," 100.

22. Lange, "The Law, the Prophets," 76.

make him an archetype of the (potential) martyr. This may be reflected in the author's emphasis on Isaac's "endurance," which implies volition, as well as his refusal to flinch under his father's knife-bearing hand, again implying equal commitment to fulfilling the action: "Remember whence you are, and by the hand of what father Isaac endured being sacrificed on account of piety!" (13:12); "Isaac . . . did not cower in regard to his father's sword-bearing hand bearing down on him" (16:20).

Fourth Maccabees 18:11 shows signs of creating distance from other traditional developments that assert that Isaac was in fact killed. The use of the present participle ὁλοκαρπούμενον rather than the perfect or aorist is significant: "He read to you about . . . Isaac as he was in the process of being offered as a burnt offering." This nuance is frequently missed, as in the NRSV, which translates "Isaac who was offered as a burnt offering" (an error that appears also in the ESV and CEB because of my own failure to notice the aspect of this participle earlier). One can hardly blame Seth Ehorn, then, for his comment that "It is interesting that the reference here is to the story of 'the one offered as a burnt offering, Isaac [τὸν ὁλοκαρπούμενον Ισαακ]' (4 Macc. 4.11). Leaving out the fuller detail that Isaac was not actually sacrificed is rhetorically useful in this context where death will not be eluded."[23] Ehorn, like the translators of the NRSV and my own perpetuation of this error in the ESV and CEB, translates the participle as if it were an aorist ("the one offered") rather than as a present ("the one being offered," even "the one in the process of being offered"). The present aspect points the reader away from any possible misconstrual of Isaac as in fact sacrificed, a misunderstanding that an aorist or perfect participle could permit.

Just as Isaac considered it just to give up his body as a sacrifice to God if obedience to God required it, and just as he walked in line with that high ideal, and just as Isaac proved himself worthy to be Abraham's son by being willing to give up his life if God required it (13:12), so the mother's recollection of this example once again challenges her sons, and by extension the audience, to do the same. From Abel to Isaac we also take the step from pious (and probably unwitting) victim of violence to voluntary self-offering for the sake of piety in the face of violence.

The story of Joseph (Gen 39:7–23, esp. 39:20 and 40:3) recalls the model of a man who refused to violate a particular commandment of God (the prohibition of adultery) even though doing so would save him from intense marginalization (prison). The brothers learned from him to imitate his willingness to suffer deprivation rather than choose what might seem the easier path of transgressing one of God's commands. The three examples of Abel,

---

23. Adams and Ehorn, "Composite Citations," 120.

Isaac, and Joseph taken together teach that pious commitment to God, far from providing insurance against pain and hardship, can lead directly to the experience of deprivation and death, while also moving to increasing levels of intentionality in choosing that path of costly commitment.

The example of the "zeal of Phinehas" (18:12; see Num 25:6–13) at first seems out of place here. Phinehas was, after all, celebrated in earlier Second Temple Period literature as the archetype of the militant Maccabean revolutionary (see 1 Macc 2:24–26, 54). Ben Sira, however, crafts a portrait of Phinehas that does not highlight the violent form that the expression of his zeal took: "Phinehas son of Eleazar ranks third in glory for being zealous in the fear of the Lord, and standing firm, when the people turned away, in the noble courage of his soul; and he made atonement for Israel" (Sir 45:23, NRSV). The author of 4 Maccabees would no doubt flesh out the picture of Phinehas's zeal similarly. He was a picture of "standing firm, when the people turned away," and thus also an example of joining "courage" to "piety." The essence of Phinehas's accomplishment was, moreover, to stem the tide of idolatry and assimilation among the Hebrews. The brothers displayed the same zealous vigilance (if not vigilantism) among themselves by keeping *one another* faithful in the face of enticements and coercive pressures to do otherwise (13:9–18). Each of the martyrs, in dying, contributed to the renewal of covenant loyalty among themselves and among the people as a whole (6:19; 9:23–24; 13:9–18; 16:16–23; 18:4).[24]

The final paradigmatic examples come from the book of Daniel—Hananiah and his companions facing the trial of the furnace (18:12; Dan 3:1–30, esp. 3:24) and Daniel in the lion's den (18:13; Dan 6:1–28). The author gives clear evidence of knowing this book in the Old Greek tradition. At both 16:21 and 18:12, he refers to the three young men as "Ananias and Azariah and Misael," the names given, and given in this order, in the Old Greek of Dan 3:24 (the introduction to the Prayer of Azariah) and 3:88 (in the third-to-last verse of the "Song of the Three," there in both the Old Greek and the pre-Theodotion text traditions). According to Schaller, we find here "the first

24. Phinehas's act of zeal for God and God's Law propitiated an angry God offended by the disobedience of the people as a collective (Num 25:11): "Phinehas son of Eleazar, son of Aaron the priest, has turned back my wrath from the Israelites by manifesting such zeal among them on my behalf that in my jealousy I did not consume the Israelites." Such a paradigm teaches that remarkable acts of covenant loyalty could have atoning benefits for the people as a whole, a paradigm on which the martyrs clearly rely (e.g., 6:37–39; 9:24; 12:17) and that the author has already affirmed in his peroration (17:20–22). The larger story of Phinehas may have helped to nurture this understanding. The honors that God heaps upon Phinehas after his display of zeal also foreshadow the post-zeal (post-mortem) honors that grace the martyrs (17:5; 18:23).

clear witness to the expanded edition of the Book of Daniel" ("das erste klare Zeugnis für die erweiterte Fassung des Danielbuches").[25]

The escalation from previous examples is evident in the explicit choices being made by these exemplars—obey a *foreign* power's dictates concerning religious practice (whether the promotion of a particular cult, as in Daniel 3, or the repression of one's customary religious practice, as in Daniel 6) or face the death penalty under increasingly gruesome circumstances. The story of the three youths in Assyria provides the closest prototype thus far for the seven brothers' situation of having to resist the impious demands of a tyrant and his coercive measures. Daniel similarly refused to alter his practice of piety for the sake of a human king's capricious decrees, continuing his practice of thrice-daily prayer—and that before an open window—despite the thirty-day moratorium decreed against praying to any god beside the ruler (Dan 6:1–28). Rather than violate the prohibition against idolatry or obey the proscription of their pious practices, the three young men and the aged Daniel bravely face the prospect of death, whether by fire or by the mouths and claws of lions. The three particularly display the solidarity and unity of purpose that came to be required of the seven, as well as the boldness of speech before a "tyrant" that characterized the seven brothers, collectively in 4 Macc 9:1–9 and individually each in their turn: "If our God whom we serve is able to deliver us from the furnace of blazing fire and out of your hand, O king, let him deliver us. But if not, be it known to you, O king, that we will not serve your gods and we will not worship the golden statue that you have set up" (Dan 3:17–18, NRSV). Just as the resolve of these three (or Daniel, for that matter) did not depend on the prospect of deliverance but rather on their absolute loyalty, so the mother's recollection of their example directs the resolve of her seven sons toward their commitment to virtue and to remain loyal to God. Indeed, the brothers do not even anticipate the possibility of deliverance on this side of death, looking only to the rewards for the pious in eternity.

At this point, the speech moves from a list of paradigms to a chain of scriptural quotations. The order of the quotations appears to be not haphazard but purposeful, as the author builds up a "case" on the strength of written authorities that would support a person facing, and choosing, endurance of hardship for the sake of covenant loyalty.[26] First, the author recites LXX Isa 43:2 in a slightly abbreviated fashion: "He reminded you also of the scripture of Isaiah which says, 'and if you cross through fire,

---

25. Schaller, "Textzeuge," 330.

26. Schaller, "Textzeuge," 326–28, provides a helpful synopsis of the LXX citations in 4 Maccabees against the wording in the books cited.

a flame will not consume you" (4 Macc 18:14). Isaiah 43:2 reads καὶ ἐὰν διέλθῃς διὰ πυρός οὐ μὴ κατακαυθῇς φλὸξ οὐ κατακαύσει σε. The author has omitted οὐ μὴ κατακαυθῇς and transposed διέλθῃς and διὰ πυρός, perhaps to emphasize the "fire" that has been so prominent in the scenes of torture by placing it first.[27] The verse might also have been suggested to the author as a starting point for his catena of citations by the recollection of the example of the three young men "in the fire" (18:12; cf. 13:9; 16:3, 21). They indeed passed through the fire and were not consumed. This fact points to a tension in the tradition that has already been resolved by the time the author of 2 Maccabees placed such a strong emphasis on the resurrection of the bodies of the martyrs: why were not *these* martyrs also preserved from the flames? The author of 4 Maccabees anticipates the answer that would be provided by later Christian theologians: the three young men were saved from the fire; the Maccabean martyrs were saved through the fire and preserved for eternal life in God's presence (see 4 Macc 17:1–6).

Isaiah 43:1–4 is part of a larger passage that had detailed the people's disobedience and God's chastisement of Israel (see Isa 42:18–25). It is thus highly appropriate to the martyrs' situation as the author has constructed it. The leaders of Jerusalem had led the way toward rebellion against God's covenant, resulting in the pouring out of God's anger upon the nation (see 4 Macc 4:15–26; cf. Isa 42:25). The martyrs, however, who stand fast by piety in the midst of the flood and fire that has been let loose upon them, receive God's assurance that they will indeed be redeemed by God and not utterly overwhelmed by the flood or consumed by the fire. Dupont-Sommer finds the order of this and the following recitations problematic, re-arranging the text so that the citations follow canonical order.[28] However, the recitations are skillfully placed in the current sequence by the author to construct a certain movement that is salient to the subject matter. The catena begins with a verse that acknowledges the reality of the fiery trials that come even upon the faithful, but also gives assurance that, in some sense, those fiery trials do not threaten the *ultimate* integrity of the faithful person's being, which is kept by God, even if not in the manner of the deliverance of the three young men in Babylon. They may indeed be "burned to the very bones" (4 Macc 6:26), but they are not thereby ultimately "consumed." The audience knows this, and is able to read Isaiah thus, by this point in the discourse since the author has already narrated the mother and brothers' entrance into an immortal life in 17:1–6.

27. The author's recitation corresponds to no known variants in the LXX tradition, suggesting that he himself has given it its shape here.

28. Dupont-Sommer, *Quatrième Livre*, 155.

The mother next recalls the father reciting the first stich of LXX Psalm 33:20 in 4 Macc 18:15. Departing from the syntax used to introduce the citation in 18:14 (but ultimately depending on it to give clear sense to what follows), the author uses metonymy in this and the following verses, referring to the author for the text produced by the author ("He sang to you the hymn-writer David" rather than "he sang to you the hymn written by David," much as an organist might be said to "play Bach"). The five Greek words recited by the author—πολλαὶ αἱ θλίψεις τῶν δικαίων ("many are the afflictions of the righteous")—attest to the fact that those who would remain "just" in regard to keeping faith with God and God's Law will encounter many trials or afflictions in the course of life in a world opposed to God. As such, the recitation provides a maxim, a generalized truth, reflected already in the stories of Abel, Joseph, the three young men, and Daniel (and, from another vantage point, Isaac, in a story where the source of the trial was not the vicious passions dominating the unrighteous but rather God's desire to prove the genuineness of Abraham's loyalty). This has the effect of preparing the righteous to expect affliction, so that the negative experiences they encounter will not disconfirm their world view (according to which observance of the covenant means enjoying God's favor and the promise of ultimate reward—it is significant in this regard that the *tradition* itself is shown to anticipate these experiences of trial) nor undermine their confidence that they are in fact walking in line with God's good pleasure.[29]

Ehorn suggests that the author "is highly selective—the citation stops just short of assuring the reader/listener that 'from all their afflictions [God] will rescue them [καὶ ἐκ πασῶν αὐτῶν ῥύσεται αὐτούς]' (Ps. 33.20b; cf. 33.5, 7, 18),"[30] perhaps on the ground that "the confession καὶ ἐκ πασῶν αὐτῶν ῥύσεται αὐτούς would have rung hollow in a text where *hoi dikaioi* were by no means 'rescued', but rather met the fate of martyrs."[31] The Psalms, however, would have been among the most familiar parts of Scripture for the audience, given their regular use in public worship, and thus it would be nearly unavoidable that the hearer of this passage would mentally supply the remainder of the verse: "and out of them all he [God] delivers them [the righteous people]." Similarly, I imagine it would be difficult for me to write "Weeping may endure for a night" without the scripturally literate reader completing the verse. This is a refrain recurring throughout the Psalm, moving from the psalmist's own experience of

29. See 1 Thess 3:1–4 for an example of similar "advance preparation" for hostility so as to disarm its power to erode confidence and commitment.

30. Adams and Ehorn, "Composite Citations," 121.

31. Stanley, *Paul and the Language*, 318.

deliverance to his generalization on this basis to statements about the "way God works" on behalf of all the righteous:

"from all my sojourning he rescued me"

ἐκ πασῶν τῶν παροικιῶν μου ἐρρύσατό με (LXX Ps 33:5)

"from all his trials he saved him"

ἐκ πασῶν τῶν θλίψεων αὐτοῦ ἔσωσεν αὐτόν (LXX Ps 33:7; still self-referential)

"from all their trials he rescued them"

ἐκ πασῶν τῶν θλίψεων αὐτῶν ἐρρύσατο αὐτούς (LXX Ps 33:18)

"from them all he will rescue them"

ἐκ πασῶν αὐτῶν (namely, αἱ θλίψεις τῶν δικαίων) ῥύσεται αὐτούς (LXX Ps 33:20)

These repetitive statements of God's rescue establish a clear expectation of temporal sequence: the righteous are afflicted; the Lord takes notice; the Lord delivers them. By invoking this psalm with a brief recitation, the author has also created the possibility—indeed the probability—that the reader/hearer will bring the inner logic of the psalm into his or her experience of the text, a logic that leads one firmly to anticipate God's rescue of the righteous in one form (temporal safety) or another (reward beyond death).[32]

The first two citations underscore the fact that even the righteous, and perhaps especially the righteous, will not escape facing trials on account of their virtue, even as had proven true in the cases of Abel, Isaac, and Daniel and his companions. They also affirm, however, that God will ultimately preserve the righteous despite those trials. As the catena progresses, the mother specifies in what way these early affirmations concerning outcomes prove true, such that the promises attached to the covenant itself (see the climactic recitation from Deuteronomy) prove trustworthy and, therefore, dependable information on the basis of which to evaluate advantage.

---

32. The veracity of the psalmist's claims is openly threatened at one point by the experience of the martyrs. The claim that "the Lord guards all their bones; not one of them will be broken" is belied by the experience of these martyrs whose bones are directly targeted and frequently broken throughout the drama. The author's ability to invoke LXX Ps 33:20 without fear that LXX Ps 33:21 will cast doubt upon his emerging argument from Scripture shows how completely he and his audience have accepted that the fulfillment of such promises may be naturally transferred from this life and the well-being of this physical body to the life beyond death.

The author again refers to the text metonymically by its author, introducing a "saying of Solomon" simply as "Solomon,"[33] and reciting in 18:16 the first part of LXX Proverbs 3:18 (ξύλον ζωῆς ἐστι πᾶσι τοῖς ἀντεχομένοις αὐτῆς) with some variation. In both the original Hebrew and the Greek Bible, Prov 3:18 points to Wisdom as the subject of this sentence: "*She* is a tree of life for those remaining loyal to her." While the subject of ἐστι might at first blush be ambiguous, the reference to a female entity in τοῖς ἀντεχομένοις αὐτῆς would clarify this in favor of a female subject. Read in context, there would be no doubt that Wisdom was meant. The author of 4 Maccabees has altered the second half or the saying, however, perhaps influenced by the wording of Prov 1:7 (also Ps 110:10): "reverence for God is wisdom's beginning and good sense for all those who practice it"(ἀρχὴ σοφίας φόβος θεοῦ σύνεσις δὲ ἀγαθὴ πᾶσι τοῖς ποιοῦσιν αὐτήν, i.e., σοφίαν). "Doing wisdom" and "holding fast to (remaining loyal to) Wisdom" are both interpreted by the author of 4 Maccabees as "doing God's will," that is, as revealed in God's commandments which have figured so prominently throughout this oration. Such an interpretation of the proverb is entirely consonant with Ben Sira's identification of "Wisdom" with the keeping of the Torah (Sir 1:26; 19:20; 24:23). Thus "those who do his will" (τοῖς ποιοῦσιν αὐτοῦ τὸ θέλημα) are now the beneficiaries of this "tree of life." With the shift from αὐτῇ to αὐτοῦ, the author has also changed the implied subject of the sentence. It is likely that the audience will hear "God" (the "he" whose "will" merits doing) now as the subject of the verb ἐστίν.[34] Alternatively, it would also be *possible* to read this ἐστίν simply as "there is [a tree of life]," and therefore, "those who do God's will have a tree of life."

However one resolves the question of the subject, the argumentative force is clear. In the midst of the "many trials" that afflict the righteous and threaten their well-being, God provides a "tree," an image of stability and safety, that moreover provides assurance of deliverance and survival ("life"), even if this will not take the form of continued enjoyment of the goods of *this* life, since making the possibility of "life" available to people who have already been living *this* life suggests a life beyond this existence as the sphere of God's promise. The obvious connection of this image with the Garden of Eden in Gen 3:22, where eating the fruit of the "tree of life" meant immortality, which is in turn the reward held before the eyes of the

33. The verb chosen by the author here (τὸν Σαλομῶντα ἐπαροιμίαζεν, 4 Macc 18:16) recalls the title and genre of the collection from which he quotes (παροιμίαι Σαλωμῶντος, Prov 1:1; so Schaller, "Textzeuge," 327).

34. Dupont-Sommer, *Quatrième Livre*, 156; Hadas, *Maccabees*, 241; Klauck, *4 Makkabäerbuch*, 755.

Torah-observant in 4 Maccabees as well (e.g., at 17:12), helps move the inferential process in this direction.[35]

The mother goes on to recall how her husband had "rendered credible the [question of] Ezekiel," reciting Ezek 37:3 ("Will these bones live?" εἰ ζήσεται τὰ ὀστᾶ ταῦτα;) with the addition of the detail that the bones were ξηρά ("dry"), readily supplied from the immediate context (Ezek 37:2, 4; 4 Macc 18:18).[36] This question is especially appropriate to recite in the aftermath of the tortures (even though the speech itself must, in terms of the narrative's chronology, temporally precede the tortures faced by this family), for the audience has looked out by this point in the narrative, as it were, on a courtyard full of dismembered corpses (see, e.g., 15:15, 20) and was left to wonder, with Ezekiel, if there will be any future for these individuals. By bringing in this quotation, the author has clarified the meaning of the Scriptures previously recited, showing that the Scriptural tradition taken as a whole leads its adherents to expect that the "many trials" that face those who would remain "just" toward God could indeed lead to death. Thus the promise that the "fire will not consume" the faithful is not disconfirmed when the faithful are in fact burned to their very bones, as was Eleazar (4 Macc 6:26). The ability of the fire to consume the flesh of the faithful does not signal its ability to consume the faithful themselves, for God is able to keep their lives into eternity, as the climactic verse in this catena will conclude.

The final link in the chain is a reference to the Song of Moses in Deuteronomy ("the Song that Moses taught," 4 Macc 18:18; compare LXX Deut 31:30: "and Moses spoke into the ears of all the assembly of Israel the words of this song"). The author offers this last recitation explicitly as the evidence (γάρ) by means of which the father confirmed the truth of, and therefore the hope communicated by, Ezekiel's vision of dead bones receiving new life from God.[37] The Song of Moses is an important song in other texts reflective of high tension between group and society, as in

35. It is also suggested by the emphasis on renewed access to the tree of life in at least one vision of the renewal of creation (i.e. Rev 2:7; 22:1–2).

36. This is, incidentally, the only point at which the author makes room for the resurrection of the dead in his discourse, which is even muted here in deference to the author's predilection for speaking instead of the immortality of the soul. I do not regard it unlikely that the same author who promotes the latter would refer to a verse that suggests the former, any more than Paul or the author of Revelation find it important to be entirely consistent on this point.

37. Technically, the quotation is only partially derived from the Song of Moses itself (Deut 32:1–43). Some material comes from the epilogue immediately following the song (Deut 32:47), some from the climactic exhortation of the statement of the law itself (Deut 30:15–20).

Rev 15:1–8, and as a whole is singularly appropriate to the narrative of 4 Maccabees. The Song speaks of God punishing Israel for turning to idols (32:15–25), presumably by using Gentile nations as agents of punishment (32:21, 27). God, however, vindicates Israel before bringing them to complete destruction and thus has "compassion on his servants" (32:36–43). To this vindication and vengeance upon Israel's enemies, the final verse adds the note that God purifies the land for God's people (32:43c). This is, in effect, the template for 4 Maccabees, with the martyrs serving both as the turning point between wrath and compassion/vindication and as the medium for purification (see 1:11; 17:21).

The first half of this recitation comes from Deut 32:39. The word order in this particular quote is highly significant. It is read by the author as a temporal sequence rather than merely as a balanced expression of God's power to give and/or take away life: "I kill and [then] I make alive" becomes scriptural warrant for the belief in the resurrection or post-mortem survival of the martyred faithful. This is how, indeed, the martyr can pass through the fire (cf. Isaiah 43:2, recited in 18:14), suffer the utter consumption of his or her body, and yet not in fact be "consumed" in any ultimate sense. This is how the martyr, as the "just" or "righteous person" who will not break faith with God, can face the "many trials" (LXX Ps 33:20) and still anticipate the deliverance that provides the steady pulse of the repetitive texture of Psalm 33 (34).

The second part of the quotation is a blending of LXX Deut 32:47 with LXX Deut 30:20,[38] two verses that are substantially paraphrases of one another:

> "This (fem.) is your (pl.) life and you will live many days on account of it" (αὕτη ἡ ζωὴ ὑμῶν καὶ ἕνεκεν τοῦ λόγου τούτου μακροημερεύσετε, LXX Deut 32:47);

> "This (neuter) is your (sg.) life and the length of your days" (τοῦτο ἡ ζωή σου καὶ ἡ μακρότης τῶν ἡμερῶν σου, LXX Deut 30:20)

> "This (fem.) is your (pl.) life and the length of your days" (αὕτη ἡ ζωὴ ὑμῶν καὶ ἡ μακρότης τῶν ἡμερῶν, 4 Macc 18:19)

The author of 4 Maccabees has combined these, reciting αὕτη ἡ ζωὴ ὑμῶν verbatim from Deut 32:47 and καὶ ἡ μακρότης[39] τῶν ἡμερῶν verbatim from

---

38. So also Dupont-Sommer, *Quatrième Livre*, 155; Hiebert, "Greek Pentateuch," 252.

39. Codex Alexandrinus reads μακαριότης ("blessedness") for μακρότης ("length"). This could be the result simply of a scribal error; it could result from a scribe's reaction

Deut 30:20. Deut 30:20 identifies the source of this life to be loving God, obeying God, and holding fast to God (i.e., choosing life by keeping the commandments, as the larger passage of Deut 30:15–20 forcefully urges); Deut 32:47 connects this life more explicitly with the performance of the words of the law in the lives of the Hebrews. Most appropriately for the setting in 4 Maccabees 18, this latter text enjoins upon the hearers to teach the words of the law to their children, that they might also "guard and do all these words," the very thing that the father of the seven is remembered to have done (18:10). Doing the Law and contributing to the preservation of the Jewish way of life, then, is clearly envisioned as the path to the life that stretches beyond death.[40]

In 4 Maccabees, "life and length of days" is no longer limited to "living in the land" located across the Jordan (as explicitly in Deut 32:47, the land sworn to Abraham, Isaac, and Jacob in Deut 30:20), but transferred to immortal life in the presence of God. The final (carefully crafted) recitation affirms that God gives life even to the dead, allotting "life and length of days" to the just, whether in this life or the life beyond. Aligning oneself with God, then, by honoring and diligently obeying God's Law is the prudent course of action in the face of any trial that might present itself, even if that trial is life-threatening in a temporal sense (as it certainly was for the martyrs). As part of his argument for rearranging the material in this passage, such that 4

---

to recognizing the theological problem of promising "length" of life to martyrs without *also* recognizing how the author is addressing this problem in this very verse.

40. Ehorn (Adams and Ehorn, "Composite Citations," 122) argues that 4 Macc 18:19 is a composite citation *only* of Deut. 32:39 and 30:20. He asserts that the change from the neuter τοῦτο to the feminine αὕτη "was required by the insertion of the citation into its new literary context, which in turn argues against the more complex compositional proposals suggested by deSilva and Hiebert" (Adams and Ehorn, "Composite Citations," 124). Ehorn does not specify what in the new context necessitates such a change. One might surmise that he is thinking of agreement with ἡ ζωή, though such agreement was not "required" in Deut 30:20 (τοῦτο ἡ ζωή). An examination of 4 Macc 18:17–19 suggests no feminine antecedents to which this pronoun should refer and, therefore, on the basis of which it should have been altered from τοῦτο to αὕτη. If anything, the reverse is true: preserving the neuter form as found in Deut 30:20 would have better suited the context, in which the immediate antecedent would be the proposition, "I kill and I make alive," even as the neuter τοῦτο in Deut 30:20 functions as a generic "stand in" for the preceding material rather than a particular nominal antecedent. Ehorn explains the shift from the sg. σου in Deut 30:20 to the pl. ὑμῶν on the basis of its situational propriety: the text "refers now to the mother and her sons." The result is as he suggests, but the question remains whether the author achieved this result by introducing two purposeful changes into Deut 30:20 (thus making it independently identical to the expression in Deut 32:47) or by simply incorporating the parallel statement in Deut 32:47 as the more useful in this setting. The latter strikes this author as by far the simpler and more likely solution.

Macc 18:18–19 should precede 18:14–17, Dupont-Sommer asserts that the "for" (γάρ) in 4 Macc 18:19 does not provide a suitable rationale for 18:18, though it does for 18:13.[41] In this he is surely mistaken, as the constructed citation from Deuteronomy very well provides justification for the implied answer to the question, "Shall these bones live?" (18:18), the answer that the father "rendered credible" by not forgetting to teach "the Song that Moses taught." The dead righteous shall yet meet with justice—they shall enjoy the covenant blessings of (exceedingly) long life—in God's providential care, "*for* I kill and [then] I make alive."

The Author's Greek Bible

The foregoing examination of 4 Maccabees 18:6–19 permits a number of observations concerning the author's Greek Bible and his use thereof. In this passage, he approaches the corpus as a resource for paradigms and propositions on the basis of which wise judgments may be reached. He exhibits a canonical approach to Scripture—not in the sense of necessitating a closed canon, but in the sense of reading individual texts in the context of a larger body of sacred writings that become mutually interpreting. Following this approach, individual texts that lived experience might tend to disconfirm, and whose authority and continued life in the community of faith might thereby be put in jeopardy, are placed in a broader interpretive context that invites new readings and grants new life to them. Especially interesting in this regard is the author's presentation of a (composite) text from Deuteronomy as the rationale and evidence providing support for (the implied answer to a question in) Ezekiel—and the ways in which the citations leading up to the text from Deuteronomy anticipate and render plausible the reinterpretation of the promise of "life and length of days."

If 4 Macc 18:11–18 is meant to exemplify the claim made by the mother in 18:10, then the author uses "the Law and the Prophets" as an inclusive title, since exemplars and texts from the "Writings" (Psalms, Proverbs; Daniel if considered from the categorization of the Hebrew Bible) are prominently featured in the mother's recollection of the father's instruction of their sons in "the Law and the Prophets." It is unlikely, however, that we should regard the *absence* of citations from representative sections of the (later) canon as evidence for the limitations on the author's canon. Thus I would disagree with Lange when he suggests:

41. Dupont-Sommer, *Quatrième Livre*, 155.

That the books of 1 Samuel-2 Kings do not occur in the father's curriculum although the author of *4 Maccabees* was familiar with them could thus hint to the idea of canonical exclusivity in *4 Maccabees*. This is even more probable as the persecution of Elijah which is described in 2 Kgs 19:1–8 would have been a fitting role model for the seven martyred sons and could thus have been easily a part of the father's curriculum. Hence, *4 Maccabees* seems to consciously exclude at least the books which were later labeled the former prophets from what it regards worthwhile to be taught. Both the Pentateuch and the book of Daniel are part of the father's curriculum while none of the books of the deuteronomistic history are.[42]

This seems a tenuous conclusion to draw in the face of the author's own extensive use of the story of 2 Sam 23:13–17//1 Chr 11:15–19, a reference of which Lange is well aware.[43] The rationale for the author's decision not to include a story from the Deuteronomistic History in the summary of the father's teaching must be sought elsewhere than the author's view of the authority of these texts, given his use of the story of David's thirst alongside and, indeed, as in many ways the *climax* of his own proof from Scripture of the efficacy of the educative formation of the Torah-observant way of life for equipping those so formed to master their passions for the sake of choosing a virtuous path (1:30b—3:18, a first series of proofs or evidences offered in support of the thesis of 1:1, 13 after the preliminaries of 1:15–30a, themselves announced in 1:14).[44] It is, moreover, quite disputable that 1 Kgs 19:1–8[45] would have supported the theme of 4 Macc 18:10–18 sufficiently well to have been included, independent of the author's opinion of the authority of the historical books. The author's goals for these citations was not, after all, to exhibit the breadth of his scriptural canon, but to give the impression that the whole of the scriptural witness works together to motivate commitment to virtue—particularly the virtue of justice toward God, or "piety"—in the face of any and all incentives to loosen or even abandon this commitment, and thus that the Torah-trained reason is indeed master of the passions from within and without.

42. Lange, "'The Law, the Prophets," 78.

43. Lange, "'The Law, the Prophets," 78: "This is all the more astonishing as the story of David's thirst in 2 Sam 23:13–17 (cf. 1 Chr 11:15–19) is referred to in *4 Macc* 3:6–18 as exemplary behavior.

44. See, further, chapter 4 above.

45. Lange writes "2 Kgs," but he clearly intends the narrative of Elijah in the aftermath of the slaughter of the priests of Baal.

Part 3

The Legacy of 4 Maccabees

7

The Human Ideal, the Problem of Evil, and
Moral Responsibility in 4 Maccabees

Like the Scriptural texts that form the authoritative basis for theological
and ethical reflection, parabiblical texts often also attempt to wrestle
with some of the most basic questions of human existence before God. They
do so, moreover, alongside us on the basis of the same, shared Scriptural
heritage. Our spiritual forebears in early Judaism and the early church have
much, therefore, to contribute to our own ongoing attempts to struggle with
the large questions that occupy—even plague—the minds of every person at
some point, if not at many points, in his or her existence: What does it mean
to be fully human? Whence does evil intrude upon human experience, and
where does the responsibility for evil lie? Where is God in the midst of the
experience of evil? How can "good" be restored? What is the meaning and
significance of death? What role do convictions about life beyond death play
in the confrontation of evil in human experience?

The following essay seeks to probe 4 Maccabees to discover its author's
answers to these questions. Even though this text stands in the outermost
fringes of the Christian Old Testament canon (and is nowhere to be found
in the landscape of the Jewish canon) it focuses on such central questions
of what it means to be human in relationship to God in the midst of life's
struggles, both internal and external. As the author of 4 Maccabees explores his "quintessentially philosophical principle" (φιλοσοφώτατον λόγον),
namely "if pious reason is master of the passions" (4 Macc 1:1), he creates an
ethical-theological treatise that responds quite directly to these existential
and theological questions in ways that merit full consideration by his spiritual descendants as they wrestle with the same.[1]

---

1. The historical setting of 4 Maccabees remains somewhat contested, though all
positions currently advocated fall within the period of the early Principate, between
Augustus and Hadrian (see discussion in deSilva, *4 Maccabees: Introduction and*

The Human Ideal in 4 Maccabees

The author of 4 Maccabees gives explicit expression to his view of the human person: "When God fashioned humanity, he implanted humanity's passions and habits, and at that time enthroned the mind, the sacred governor, over all things through the power of discernment. And to this faculty he gave the Law. Governing one's life according to the Law, the mind will rule a kingdom that is self-controlled and just and good and courageous" (2:21–23). The author calls to mind the creation account of Genesis 2:7–9, where God formed human beings and engaged in planting (i.e., the garden of Eden), and he shapes this story in ways that align with the writings of other Hellenistic Jewish philosophers. The starting point for the author's understanding of what it means to be human is his conception of God as creator, with the human being understood first and foremost a "creation," thus conceptualized entirely in relationship to God with a particular debt to God.[2] The "good" person understands and fulfills this debt, a foundational premise in the thinking of the martyrs throughout the narrative (see 13:13; 16:18–19). The "evil" person ignores or fails to understand this debt, and so acts unjustly toward his or her maker. All "evil" stems, in this regard, from a failure of reciprocity, a subset of "justice" in Greco-Roman discourse. This will be explicitly expressed in regard to Antiochus in 12:11–12.

As created beings, human beings possess an inherent, intelligent design—there is an inherent order in their creation and an ideal for their proper functioning. God planted both "passions" ($\pi\acute{\alpha}\theta\eta$)—a term including emotions, drives, and sensations[3]—and "inclinations" (or "character traits," $\mathring{\eta}\theta\eta$) in the human being, setting the mind over these other faculties as their governor.[4] The author's development of the creation story of Genesis (God as "planter") recalls Philo's insistence on reading it in terms of God's

---

Commentary, xiv–xvii), with a preference for the later half of that period (see Dupont-Sommer, *Quatrième Livre*, 75–85; Klauck, *4 Makkabäerbuch*, 668–69). The provenance is also not certain, though van Henten ("Jewish Epitaph") has advanced a cogent argument for a provenance somewhere between Asia Minor and Syrian Antioch.

2. Greeks and Romans were well aware of the debt of gratitude owed to the gods for sustaining human life. Aristotle (*Eth. Nic.* 8.14.1 1163b15–18) writes that "requital in accordance with desert is in fact sometimes impossible, for instance in honoring the gods, or one's parents. No one could ever render them the honor they deserve, and people are deemed virtuous if they pay them all the regard they can."

3. Klauck, *4 Makkabäerbuch*, 688.

4. The author takes as his theme a topic that is, indeed, "quintessentially philosophical" (1:1). Several authors regarded reason's ability to master the passions as the heart of ethical philosophy (see *Aristeas* 221–222, 256; Plutarch, *Virt. mor.* 1 [*Mor.* 440D]; *Phaedo* 93–94).

planting of the interior faculties of the human being rather than a physical garden spot (*Leg.* 1.43–55). From this model of the human being, it is clear why the author disagrees with the position held by the majority of Stoic philosophers, namely that the πάθη themselves are evils.[5]

The ability to "feel" was created and pronounced "good" by God. People therefore need to control and channel their feelings so that these feelings support those courses of action that align with God's good purposes for them, rather than attempt to eradicate them.[6] The author therefore censures the gluttonous person who sets out a feast only for himself or herself, since he or she channels the desire for and experience of pleasure in food toward self-indulgence (2:7). Those who set a feast for the purpose of inviting their friends and share their food with the poor use the enjoyment of food to support the creation of community and the sustenance of the life of the needy, and thus use pleasure to undergird and motivate God's higher goals for people. The Stoic goal of "passionlessness" (ἀπάθεια) is neither possible nor advantageous, for it sets itself against God's design for the human person in community.

The author also differs from Jewish writers who speak of the "evil inclination" as something that God planted in the human person or that took root as a consequence of Adam's transgression (see 4 Ezra 3:12–17). He does not speak of the *yetzer ha-ra'* when he speaks of "inclinations."[7] Contrary to such anthropology, he does not identify a single, unified power that wages war against the human will. There is no agonizing over the power of the evil inclination and the futility of struggle against it, as in 4 Ezra. The odds are not stacked against human beings fulfilling their created design. "As many as attend to religion with their whole heart" are able to master the passions (7:18). The author's conception of "inclinations" has

5. Townshend, "Fourth Book," 668. The classical Stoic goal was ἀπάθεια, the absence of the experience of emotion (Seneca, *Ep.* 116.1; Cicero, *Tusc. Disp.* 3.22; 4.57), though some Stoics, like Poseidonius, and the Peripatetics taught that the passions were to be controlled and moderated, not destroyed (Renehan, "Greek Philosophic Background"; Stowers, "4 Maccabees," 846). The author of 4 Maccabees clearly aligns himself with the latter school, as would Plutarch, according to whom "mastery and guidance" of the emotions by reason is the goal of the sage (*Virt. mor.* 4 [*Mor.* 442C; *Mor* 443D]).

6. Klauck, *4 Makkabäerbuch*, 699.

7. *Contra* Hadas, *Maccabees*, 156. Dupont-Sommer (*Quatrième Livre*, 51–52) finds traces of this doctrine in the "malicious disposition" (ἡ κακοήθης διάθεσις, 1:25) that the author claims to inhere even in the experience of pleasure, but it is not at all clear that this phrase ought to be translated "inclination to evil" as opposed to "spiteful" or "corrupting attitude." The author does not share the Cynic view that pleasure is the root of all the passions and vices (*contra* Dupont-Sommer, *Quatrième Livre*, 52), but rather the Aristotelian view that both pleasure and pain are equally deep roots in this regard (see 1:21–23, 28; Aristotle, *Rh.* 2.1.8; *Eth. Nic.* 2.5.2 1105b21–24).

much more in common with Aristotle's, as, for example, in regard to the proclivity of the young for sexual intercourse (compare 4 Macc 2:3 with Aristotle's discussions of age-related inclinations in *Rhetoric* 2:12). The challenge facing the individual is to control and cultivate the inclinations and the passions implanted by God for good, rather than allowing them to lead one into vice (and, therefore, evil).[8]

Fourth Maccabees articulates an anthropology very similar to Philo's: "scripture being well aware how great is the power of the impetuosity of each passion, anger and appetite, puts a bridle in the mouth of each, having appointed reason as their charioteer and pilot" (*Leg.* 3.118). His conception of the mind as the faculty appointed as "governor" (ἡγεμόνα) among the "senses" (αἰσθητηρίων) also aligns closely with Zeno's psychology, which affirms "the soul to consist of eight parts, dividing it into the governing principle, the five senses, the faculty of speech, and the procreative faculty" (translation mine).[9]

The mind is thus charged with maintaining control over the "passions and inclinations" (τὰ πάθη, τὰ ἤθη) so that the person continues to walk in line with what is good and virtuous. The passions and inclinations are like plants, each having many offshoots; reason, or the mind, is "the chief gardener, cleaning and pruning and binding and watering and irrigating in every manner," with the result that it "reclaims the forests of the inclinations and passions, for reason is the governor of the virtues, but it is the absolute master of the passions" (1:29–30). Reason gives every shoot the proper treatment. It must cut back the excess of certain passions, so that they function well within their proper boundaries rather than driving the individual to transgress those boundaries in their excess. The image of reason "binding" others calls to mind the practice of tying plants to a stake to help them grow straight and upright, suggestion that reason must work to incline some passions in their proper direction and to keep them from growing in twisted directions. Reason even nurtures other passions,[10] perhaps the strongest indication that the author has a positive evaluation of some emotions and

8. In this regard, it is significant that Jewish youths do *not* prove inferior to their passions, as Aristotle observes to be the tendency among youths (*Rhet.* 2.12.3), but rather are empowered by their observance of Torah to master any passions, whether the drive for intercourse (2:2–3) or pain (chapters 8–12, *passim*).

9. The text is given in Pearson, *Fragments*, 142. See also Arnim, *Stoicorum*, 1.39, as well as the similar conceptualization of the component faculties of a human being in Philo, *Opif.* 30.

10. Townshend ("Fourth Book," 668) points this out as he calls attention to the difference in nuance between ἐπάρδων and μεταχέων. The latter refers to irrigating in general, but the first to giving careful attention to making sure that water gets to each plant, giving each the proper amount of nourishment.

desires as aids to virtue. The garden is rank with weeds and thorns but it is also rife with potential for beauty and order.

Such imagery was familiar among discussions of reason's task in regard to the passions. Plutarch, for example, writes: "The work of reason is not Thracian, not like that of Lycurgus—to cut down and destroy the helpful elements of emotion together with the harmful, but to do as the god who watches over the crops and the god who guards the vine do—to lop off the wild growth and to clip away excessive luxuriance, and then to cultivate and to dispose for use the serviceable remainder" (*Virt. mor.* 12 [*Mor.* 451C]). Philo interprets Noah's work at farming in a similar manner, seeing here the lesson that

> like a good farmer, the virtuous man eradicates in the wild wood all the mischievous young saplings which have been planted by the passions or by the vices, but leaves untouched all those that bear fruit, and which may act as a wall and prove a firm defense for the soul. And, again, among the trees capable of cultivation he manages them in different ways, and not all in the same way: pruning some and adding props to others, training some so as to increase their size, and cutting down others so as to keep them dwarf. (*Det.* 105; see *Leg.* 1.47)

In the properly ordered person, reason (or the mind) keeps the passions in check so that the latter do not propel a person into the actions (the evils) that such impulsive drives as anger or malice promote (3:3–5). The consistent practice of virtue—of self-control, justice, courage, and prudence—promotes well-being in human experience. It is through vice—gluttony and lust, anger and malice, fear and pain—that evils break into human experience (1:3–4).

Torah and the Human Ideal

The Creator God has not left the human mind to its own devices, nor given it a role to fulfill without the proper guidance and empowerment. "To the mind, God gave the Law" (4 Macc 2:23). Only if a person submits his or her mind to the directives and principles of the divinely-given Torah will his or her reason keep the upper hand over the passions and inclinations. Plato had held to a similar view of the purpose of all "law" and "convention," namely that it was to be a guide for the mind to identify when the passions that pushed one to acts contrary to the law needed to be put in check (*Gorgias* 504D). The author of 4 Maccabees now claims this function for the Jewish Law, and further claims that this Law alone proves a reliable guide and support to reason in its task. The author speaks of Torah as, in effect, an operator's manual for the proper maintenance of the human being. Eleazar explains: "we do not eat unclean food, for, believing of God that he established the law, we know that the Creator of the world has shown sympathy toward us in accordance with Nature (κατὰ φύσιν) by giving the law. On the one hand, he permitted us to eat the things that would be the best suited (τὰ ... οἰκειωθησόμενα) to our persons, but, on the other hand, he forbade us to eat the things that would be adverse" (5:25–26).

Eleazar uses a term here (τὰ οἰκειωθησόμενα) that recalls earlier Stoic discussions about living in accordance with Nature. In his life of Chrysippus, Diogenes Laertius writes that "nature in constituting the animal made it near and dear to itself; for so it comes to repel all that is injurious and give free access to all that is serviceable or akin (τὰ οἰκεῖα) to it" (*Vit.* 7.85).[11] According to the author of 4 Maccabees, the Jewish sage discovers in the Torah what Stoics believed Nature to implant in its creatures, namely reliable knowledge of what is contrary to one's well-being and what conduces to the same.[12] Far from being contrary to the goal of living "according to nature" prized by the Stoic philosopher, as Antiochus had criticized the prescriptions of the Torah (5:9), the giving of the Torah was itself done "in accordance with Nature" as from a divine parent who makes provision for the child's education and upbringing. Following the directives of Torah affords a superior path to discovering what was truly in accordance with Nature, since the same God who had created the "world order" that was "Nature" also gave the Torah.[13] The Torah is the God-given resource (5:25–26) to enable created beings to live in line with their creator's ordering of their persons (2:21–23).[14]

11. Stowers, "4 Maccabees," 850.

12. In regard specifically to the dietary regulations of the Torah, the author appears to have embraced Philo's view that the Law forbids certain meats precisely because they are so succulent and apt to provoke gluttonous loss of self-control (1:31–35; Philo, *Spec.* 4.100).

13. Redditt, "Concept of *Nomos*," 257. Torah's superiority to nature as a guide to virtue will be made even clearer in the narratives that follow. Love for one's offspring and love for one's siblings, both natural affections, would have moved the seven brothers and their mother to abandon loyalty toward God for the sake of preserving one another's lives and sparing each other grief, were they not committed first of all to a higher guide than Nature (see 13:27; 15:25). Following the leading of Nature rather than the leading of Nature's Creator in the divinely-revealed Torah would have left them vulnerable to faltering at a critical juncture (7:18–19; 9:18).

14. Torah will also be shown to be a more reliable guide to virtue than Nature in the mother's exemplary attitude (15:25). The author dramatizes the mother's internal struggle using the familiar image of the council chamber. "Nature," the Stoics' guiding principle (and the final authority in Antiochus's reasoning, as represented in 5:8–9),

The author gives extended consideration to how particular commandments within that Law assist reason to tame and master particular unruly passions (1:31–2:19) as evidence for his claims about the human potential for virtue and the value of the Torah in the pursuit of virtue. The ability of pious Jews to follow particular statutes of Torah provides the proof that reason can master the passions by the power of self-control (1:31–35; 2:1–6), but the Torah also provides the discipline—the exercise regimen—that trains and empowers a person's reason to overcome his or her inclinations and desires (2:7–9a, perhaps also 9b–14). Doing conscientiously what Torah stipulates makes one work against one's own greed or stinginess, or against one's feelings of dislike or enmity. The variegated commandments of Torah reflect the diversity of cultivating techniques envisaged by Philo and listed in 4 Macc 1:29: following the particular commands is the way to prune excess and cultivate virtue according to the different requirements of each passion. Praising the value of the formative discipline (παιδεία) given by the Torah, Eleazar proclaims: "it thoroughly teaches us moderation so that we restrain all pleasures and desires, and it thoroughly teaches us courage so that we endure every pain willingly, and it instructs us in justice so that we render what is due in all our interactions, and it thoroughly teaches us piety so that we revere the only existing God in a manner befitting his greatness" (5:22–24).

The author of 4 Maccabees is entirely positive about the capacity of the human being to do what is good. The fact that the Law says "you will not covet" is, for him, sufficient proof that human beings are able not to covet (2:6, citing Exod 20:19; Deut 5:21). There is none of Paul's agonizing over how the commandment prohibiting coveting aroused all manner of covetousness in him (whether Rom 7:7–24 is to be taken as a reflection of Paul's pre-Christian life, his post-conversion life, or the hypothetical struggles of the persona he adopts for a "speech in character"). Rather, the author assures those who adopt and live in line with this internal hierarchy (Torah guiding the mind; the mind controlling the passions and inclinations) will

---

urges the mother to slacken in her courage, violate the demands of piety, and tell her sons to save themselves. Redditt ("Concept of *Nomos*," 256) draws a distinction between the meaning of φύσις in 4 Maccabees' discussions of love for siblings and offspring from its meaning as a "structure in harmony with which men [*sic*] ought to live" (as in 4 Macc 5:8–9). The latter, however, is the same φύσις that implants love for offspring and love for siblings in human hearts. To make a distinction would be to miss the significance of the argument of the author of 4 Maccabees that Nature remains insufficient as a guide to virtue, since the generally positive feelings of parental and fraternal love implanted by Nature (as in Plutarch, *Am. prol.* 3 [*Mor.* 496A]), and for which feelings Nature pleads in 4 Macc 15:25, would have led the mother to perpetrate evil against God and, thus, her nation as well.

attain the ideal of the Greek sage. They will reign as kings and queens (see Diogenes Laertius, *Vit.* 7.122; Philo, *Migr.* 197) over a well-governed domain in which each of the cardinal virtues flourishes.[15]

The picture of Torah as training in virtue and an exercise program for the rational faculty dominates the opening three chapters of 4 Maccabees. There is a second dimension to Torah, however, which comes to the fore alongside this first dimension once the author begins his "narrative demonstration" of his thesis (3:19). As we will explore shortly, this second dimension introduces some complications in what is otherwise an individual and potentially universal formulation of the problem of evil and its resolution. The Torah is also the covenant agreement with God, the terms of an alliance to which the ancestors of the Jews bound themselves by oath (5:29). As an agreement made between God and the *people*, not between God and individual persons, the problem of evil is complicated as a guilty *people* suffers the punishment stipulated in the covenant for breach thereof while innocent *persons* suffer as part of that people.

The Problem of Evil

Some definition of what is meant here by "evil" seems to be in order, although I will not pretend that it is a philosophically adept definition. I find that people are not so much concerned with the problem of "evil" as an abstract power or idea as with the problem of "evil" as the actual experience of undeserved misfortune, unhappiness, or loss. Questions about the problem of evil arise when what we would seek or choose for ourselves (the pleasant and happy future we envision for ourselves and ours, and towards which we strive) does not come about, but rather its opposite, or when what we would wish to avoid for ourselves and ours comes upon us from without. The problem also arises when we witness others falling into either of these situations through no fault of their own. In short, the problem of evil arises primarily when we inflict harm or harm is inflicted upon us, "harm" being broadly defined.

---

15. See also Arnim, *Stoicorum*, 3.617–619. To what extent does the author of 4 Maccabees exhibit ethnocentrism in his formulation of the problem of human existence and its solution? On the one hand, there are some rather exclusivist claims made on behalf of Jews. "The children of the Hebrews *alone* are invincible on behalf of virtue" (9:18). On the other hand, Gentiles are not *intrinsically* debased qua Gentiles (as appears to be the case in Wisdom of Solomon's depiction of the Canaanites, who were beyond redemption, 12:10–11), but only insofar as they have not "attended to religion with a whole heart," a path that is theoretically open to all (7:18–19).

For the author of 4 Maccabees, with his theocentric view of human experience, evil is also—and especially—the violation of what God would seek or choose for human interaction and for human relating with Deity. Evil is that of which God does not approve. In the Jewish Scriptures, the constant refrain "he (or they) did what was evil in the sight of the Lord" shows that the regular reference point for "evil" as opposed to "good" was alignment with God's standards for human behavior (accessible in the Torah, the codification of the same). This dual perspective on evil—the human and the divine—may offer a way into the dual sources of evils breaking in upon human experience in 4 Maccabees: (1) the evil that results from individual humans, often large collections of individual humans, not living in alignment with their created ideal (i.e., with God-centered reason ruling the passions); and (2) the evil that results as the experience of divine punishment for violation of God's covenant (or disregard for God's claim upon the human being as creator and giver of life). The two exhibit a fundamental unity, however, since God's Torah (that is, living in line with Torah) is the path to avoid both evils, fulfilling both the human ideal and the covenantal ideal.

As 4 Maccabees opens, the problem of evil is presented as largely an interior issue. This will change somewhat in 3:19–18:24, when the issue of the consequences of covenant disobedience and divine punishment are raised, but even there the roots of evil are interior to human beings. There is a striking absence of spiritual causes of evil in 4 Maccabees. After reading 1 Enoch, Daniel, *Testaments of the Twelve Patriarchs*, or even Tobit, with their presentations of fallen angels, demonic spirits, and spirits of error or spirits of truth taking possession of a human's will,[16] 4 Maccabees seems to come from another world entirely—a highly rationalized and demythologized world. There are no evil angels, no giants, no forbidden knowledge, no spirits entering human being or enticing them away from the righteous path.[17] An-

16. According to 1 Enoch, evil enters the world chiefly through the activity of rebel angels who leave their realm to mate with human females, impart forbidden knowledge (e.g., about metallurgy, thus providing the means to create deadlier weapons, feeding wrath and violence, and to refine precious metals, stoking greed and covetousness), and sire a race of giants that wreak havoc on humankind (1 Enoch 6–16; cf. Gen 6:1–4). In Tobit, a particular fallen angel, Asmodeus, oppresses a virgin, killing her husbands out of a desire to possess her himself (Tob 3:7–8, 17). In the *Testaments*, spirit beings directly enter human beings and act upon their moral choices, whether for virtue or vice (see, e.g., *T. Reub.* 2.1—3.9).

17. There is one reference that might contradict this observation. In the mother's closing speech, viewed by many scholars as a secondary addition to the text (Freudenthal, *Flavius Josephus*, 155–56; Deissmann, "Das vierte Makkabäerbuch," 175; Dupont-Sommer, *Quatrième Livre*, 152–54; Rost, *Einleitung*, 81), the mother claims that she was not overcome by the "seducer or corruptor on a deserted plain" (18:8a), recalling the

gels appear in the narrative only once, at the end of the Apollonius episode
(4:10–11), a story taken over and adapted from 2 Maccabees (where angels
play a more prominent role), and in the author's recollection of the episode
of Aaron halting the plague (7:11), which reflects the midrashic tendency to
imagine an angelic figure spreading the plague among the congregation of
Israel (compare Num 16:41–50 with Wis 18:20–25).[18]

The primary source of evil is a person's failure to maintain the God-or-
dained order within, as the author spelled out this order in 1:29–30; 2:21–23.
Evil enters the sphere of human experience as a person allows the passions
to overflow their bounds and to become the driving force in his or her decisions and actions. As the individual is overcome internally by a particular
emotion, desire, or sensation, behavior that is destructive of well-being—of
one's own or that of others or both—results and "evil" is experienced. The
major battle is an internal one, as in 4 Ezra, where the whole point of life
is to win the battle against the evil inclination (4 Ezra 7:89, 92, 127–129)
or in Epictetus (*Ench.* 1.1) or Seneca (*De Constantia* 3.3–5; 5.1–5), where
ultimately there is no evil that can be inflicted from without, as long as one's
goals and expectations for life in this world are set just right.[19]

Fourth Maccabees 2:15–20 provides a diptych of examples. When faced
with a challenge to his authority, Moses does *not* respond out of his anger
against Dathan and Abiram. He does *not* become an agent of self-motivated
violence and harm. Levi and Simeon, on the other hand, allow their anger to
gain the upper hand, and the result is the massacre of the males of Shechem.
For the Shechemites, this was an experience of overwhelming evil—the

---

case law in Deut 22:25–27 which speaks of a man accosting a woman at some distance
from an inhabited place, but here again it is a matter of another human being failing to
master his own passions. In the next phrase, however, she adds that "the seducer, the
snake of deceit" did not "defile the purity of [her] virginity" (18:8b). This appears to
refer to a reading of Genesis 3 in which the serpent, possibly acting out the intentions
of Satan, seduces or deceives the woman in the Garden (Gen 3:13).

18. While Dupont-Sommer (*Quatrième Livre*, 44) may be correct to claim that the
author does not "repudiate" contemporary Jewish ideas concerning angels, he is certainly far more conservative in his appeals to their impact on the human situation and,
especially, human moral choice.

19. The tortures, far from being experienced as an absolute evil, are turned into
"splendid favors" because they give the martyrs the opportunity to show the depth of
their dedication to the Torah-driven life and the mastery of the passions that this life
has nurtured. The only real evil or injury that the martyrs can suffer is what they might
do to themselves by breaking faith and yielding to the passions of fear, pain, and the
like. As the brothers declare in unison, "Even if you kill us because of our godly character, don't think that you can truly harm us by these tortures. We will gain the awards
of moral character through this suffering, and we will be with God, for whose sake we
suffer" (9:7–8).

violent end of many innocent lives (only Shechem himself, ostensibly, had been guilty of assault on Dinah) and the mourning of those lives by surviving wives, mothers, and children. "Cursed be their anger," indeed!

Where evil comes upon a person from without, it stems ultimately from another person's failure to discover and maintain this divine ordering of the inner person (often along with ignorance of *how* to achieve this ordering, seen, for example, in Antiochus IV's ignorance of the value of Torah—hence it is all "madness" or "stupidity" to him, 5:7; 8:5; 12:3). The rape of Dinah was an experience of evil born of Shechem's failure to master his lust (as opposed to Joseph's positive counter-example in 4 Macc 2:2–4), allowing the passion to propel him to an impulsive act of violence against Dinah. But Levi and Simeon's response was of exactly the same kind from the same disordered source.[20]

Ultimately, the same source drives Israel's enemies throughout the story of 4 Maccabees. Antiochus and his soldiers are "savage," "inhumane," driven by anger and rage to mistreat the Judean prisoners more and more brutally.[21] Antiochus is a placard example showing the vital importance of mastering the passions by portraying the horrific evils that can result where these are *not* mastered (and, in regard to his self-understanding as a human being, also the terrible consequences of failing to know oneself as *creature* of the One God, the same God who created Antiochus's fellow human beings in Judea). He is himself driven by a particular passion afflicting the soul, namely "arrogance" (1:26; cf. 4:15). He lacks the humility that comes from acknowledging one's own fragility, and thus one's essential kinship with all other human beings who live within the limits of the same fragility (see 12:13), and therefore he thinks it right to inflict physical harm in the extreme. He lacks the humility that comes from acknowledging that the will and rule of God is superior to one's own, and that one's first duty and that of others is to God's will and rule. This is made explicit in 12:11, but emerges also earlier in 5:13 and 8:14, where Antiochus expects God to excuse transgression of God's divine commands under compulsion while Antiochus enforces his own commands without giving room to the Jews for being "compelled" by a higher law to disobey his commands.

20. The author of 4 Maccabees takes a much different view of this episode than one finds, for example, in *Testament of Levi*, where Levi acts on divine commission to take vengeance against Shechem (*T. Levi* 5:1–4) and Jacob is ignorant of God's will in this situation (*T. Levi* 6.6–8), or in Judith, where Simeon is similarly commissioned by God (Jdt 9:2–4). Fourth Maccabees is more conservative in remaining aligned with the perspective of Gen 49:7.

21. Thus, rightly, Moore and Anderson, "Taking It Like a Man," 254; see also deSilva, "Using the Master's Tools," 108–10.

Antiochus is impelled to act by his own passions, which is a bitter indictment of his fitness to rule.[22] "In exceedingly violent passion he gave orders to bring others from the captives of the Hebrews" to be tortured, this anger coming from his defeat by Eleazar, his frustration at his own inability to coerce an elderly man to obey (8:2).[23] It is Antiochus's passion (anger) that stands behind the order "to torture them still more cruelly" (8:2), as if to communicate that Antiochus's raw, unchecked passion was being translated into violence and evil enacted upon the bodies of other persons. He warns the seven brothers: "If you move me to anger by your disobedience, you will compel me to destroy each and every one of you with terrible punishments through tortures" (8:9). The brothers cannot be compelled to do evil by the fiercest tortures, but Antiochus can be compelled by his own anger (aroused by the imagined affront of people obeying their God rather than him) to have human beings like himself shredded, dismembered, and killed. The brothers' declaration of loyalty to their own ancestral way of life and indictment of Antiochus for his ultra-violence against them leaves him "indignant" and "infuriated" (9:10). This fury becomes active in the tortures applied to the brothers (9:11). Antiochus's soldiers transform themselves into animals in their equipment and actions: they become "leopard-like beasts" (9:28), ripping and tearing into their prey. The torturers themselves are piqued by the third brother's freedom of speech and their embitterment fuels their violent treatment of the young man (10:5). In a world in which not everyone is committed to the mastery of the passions, to the regulation of one's own conduct by the cardinal virtues, and to living in awareness of one's creatureliness, it is sometimes necessary to "die for the sake of virtue" (1:8) or "for the sake of nobility of character" (1:10).

The solution to the problem of evil, insofar as a solution lies in the hands of any individual, is entirely straightforward, namely ordering one's inner life, one's inner being, through the discipline provided by Torah. The solution takes effect "as soon as a person adopts a way of life in accordance with the Law" (2:8, NRSV), since the Torah at once constrains a person to act in ways that are just, generous, and the like (2:9–14). Where people resist this solution, evils will still burst forth into human experience, but the solution lies ever close at hand, within the grasp of every person. The only way

---

22. Greco-Roman philosophers were adamant in their affirmation that only the person who could rule himself or herself was competent to exercise rule over other people (Plato, *Gorg.* 491D; Xenophon, *Oeconomicus* 21.12; Dio Chrysostom, *Or.* 62.1). See, further, Moore and Anderson, "Taking It Like a Man," 253–54.

23. Moore and Anderson ("Taking It Like a Man," 264) rightly observe that the dynamics of honor and shame are at work in this public contest, and that Antiochus has been shamed by his failure in round one against Eleazar.

THE HUMAN IDEAL, THE PROBLEM OF EVIL, AND MORAL RESPONSIBILITY

in which the individual can contribute to the solution, beyond appropriately ordering his or her life, is to witness to the value of Torah and the virtue of the Torah-guided life in the hope that others will be persuaded to become part of the solution rather than the problem, as these early martyrs—these "witnesses"—do (4 Macc 16:16).

The author of 4 Maccabees does not leave everything quite so simple, however. Within the narrative world, there is another source from which "evils" break into human experience—namely from God as divine punishment. Under Onias III, Judea enjoys the covenant blessings promised in Deut 28:1–14, expressed here in terms of "experiencing deep peace because of their loyalty to the Law, and getting along well" (4 Macc 3:20–21). Onias's brother Jason, however, breaks the covenant agreement: he "changed the nation's way of life and altered its form of government in complete transgression of the Law," and, thereby, exhibited scorn for the Law (4:19–21). This, in turn, provoked "divine justice," which had warned long ago that disobedience toward or breaches of the covenant would bring severe punishment upon the disloyal nation as a whole (Deut 27:15—28:68). In consequence, then, "Divine Justice . . . caused Antiochus himself to war against them," even as Deuteronomy promised that God would bring down upon a disobedient Israel "a grim-faced nation" that would show regard neither for the old or for the young (Deut 28:49–50; 4 Macc 4:21). Antiochus specifically tries to destroy any remaining loyalty to the Law among the people (4 Macc 4:23–26). In stark opposition to the priestly elite, however, the "regular" people are disposed to be executed before breaking faith with the covenant agreement.

When are "evils" *evil*, and when are "evils" *justice*? When are they the consequences of one's own evil, or the evil (the injustice) in the decisions and actions of the people in whose midst one lives? The experience of persecution under Antiochus is, under the terms of the covenant, "just" as a consequence of the nation's departure from the covenant and forfeiture, therefore, of the protection of their divine Patron. A particular problem raised implicitly by the author, however, is the problem of the intense and brutal suffering of the most innocent Judeans—the ones most faithful to God and least deserving of being objects of divine punishment. Where is the justice in *their* experience of evils? Reading through 4 Maccabees, one must ask: Is God in Antiochus and Antiochus's horrific treatment of the Judeans? Is God behind the tortures? The author appears to be, again implicitly, aware of this problem, for he is at pains to demonstrate that their fate is not, in fact, an "evil." They are not overcome; they are not injured; they maintain their virtue intact. Here afterlife will play an important role: it is the ground for affirming, ultimately, that God is not unfair, that mastering the passions *is* ultimately advantageous (and *absolutely* so).

Where was God when these brothers were being twisted on wheels, burned over fires, and hacked into pieces? The author of 4 Maccabees would answer that God was in the giving of the Torah (2:21–23) that allowed Eleazar, the seven brothers, and the mother of the seven to overcome the tyrant's attempts to compel them to act against the good, holding firm to their convictions and successfully maintaining the freedom of their wills. God was in the hope that each had of entering into life beyond death as the reward for a life well-lived, the reward for ordering one's life in God's way rather than becoming a source of evil and vice oneself.

The solution to this facet of the problem of evil, however, is closely compatible with the solution to the problem in regard to the individual. According to Deuteronomy 30:1–5, a revival of obedience among the people would bring about a restoration of the covenant blessings for the whole nation. The martyrs offer representative obedience, but as it is complete obedience—obedience unto death—they cherish the hope that it will weigh more heavily in God's estimation than the disobedience of the priestly aristocracy (6:27–29; 9:24; 17:20–21). Their extreme display of loyalty to the covenant, testifying to the covenant's value in the sight of their neighbors, reawakens commitment to such obedience in a broader public (18:4). Their individual commitment to maintain the divine ordering of their inward person, mastering the passions that would draw them away from the just path of loyalty to the covenant God, also contributes to the reversal of the experiences of evils plaguing the nation as a whole.

The Problem of Death

The author does not speak of death as a tragic loss. Instead, he speaks of it positively as a "faithful" or "reliable seal" upon one's life. Praising Eleazar after recounting his martyrdom, he exclaims: "O man of blessed old age and respectable gray hair and life lawfully lived, whom the trustworthy seal of death perfected!" (7:15). The author reflects the logic of the sober maxim that closes Sophocles's *Oedipus Tyrannus*: "call no mortal happy until he is dead, free from pain." Oedipus was someone all people considered blessed by the gods, but in a single day tragedy turned all his joy into sorrow. Similarly, a person may have lived a long life with a spotless reputation for virtue, but in a single day some weakness of character could bring all of that to ruin, as indeed any such weakness would have done on that day before Antiochus. Life is a trial—a "noble contest" (16:16)—and one's virtue is always at risk until death imprints its seal upon a completed life. Eleazar's virtue was not "perfect" and beyond the possibility of ruin until his virtue was no longer vulnerable to being threatened or assailed. Death placed a "seal" upon Eleazar's virtue insofar as, prior to death, he had not besmirched it and now, after death, there was no possibility that Eleazar would ever pollute himself. Indeed, in his particular circumstances, the fact that he died at all sealed his victory, for it meant that at no point did he yield to the feelings of pain being inflicted upon him. By dying honorably, the honor of his life would forever remain intact. Thucydides similarly speaks of death as a "seal" when Pericles calls the deaths of the fallen soldiers the "seal" upon their virtue (*Hist.* 2.42): those who had shown courage to the point of death held that reputation securely and would never again be tempted to cowardice.[24]

The author opened his encomium on Eleazar expressing the same view of death, though using more colorful, nautical metaphors: "For just as an excellent navigator, the reason of our father Eleazar, steering the ship of piety in the open sea of the passions, assailed by the tyrant's threats and flooded by the high waves of the tortures, in no way turned the handles of the rudder of piety until it had sailed into the harbor of immortal victory" (7:1–3). Sophocles described a political king using the image of a pilot steering a ship (*Oedipus tyrannus* 689–696; *Antigone* 994–995). It was readily available to be applied in the extended sense to the mind or the reason as the governing faculty "enthroned" among the senses (4 Macc 2:21–23). The author of 4 Maccabees shares this application in common with Philo, reminding us again of his alignment with other Hellenized Jewish authors:

> As a ship holds on to her right course when the pilot has the helm in his hand and steers her, and she is obedient to her rudder, but the vessel is upset when some contrary wind descends upon the waves and the whole sea is occupied by billows; so when the mind, which is the charioteer or pilot of the soul, retains the mastery over the entire animal, as a ruler does over the city, the life of the person proceeds rightly. (*Leg.* 3.223–224; see also *Leg.* 3.118; *Migr.* 6)

In Eleazar's situation, the only safe anchorage at the end of his rough voyage was, in fact, death (7:3). If his journey had ended in any other way, that is, as a consequence of acquiescing to Antiochus's demand, Eleazar would have made a shipwreck of his piety. The image of the harbor also reminds the hearers and readers that such a death is not something to be feared. In Eleazar's case death was the transition to unending life with God and the enjoyment of everlasting peace at the end of a harsh storm.

24. See also Epictetus on the death of Menoeceus in *Diatr.* 3.20.4–6.

Death can be a "glorious" (10:1) or "a privileged" experience (10:15; cf. 12:1) when it is the result of maintaining virtue, keeping the proper ordering of oneself intact—even more, or at least in parallel, when it is the result of maintaining covenant loyalty with God, which is, for the author, the equivalent of ordering one's life properly by "pious reason" (cf. 1:15–17; 2:21–23). When death is the result of *not* breaking faith with God, it is a "noble death," since it is embraced as the means by which to give back to the creator God proportionately as one has received from God, namely life itself (12:14; 13:13; 16:18–19). Though the death is unjustly inflicted, dying itself is an act of justice (δικαιοσύνη). Death becomes a gift to God of the full measure of grateful response and covenant faithfulness.

The author also presents the possibility that death is a witness or a testimony. The mother summons her seven sons to bring forward evidence on behalf of the nation, using a technical term from the Attic law courts—διαμαρτυρία, "evidence given to prevent a case from coming to trial" (16:16).[25] The use of the term asserts that more is on trial here than the martyrs themselves; more is at stake than their own lives. The martyrs' response to Antiochus's demands will bear witness to the nation's character and, in particular, to its commitment to the covenant relationship initiated by God at Sinai. It is possibly in this context that the author intends the more precise meaning of διαμαρτυρία: the martyrs' evidence of fidelity to the covenant now would prevent God's covenant law suit from coming to trial, as it were, in which God would declare the covenant null and void on account of Israel's disobedience. The martyrs' obedience unto death brings sufficient "evidence" to the contrary. In this regard, death becomes a testimony, a witness. On the one hand, it is a witness to other human beings (here, Antiochus) concerning the nobility and value of the Jewish way of life as a way in which to live and die in integrity, aligned with the created order and purpose of the human being. It is also, however, a witness to God, affirming the value that Jews placed upon the covenant and upon honoring the covenant, counter-evidence to be weighed against the acts of the priestly elite under Jason.

Life beyond Death and the Contest against Evil

The author's view of death depends entirely on his convictions about the afterlife. Death can be embraced as a harbor because this harbor lies on the shore of a new and deathless life. For those who die in a state of—and all the more on account of—covenant loyalty (16:13), death becomes the gate

25. This meaning is given in Liddell and Scott, *A Greek-English Lexicon*, 403, col. 1.

through which one passes into immortality. For the author of 4 Maccabees, convictions about the afterlife play a major role in positioning the individual to confront evil, to align with the solution to evil rather than contribute to the problem through perpetrating injustice (either against others or against the creator God). These convictions are essential to properly weigh advantage and, thus, make one's decision in favor either of "pious reason" or of the direction in which the passions drive one.[26]

The author suggests possible responses that the brothers (8:17–26) and the mother (16:6–11) could have made (but did *not* make) in their circumstances had they been of weaker character. In these hypothetical speeches, the situation facing the martyrs is seen and evaluated strictly from the perspective of this temporal life, with no consideration given to a life beyond death. Death means only "removal from this most pleasant life" and "deprivation of this delightful world" (8:23). It means utter loss and the negation of all one's efforts on behalf of the deceased, poignantly expressed in the lament the mother *could* have uttered, but did not, speaking of giving birth "in vain," of nurturing the boys "to no purpose," and of enduring ultimately "unfruitful" pregnancies (16:7 [3x], 8, 9). Seeing death as the end of one's being, the author suggests, would have undermined the martyrs' commitment to virtue and their ability to master their passions for the sake of acting virtuously.

The author makes an explicit statement to this effect at the conclusion of his eulogy for Eleazar:

> Some people might say, perhaps, "Not all control the passions, because not all keep their reason prudent." But as many as have a care for piety from the whole heart—these alone are able to restrain the passions of the flesh, trusting that they do not die to God, just as neither our patriarchs Abraham and Isaac and Jacob did, but live to God. Therefore, for some people to be seen indeed to be ruled by the passions on account of the weakness of their reason contradicts this in no respect. For who, philosophizing with reference to the whole rule of philosophy, and trusting God, and knowing that it is blessed to endure every pain on account of virtue, would not control the passions on account of religion?! (7:18–22)[27]

26. The author shares this conviction with his source (2 Maccabees), although he consistently portrays afterlife in terms of the survival of the soul in a state of blessedness rather than in corporeal terms (i.e., as physical resurrection, as in 2 Macc 7:9, 11, 14). See Dupont-Sommer, *Quatrième Livre*, 44–47.

27. See also 16:24–25: "the mother of the seven persuaded each one of the sons to die rather than disobey the commandment of God, but also, moreover, with them

Both Roman and Hellenistic Jewish authors promoted the view that absolute commitment to virtue could only be achieved where the sting of death (and, thus, the fear of death) was removed. Seneca, for example, wrote: "If it is realized that death is not an evil and therefore not an injury either, we shall much more easily bear all other things—losses and pains, disgrace, changes of abode, bereavements, and separations" (*Constant.* 8.3). Josephus recognized that his fellow Jews were able to endure martyrdom only because they held firm their conviction that "they shall come into being again, and at a certain revolution of things receive a better life than they had enjoyed before" (*Ap.* 2.217–218). Belief in life beyond death radically changes a person's evaluation of what is "advantageous" (or, in terms of a category invoked previously by Antiochus, "what is truly beneficial," τὴν τοῦ συμφέροντος ἀλήθειαν, 5:11). The hope of a blessed eternity makes the endurance of any temporary disadvantage required to attain everlasting good the more expedient course of action. For this cause, the author insists that "pious reason," "reason that operates taking piety into full account," is the force that can overcome any passion or inclination (1:1). Those who do weigh advantages and disadvantages in light only of the present life are vulnerable to being mastered by their passions, especially the passions of fear and pain in the cases of the martyrs (7:20). Anyone who looks to eternity, however, *can* live a well-ordered life and avoid perpetrating evil. Thinking about life according to the "*whole* canon of philosophy" (7:21) includes taking life beyond death into account in one's choices.

The promise of life with God beyond death, then, is an important incentive to dying in alignment with the Torah, the covenant agreement with God. It is this promise that provides the essential support for *absolute* mastery of the passions, since no breach of virtue (whether urged by the promise of pleasure or the compulsion/pressure of pain) would ever seem advantageous, while virtue (as alignment with the Torah) would always present itself as advantageous. Belief in life beyond death—and the possibility of securing the quality of that life beyond death in the here and now (whether good or ill)—redefines

---

knowing these things—that those dying on account of God continue to live to God, just as Abraham and Isaac and Jacob and all the patriarchs." Compare Mark 12:26–27// Matt 22:32// Luke 20:37–38. Both the author of 4 Maccabees and Jesus appear to presume a traditional exegesis of Exod 3:6. Grimm ("Viertes Buch," 332) regards 7:19 to be a doublet of 16:25 and suggests excising the former passage. This reflects more the tendency of nineteenth-century scholars to prefer their edited versions of texts to actual necessity. The verse fulfills an expected function in its place, providing a rationale for the claim made in 7:18; moreover, it conforms to the general repetitiveness of the author's style (compare, for example 6:31–35 with 13:1–5; see also Dupont-Sommer, *Quatrième Livre*, 117).

advantage and the weighing of relative advantages, as the author prominently
displays throughout his narrative demonstration.

The brothers consider Antiochus's "pity, which offers safety at the cost
of breaking our Law, to be more bitter than death" (9:4)—"more bitter than
death," because transgression brings punishment worse than death, from
which there is no release *in* death (see 13:15). Yielding to one's passions poses greater danger to oneself (3:15; 13:14–15), since such yielding inevitably
leads to provoking God, violating justice toward one's creator and superior
covenant partner. On the basis of their assurance that they "will be with
God, on whose account [they] are suffering," enjoying "the rewards given
to moral character," the brothers tell Antiochus that, "even if you are able to
kill us because of our godly character, don't think that you can truly harm
us by these tortures" (9:8–9). But it is in his discussion of what was going
on inside the mother's mind that the author gives fullest expression to the
importance of a firm belief in life beyond death for mastering one's passions
and remaining aligned with God's vision for the human being.

The central process of deliberation in ancient rhetoric involved weighing the respective advantages of two possible courses of action. The more
advantageous course conduced to greater safety ("the avoidance of a present
or imminent danger") and to greater honor than the alternatives (see *Rhet.
Her.* 3.2.3; Quintilian, *Inst.* 3.8.33). It was in the weighing of advantages and
disadvantages that the virtue of "wisdom" primarily manifested itself (*Rhet.
Her.* 3.3.4). Orators would be sensitive to contrasting short-term gain before
long-term pain with its converse; it would fall mainly to philosophers (like
Plato at the conclusion of the *Gorgias*) and to speakers in the Jewish and
Christian minority cultures to transpose this to an otherworldly venue in
which one might choose hardship in this life for the sake of security in the
life of the world to come or the life beyond death (see, for example, Susanna
22–23; 2 Macc 6:26; 2 Cor 4:16–18; Heb 11:24–26).

In the council chamber of the mother's mind, the author sets "piety
that, according to divine promise, preserves to everlasting life" against the
"temporary preservation of her sons on the terms of the tyrant's promise"
(15:2–3). Like the juror in the Greek law court, she held two ballots in her
hand, rejecting the "one [ballot bringing] deliverance that would preserve
her sons for a short time" and choosing the other ballot that, though it
brought death in the here and now for them (15:26), would give "the full
complement of her sons a new birth to life immortal" if they chose to die for
the sake of fulfilling their pious duty toward God (16:13). Her conviction
that death was not the end of a person's existence allowed her to exhibit
proper "fear of God" (15:8). She refused to provoke God by acquiescing to
Antiochus, as if his honor and his power were weightier and more worthy of

obedience than the Almighty's (15:8; see also 13:14–15). She demonstrates the virtue of "god-fearing Abraham" (15:28) by exhibiting similar "faith in/faithfulness toward God" (πίστιν πρὸς τὸν θεόν, 15:24), trusting God's promises that the righteous would enjoy a better life (15:3) and committing to remain loyal to her Divine Patron for the sake both of past and future benefits (see 16:18–19, 22).[28]

This same conviction also empowered both the mother and her sons not to perpetrate evil upon their nation. Apostasy—the willful violation of the covenant—was, after all, the purported cause of the evils that had fallen upon the inhabitants of Jerusalem as a result of Antiochus's siege and attempt to stamp out their native way of life. Yielding to the passions, violating the divine order for the individual human being, would have meant participating in the systemic evils of further apostasy, further alienating the nation from God, inviting continued experience of the evils of the covenant curses.

The individual's refusal to perpetrate evil becomes, in the author's narrative, a principal cause of the reversal of the evils that had broken into the experience of their nation and victimized many. Their individual resistance to Antiochus's demands (11:24–25) encourages a resurgence of zeal for the covenant throughout the nation, seen in the revival of covenant obedience throughout the land (18:4). Their individual commitment to maintain the integrity of their created ideal ultimately becomes the cause of the downfall of the imperial tyrant's hold on the nation (1:11).[29]

Belief in life beyond death also plays an important role in solving the problems of theodicy that the author raises by introducing the Deuteronomistic theology of history (with the possibility of the collective punishment of the people as a whole, innocent and guilty alike) into his discourse. Punishment for transgression extends well beyond the experience of the covenant curses spelled out in Deuteronomy 27–28 and lived out afresh under Antiochus. Beyond the collective, this-worldly experience of the covenant curses, there remains the individual, other-worldly experience of (reward and) punishment. This is the threat of greater punishment ("everlasting

28. On the topic of God as "Divine Patron" in 4 Maccabees, see deSilva, *4 Maccabees*, 127–31.

29. Townshend ("Fourth Book," 667) insists that the Hasmonean family would be understood as the subject of the result clause at the end of 1:11: "The spirit roused by the martyrs led to the rising headed by Judas Maccabaeus and his brethren, and so was the *effectual* cause of the Temple being purified and its service re-established." Despite such special pleading, one should rather be struck by the complete silence of the author concerning the violent resistance movement. Despite the historical problems involved with the claim, the author is intent on crediting the martyrs with the deliverance of their homeland. See Dupont-Sommer, *Quatrième Livre*, 150; Seeley, *Noble Death*, 93; O'Hagan, "The Martyr," 111–12.

torture") "awaiting those who transgress God's commandment" (13:15). Divine justice is worked out at both levels, and the other-worldly level makes up for the perceived injustices of the experiences of this life (e.g., the suffering that God's provocation of Antiochus brings also upon the Torah-observant, covenant-loyal Judeans). Because of the existence of these two levels, the martyrs' deaths can have beneficial effects for the nation in this life (6:27–29; 9:24; 12:17–18; 17:21–22), becoming, as it were, an offering to God *on behalf of* others, while their *own* experience of divine reward as a result of covenant loyalty is also secured beyond death.

The author closes his oration with several assurances that the martyrs did, in fact, enter into their hoped-for immortality:

> The moon in heaven among the stars has not been made to stand nearly as revered as you, who lit the path toward piety for the seven star-like children, have been made to stand honored in God's presence and firmly set in the heavens together with them. (17:5)

They now stand before the divine throne and live throughout the blessed eternity. For indeed Moses says, "All those who have set themselves apart for you are under your hands." (17:18–19; see LXX Deut 33:3)

> The sons of Abraham together with their prize-winning mother have been joined with the chorus of their ancestors, having received pure and immortal souls from God. (18:23)

With such visual images, the author seeks to make the hope of immortality more real for his hearers, so that they, too, would "philosophize in line with the whole canon of philosophy" (7:21), which includes living now as persons whose lives and, therefore, choices are not bounded by death. Thus they, too, will be empowered to live fully in line with the ideal imprinted in their creation and encoded in their covenant.

Conclusion

The author of 4 Maccabees promotes a view of the human being and a set of convictions concerning death and the life beyond that nurture moral accountability beyond self-interest. Antiochus is an important figure as an exemplification of failure to understand this higher accountability. His authority and power are not given to him to serve his own interests, but to serve broader interests—what the author would call God's interests. He is accountable not within the artificial lines drawn between Greek and Judean, between ruling power and reluctant colonials, but to the larger bond and higher ideal of "humanity" that should connect him with his intended victims and guide his conduct much differently.

The conceptions of the human being as "creature" of God and of a life beyond death in which obedience or disobedience to these higher ideals are rewarded and punished are elements of a world view that nurtures a higher ethos than self-interest (with its objectification of the "other") or even self-preservation. The proportionately greater temporal duration of life beyond death is a means of expressing the proportionately greater value of this higher ethos and its proportionately greater demands on the individual person.

The author claims that people who hold firm to these convictions about an afterlife, the conditions of which are determined by the decision of the divine judge, are better able to choose the virtuous course of action, that is, choose for others or for a cause greater than themselves over and above choosing for self-interest or even self-preservation. Those who lack such a hope, for whom death is truly the end, have a harder time rising above the passions (7:18–22). Indeed, according to the author of Wisdom of Solomon, the belief that *this* life is all that one has to enjoy can be a powerful inducement to self-centered living, to the intentional and programmatic indulgence of the passions, and to the perpetration of evil upon others for one's own satisfaction in this life (Wis 1:16–2:24).

There are ideals and values that are greater than our own preferences, inclinations, and desires for ourselves, ideals that call for our commitment and allow us to transcend ourselves by embodying them, even where this entails loss in terms of what we might otherwise desire for ourselves, for our own satisfaction. We might even *embrace* what we would not choose for ourselves—what from the perspective of our own desires or vision for a happy life could be accounted an "evil"—for the sake of a transcendent ideal. The deferral of self-interest and self-preservation to an arena beyond the historical sphere frees the individual from the domination of these instincts or drives for other-centered moral action, enabling moral actions that give us life, in a sense, beyond ourselves.

The author ascribes such moral power, then, to the belief in the transcendence of death since such a belief empowers the transcendence of "self" with its limitations (its self-protective and survival instincts, its fear of the loss that might ensue as the price of making the virtuous choice). I don't have to look after my own interests at the expense or to the neglect of others, as if my getting what I want out of this life is the highest priority. There is a life beyond *that* kind of life; there is One who is looking after my interests, who will ensure my ultimate fulfillment. Such convictions, in turn, empower one to resist interior inducements to perpetrate evil and the demands that systemic perpetrators of evil place on one, seeking to coerce compromise and cooperation. I am thereby freed to look after the interests of the other, or of the larger human community—truly to love my neighbor as myself.

Ultimately, such an approach to engaging the moral choices of life is in my own best interests as well, since it is a contribution to the creation of a community where others, acting in line with the same ideals, will also love *me* as they love themselves. It is an ethical ideal—and an ideal construction of the human being-in-community—that has rarely been enjoyed, it seems, in our history, but which the author of 4 Maccabees would affirm lies within the grasp of those who know themselves to have been created by God for more than the life of the self.

8

Fourth Maccabees and Early Christian Martyrdom

The Influence of 4 Maccabees on Origen's Exhortatio ad Martyrium

I n the course of his *Exhortatio ad Martyrium*, Origen retells the famous story of the martyrdoms of Eleazar, seven brothers, and the mother of the seven. While it is clear that he drew upon the version in 2 Maccabees from his verbatim recitations of the same, close study of his vocabulary, his supplements to the story, his choice of imagery, and his deployment of particular argumentative topics reveals the extent to which he also drew upon 4 Maccabees, a text that would eventually be included in the codices of the Septuagint, even though it stands today at the outermost edge of the margins of the Christian canon.[1] That 4 Maccabees should never have been a serious contender for a place in the Hebrew canon occasions no surprise. Despite the exceptional piety of its author and his commitment to the particulars of the Jewish Torah, it was nevertheless written in Greek a significant time after 2 Maccabees, a book that likewise never achieved canonical status in the synagogue. 4 Maccabees was far too late, far too distant from Hebrew culture, and far too derivative to suggest inspiration. How, then, did it attain such importance, even authority, in the Christian community by the fourth and fifth centuries that it would be included in the great Codices Sinaiticus and Alexandrinus?[2] What did it offer to the church of the second

---

1. Although published as part of the Apocrypha in the RSV, the NRSV, and the ESV, it is only included on the basis of a slim claim: the work is included in an appendix to the Greek Bible.

2. The question of whether mere inclusion in a codex of sacred writings implies canonical status has been debated, but it does seem to me to be more reasonable to regard these codices as, in fact, "Bibles" rather than merely "libraries" of useful texts.

and third centuries, that would so speak to the spiritual and pastoral needs of Christian communities as to lend it such distinction?

Origen's *Exhortation to Martyrdom* offers an important case study in regard to this question. In ways that were, somewhat ironically, not true of the author of 4 Maccabees or its first audience, Christians found themselves increasingly in situations resembling the situation of the nine martyrs whose story forms the basis of 4 Maccabees. Their story became an important resource for helping Christians come to terms with the gruesome experiences they witnessed and, increasingly, were made to share. The reasoning of the martyrs in the story, and *about* the martyrs by the author of 4 Maccabees, provided starting points for exhorting later audiences who faced actual martyrdom themselves. This study takes a modest step toward answering the questions about 4 Maccabees' history of influence raised in the opening paragraph by establishing knowledge and use of 4 Maccabees in the Alexandrian churches by 235 CE as manifested in the writings of Origen, and by detailing how Origen demonstrated the usefulness of this resource for meeting the exigencies of his own pastoral situation.

There can be no doubt that 4 Maccabees, a text written fully a century prior to Origen's flourishing and a work clearly compatible with early Christian martyrology as expressed in the letters of Ignatius and the *Martyrdom of Polycarp*, would have been theoretically available to Origen.[3] As martyrdom became a more pervasive challenge in the early church, we find increasing attention being given to the stories not only of the near-martyrs, Daniel and his three companions (Daniel 3; 6), but even more to the story of those who did in fact meet with a gruesome end during the Hellenization Crisis rather than experience miraculous deliverance. Origen's *Exhortation to Martyrdom*, written to two deacons in Caesarea during the persecution of Christian clergy by Maximin in 235 CE,[4] draws at length from the story of the Maccabean martyrs in order to encourage Christians as they continue the contest for faith. In this focus, he is joined by Cyprian in his own *Exhortation to Fortunatus* and, indirectly, by the author of the *Martyrdom of Montanus and Lucius*.

An Overlooked Resource

It is common for scholars of Origen to observe that he had 2 Maccabees in mind—indeed, that he had 2 Maccabees open before him—as the principal

---

3. See the discussion of the date of 4 Maccabees in deSilva, *4 Maccabees: Introduction and Commentary*, xiv–xvii.

4. See Früchtel, *Origenes: Gespräch*, 120 n.2; Eusebius, *Hist. Eccl.* 6.28.

resource by means of which he accesses this story. Annotations of "Scripture references" in editions and translations of the text diligently document Origen's recitations and recontextualizations of excerpts from 2 Maccabees in his *Exhortation* (particularly chapters 22–27), though none of the editions or translations surveyed included references to 4 Maccabees either in the form of in-text Scripture references (whether given as parenthetical references or as footnotes) or in indices of Scripture references.[5] This absence is understandable as a function of the nature of "Scripture references": an author or editor (or publisher!) will only "catch" and highlight references to those texts deemed to belong to the canon of Scripture, whether the canon of the one preparing the references or Origen's presumed canon. The result, however, is to mask the influence of a "non-canonical" text (4 Maccabees) upon a homiletical retelling and application of an episode from a "canonical" text (2 Maccabees), and, therefore, to mask the interplay between these two texts in Origen's retelling.

This tendency persists in several specialized studies. Winslow, for example, does not mention 4 Maccabees at all in his discussion of Origen's inspiration:

> Quoting freely and accurately from 2nd Maccabees, [Origen] weaves into the narrative vocabulary taken from the Greek Games: the martyrs are "athletes," their struggle a "contest," their accomplishments a "victory." Further, Origen underscores an element barely touched upon in the original source, namely, the freedom of the martyrs. Eleazar, for instance, he epitomizes with these words: "Who could be more eloquently praised for his death than he who, for the sake of piety, accepts death of his own free will?"[6]

Granted that the imagery of the Greek games was readily available from general cultural knowledge, from Greek philosophical ethics, and from

---

5. Origen, *Exhortatio Ad Martyrium*, PG 11:561–638; O'Meara, *Origen: Prayer, Exhortation to Martyrdom*; Früchtel, *Origenes: Gespräch*; Greer, *Origen: An Exhortation to Martyrdom*; Noce, *Origene: Esortazione al Martirio*; Hamman, ed., *Le Martyre*. All six draw careful attention to Origen's use of specific texts from 2 Maccabees. Migne, O'Meara (see *Origen: Prayer, Exhortation to Martyrdom*, 234 nn.126–33, 135, 136, 138–40, 142–49, 151, the places one might expect to find such references), Greer, and Hamman include no notice of the influence of 4 Maccabees in any form; Früchtel includes a single reference in the endnotes by virtue of quoting the title of the article by Othmar Perler on the influence of 4 Maccabees on earlier martyrological literature. Only Noce attempts to establish a handful of connections between the *Exhortation* and 4 Maccabees in the introduction (*Origene: Esortazione*, 55–57) and in the endnotes (see *Origene: Esortazione*, 171 nn. 44, 48; 172 n.49; 173 n.53; 177 n.65).

6. Winslow, "Maccabean Martyrs," 81.

the use of such imagery within the New Testament, it is noteworthy that 4 Maccabees had already combined the story of 2 Maccabees with both the range of athletic imagery that Winslow observes *and* the emphasis on the freedom of the martyr. Thus Eleazar asserts his freedom in the matters that most concern him: "You will dominate the ungodly, but you will not be lord over my reasoning on behalf of piety either by means of words or through deeds!" (4 Macc 5:38).[7] The fifth brother boldly approaches the instruments of torture before being thither led, declaring: "I have come forward on my own" (4 Macc 11:3). After their display of indomitable courage, the author exclaims: "O rational faculties, more royal than kings and freer than the free!" (4 Macc 14:2). It is all the more surprising that Winslow, though clearly familiar with 4 Maccabees,[8] does not think to include discussion of the text here, all the more as this noble "freedom" is enacted in embracing death "for the sake of piety," another prominent emphasis of 4 Maccabees (see below).

Similarly, Prosper Hartmann, who provides a fine study of Origen's theology of martyrdom in the *Exhortation*,[9] considers only the influence of 2 Maccabees. His article gives no notice of the influence of 4 Maccabees on this text beyond a reference to a brief note by Metcalfe. This is particularly important given the fact that he is investigating the *theology* of martyrdom in Origen. Hartmann has, *de facto*, eliminated the possibility that 4 Maccabees exercises such a theological influence in favor of "canonical" resources. From the other direction, as it were, studies of the *Nachwirkung* of 4 Maccabees have tended to overlook its imprint on Origen. In his excellent introduction to his translation and commentary on 4 Maccabees, H.-J. Klauck notes Origen's use of the example of the Maccabean martyrs, but not the influence specifically of 4 Maccabees on Origen's *Exhortation*.[10] The older introduction by R. B. Townshend makes no mention of the *Exhortation* at all in his section on "influence."[11] The fascinating, recent study of the role of the Maccabean martyrs in Christian texts and cult by Raphaëlle Ziadé also gives only passing attention to the influence of 4 Maccabees on Origen's *Exhortation*.[12]

---

7. Unless otherwise indicated, all translations in this chapter are by the author.

8. Later in the same article, he will speak of Gregory Nazianzen's dependence specifically on 4 Maccabees over against 2 Maccabees ("Early Christian Attitudes," 83–85).

9. "Origène et la Théologie du Martyre."

10. Klauck, *4 Makkabäerbuch*, 675 n.139.

11. "Fourth Book," 653–85.

12. Ziadé, *Les martyrs Maccabées*, 95–102. Ziadé observes that the vocabulary of "piety" recalls 4 Maccabees 5:33, 36 (p. 96, n.182), as does the pitting of piety toward God "contre les plus cruelles souffrance et les plus douloureuses tortures" ("against the

Nevertheless, there have been a few attempts to excavate the traces of 4 Maccabees in Origen's *Exhortation*. In 1921, William Metcalfe published a short note spanning two-thirds of a page citing the lack of attention given to 4 Maccabees in studies of Origen's *Exhortation*, and supplying several helpful starting points for investigating resonances.[13] While his evidence was not quite sufficient to justify his conclusion, namely that "these coincidences suggest that 'Maccabees' in the Origenist list of books of the Bible included Fourth Maccabees,"[14] it nevertheless established the importance of not neglecting this text as part of Origen's background reading. The annotated translation by Noce has affirmed several of the parallels cited by Winslow, adding a few more to the list.[15] In my first study of the *Nachwirkung* of 4 Maccabees, I give attention to the correspondences between 4 Maccabees and Origen's *Exhortation*, but not also shared in common with 2 Maccabees.[16] Ton Hilhorst has since added helpfully to the discussion in the context of his broader survey of the influence of 4 Maccabees on Christian martyr texts.[17] The present study seeks to gather the data scattered among these various resources, augment them with fresh observations, and conduct a focused and thoroughgoing investigation of the role of 4 Maccabees in the formation of Origen's *Exhortation*.

Methodological Considerations

Origen makes explicit mention of his source material at one point. When he moves from the episode of Eleazar to the episode of the martyrdom of the seven sons, he introduces them as "the seven brothers written about in [the books of] the Maccabees" (ἐν τοῖς Μακκαβαίοις, *Exh.* 23 [PG 11:592]).[18] What books does Origen have in mind? Greer resolves the question by providing a translation that points, despite the plural reference, only to 2 Maccabees, based on the obvious prominence of this particular source: "the

---

most cruel sufferings and the most grievous tortures," pp. 96–97). Beyond these observations, Ziadé follows Metcalfe in the observation that Origen's use of the rare φίλτρον was probably derived from 4 Maccabees (p. 98 n.190), together with the emphasis on the mother's battle against her own maternal affections (p. 99).

13. "Origen's Exhortation."

14. Metcalfe, "Origen's Exhortation," 269.

15. Noce, *Origene: Esortazione*, 171 nn.44, 48; 172 n.49; 173 n.53; 177 n.65.

16. DeSilva, *4 Maccabees*, 152–53.

17. Hilhorst, "Fourth Maccabees," 115–16.

18. All translations from Origen's *Exhortatio* are by the author, unless otherwise indicated.

seven brothers described in 2 Maccabees."[19] The other translations are content to leave this vague—and appropriately plural.[20] It is possible that Origen refers to 1 and 2 Maccabees, in which case one need not make too much of this plural reference. Referring to the death of Solomon in the books of Kings, for example, would not necessitate multiple treatments in multiple books, but reflects a tendency to refer to canonical books sharing a common name as a unit. However, he might well also refer to 2 and 4 Maccabees here (without the presumption that such a reference implies that 4 Maccabees already enjoyed canonical status).

A particular challenge to identifying signs of the influence of 4 Maccabees upon a Christian text such as the *Exhortatio* is the fact that early Christian authors evince a close and indubitable familiarity with the highly influential 2 Maccabees. The existence of 4 Maccabees is, indeed, itself an indication of the influence and reception of 2 Maccabees in the Jewish Diaspora of the northeast Mediterranean basin, as 4 Maccabees is clearly dependent upon the latter.[21] Second Maccabees continues to exercise the *primary* influence in Origen's account of the martyrdoms of Eleazar, the seven brothers, and the mother.[22] Origen recites the speeches of the martyrs verbatim from 2 Maccabees, weaving in recontextualizations of the descriptions of the tortures as written in 2 Maccabees as well. At several points, Origen includes details that are found only in 2 Maccabees (in *Exh.* 23, for example, the detail that the martyrs were first tortured all together with whips and cords, before being given individual "attention"; cf. 2 Macc 7:1–2).

19. Greer, *Origen: An Exhortation*, 56.

20. O'Meara, *Origen: Prayer*, 162; Hamman, *Le Martyre*, 54; Früchtel, *Origenes: Gespräch*, 96; Noce, *Origene: Esortazione*, 124–25.

21. On the use of 2 Maccabees by the author of 4 Maccabees, see deSilva, *4 Maccabees: Introduction and Commentary*, xxx–xxxi and *passim* (see pp. 289–90 for a list of references to 2 Maccabees in the commentary itself).

22. This is also the case with Cyprian's *Exhortation to Fortunatus* (*Exh.* 11). Like Origen, Cyprian recites 2 Maccabees extensively in his paraphrase of the martyrdom accounts without ever explicitly reciting—or even recontextualizing—excerpts from 4 Maccabees. In his introduction of the principal characters, however, Cyprian includes two topics that are explicated in 4 Maccabees but absent from 2 Maccabees. First, he speaks of the seven brothers as "equals alike in their lot of birth and virtues" (*Exh.* 11), a summary of 4 Macc 13:19–27, where the author introduces the topics of the brothers spending equal time in the same womb, participating in the common nurture received by their mother, and growing into the same virtues with a common purpose in order to emphasize the sympathy and fraternal affection shared (and overcome) by the seven. Second, Cyprian dwells on the mystical nature of their number, seven, beginning his rhapsody with the seven days of creation, quite probably inspired by the attention given to the same topic and its similar elaboration in 4 Macc 14:7–8.

In order to advance a case for influence, therefore, this study will employ a variation of the criterion of dissimilarity so frequently encountered in studies of the historical Jesus. We will look for signs of influence primarily in those details that 4 Maccabees does not share with 2 Maccabees (a source used both by the author of 4 Maccabees and Origen) *and* that it does not share broadly with other minority cultural literature seeking to transform experiences of hardship and marginalization into marks of nobility (e.g., through the use of athletic imagery).[23] Only after influence is established by this stricter standard may we begin to consider that Origen may have used images and language common to 4 Maccabees and other texts (for example, the enumeration of four cardinal virtues or describing death as "perfecting" one's life) as a result of reflecting upon 4 Maccabees rather than, for example, Wisdom of Solomon. Suggesting that fewer, related sources for such imagery and terminology is more probable than multiple, diverse sources would represent a reasonable application of Ockham's razor. We will begin with traces of 4 Maccabees found in Origen's retelling of the stories of the nine martyrdoms, and then to traces of 4 Maccabees in the other sections of the *Exhortation*.

Eleazar

Origen introduces Eleazar as a person "welcoming death with honor rather than life with pollution," using a phrase recontextualized verbatim from 2 Maccabees (*Exh.* 22 [PG 11:589]; cf. 2 Macc 6:19).[24] However, he prefaces

23. By "minority cultural literature" I mean the writings produced from within subcultures or counter-cultures, such as the Jewish ethnic subculture or Greco-Roman philosophical groups, especially those writings that address the need to legitimate the minority culture's views, behaviors, even existence in the face of a dominant culture (the empowered group) or the majority culture (who exercise force to some degree by sheer reason of numbers). Minority cultural literature is literature that, in some way, contributes to the ideological survival of the group and its distinctive world view and practice. It remains possible for a member of the dominant culture (for example, a Seneca) to write minority cultural literature (for example, his *De constantia sapientis*). Despite moving among the ranks of the empowered and wealthy, Seneca nevertheless writes to defend the ideology and practice of a particular group (Stoic philosophers) that runs contrary at the very least to the majority culture (for whom "reputation" and public opinion is the more important guide to conduct than considerations of moral virtue). See, further, deSilva, *Despising Shame*, 80–144, which includes a discussion of 4 Maccabees as minority cultural literature; also deSilva, "Using the Master's Tools."

24. I use here the terminology developed by Vernon Robbins (*Exploring*, 40–58) to speak more precisely about instances of intertexture. Robbins distinguishes carefully between "recitation," a quotation in which the author draws attention to the fact that he or she is importing words from another text (e.g., "as Isaiah spoke," or "as it is written"),

this introduction by identifying the "martyr" as a member of a class of persons "welcoming death on behalf of piety" (τὸν θάνατον ὑπὲρ εὐσεβείας ἀναδεξόμενος [*Exh.* 22 (PG 11:589)]). The word "piety" is not used in 2 Maccabees in regard to these martyrs' deaths, though they are said to die "for the sake of God's laws" (2 Macc 7:23; cf. 7:9). However, the identification of "virtue" in general, and "piety" in particular, as the goal of the martyr's endurance of sufferings unto death is typical of 4 Maccabees.[25] Thus, for example, Eleazar urges his fellow Judeans to die on behalf of piety, following his example (ὑπὲρ τῆς εὐσεβείας τελευτᾶτε, 4 Macc 6:22), and the martyrs are spoken of (or speak of themselves) as scorning the torments, rising above their feelings, and enduring unto death "on account of piety" (διὰ τὴν εὐσέβειαν or ὑπὲρ τῆς εὐσεβείας; see, e.g., 7:16; 9:6–7, 21, 29, 30; 11:20; 13:12, 27; 15:14; 16:13, 14, 17; 17:7).[26]

The Seven Brothers

Origen speaks of the seven brothers as "athletes for piety" on several occasions. The first brother is "the noblest athlete of piety" (τοῦ γενναιότατου ἀθλητοῦ τῆς εὐσεβείας, *Exh.* 23 [PG 11:592]), and God, the "Master of the games of the athletes of piety" (ἀγωνοθέτης τῶν τῆς εὐσεβείας ἀθλητῶν, *Exh.* 23 [PG 11:593]), encouraged them on in their contest. In the introduction to his *Exhortation*, Origen uses the phrase "a noble athlete" (γενναῖος ἀθλητής) to describe the martyr in general (*Exh.* 1 [PG 11:564]). This is a title also applied to the Maccabean martyrs throughout 4 Maccabees (6:10; 17:15, 16),[27] but not in 2 Maccabees and not by any New Testament author. Ton Hilhorst,

---

and "recontextualization," the reproduction and importation of a string of words from a source text into the new text without drawing explicit attention to the act of quoting.

25. Metcalfe ("Origen's Exhortation," 268) correctly observes the occurrence of this language at least in *Exh.* 5, where martyrs are described as people more esteeming "death with piety (τὸν μετ᾽ εὐσεβείας θάνατον) than living with impiety."

26. Boeft and Bremmer ("Notinculae Martyrologicae IV," 121 n.33) may be correct to assert that Origen's adaptation of the reason the martyrs held fast, namely "on account of love for God" (*Exh.* 25) rather than "on account of God's training and virtue" (4 Macc 10:10) shows subtly the ways in which the martyrs' examples are adapted to more distinctively Christian ideas. However, this represents more of an *addition* on Origen's part rather than a *shift away* from the less distinctively Christian idea of dying "on behalf of religion/piety" found in 4 Maccabees and expressed in more culturally specific terms in 2 Maccabees (dying on behalf of Torah).

27. See also the closely related "devotees/athletes of piety" (τοὺς τῆς εὐσεβείας ἀσκητάς) in 4 Macc 12:11. Athletic imagery is common in minority cultural literature, whether Greco-Roman ethical philosophical schools, Hellenistic Jewish literature, or early Christian texts. See the literature cited above in n.7.

using the *Thesaurus Linguae Graece*, observes that the combination καθάπερ (ώς) γενναῖος ἀθλητής is unique to 4 Macc 6:10,[28] confirming the plausibility of the proposition that Origen's language in *Exh.* 1 (ώς γενναῖος ἀθλητής) is derived specifically from 4 Maccabees, and not from the common use of athletic imagery by Stoics, Cynics, and other minority cultural groups.[29] Origen also blends this image, itself more in keeping with the presentation of the martyrs in 4 Maccabees, into his paraphrastic recitation of 2 Macc 7:11, as the third brother offers his tongue and hands to the torturers: "Forsaking these things on account of the laws of God, I hope to receive them back from God *in the way He gives them to those who are athletes of piety toward him*" (τοῖς τῆς . . . εὐσεβείας ἀθληταῖς, *Exh.* 25 [PG 11:593]).[30]

Both Origen and 4 Maccabees call attention to the fact that watching beloved brothers suffer torture and death was part of the ordeal for each of the martyrs. Thus, the brothers, "not only enduring each one his own tortures, but also by watching the maltreatment of their brothers, demonstrated the well-strung courage of their religion" (*Exh.* 23). Similarly, Antiochus tortures the first brother "with the rest of the brothers and the mother looking on, punishing the brothers and the mother by the spectacle and thinking to shake their resolve through these fearsome considerations" (*Exh.* 23). Second Maccabees does speak of this scene occurring "while the rest of the brothers and the mother looked on" (7:4), an element that Origen dutifully recontextualizes in his own narrative, but it is 4 Maccabees that explicitly draws the inference that such "watching" was part of the ordeal endured and overcome by the parties involved.

> But nevertheless, although nature and custom and the habits of
> moral excellence were heightening the affection of brotherhood
> for them, for the sake of piety those left behind endured seeing
> the maltreated brothers being tortured to death (4 Macc 13:27).

28. Hilhorst, "Fourth Maccabees," 115.

29. Plausibility rather than necessity, since the word καθάπερ is not included in Origen.

30. Origen continues to use athletic imagery throughout the *Exhortation*. The contemporary persecution is described as "the current contest" (τὸν ἐστηκότα ἀγῶνα, *Exh.* 4 [PG 11:568]) and "the present contest" (τὸν παρόντα ἀγῶνα, *Exh.* 51 [PG 11:636]), as, indeed, Origen sees "life [to be] full of contests for many virtues" with many "contestants" (πολλῶν ἀρετῶν . . . τὸν βίον ἀγώνων . . . τοὺς ἀγωνιζομένους, *Exh.* 5 [PG 11:568]). Protoctetus is Ambrose's "fellow contestant" (συναγωνιστής, *Exh.* 36 [PG 11:609]) in this contest, in which Origen calls the two to compete willingly and vigorously: "But the elect alone contend (ἀγωνίζεται) for piety" (*Exh.* 5 [PG 11:569]); "Let us contend . . ." (ἀγωνισώμεθα, *Exh.* 21 [PG 11:590]).

> The mother of the seven young men endured the torments of
> each one of her children (4 Macc 14:12).

> The mother, seeing them tortured and burned one by one, did
> not change her mind on account of piety (4 Macc 15:14).

This theme is elaborated at greater length in 4 Macc 15:15–24. It is possible
that Origen developed this theme independently from the slim notice in 2
Maccabees that the rest of the family was present to watch the torment of
each. However, the fact that 4 Maccabees developed this topic more than a
century in advance, and otherwise appears to have contributed to Origen's
Exhortation, lends plausibility to the thesis that Origen's reading of 2 Maccabees was influenced by 4 Maccabees in this particular detail.

While describing the torment of the first brother, Origen attributes
such brutality to the "savagery" of Antiochus (ὑπὸ τῆς ὠμότητος; *Exh.* 23
[PG 11:592]). The positive form of the cognate adjective ὠμός is used twice
in 2 Maccabees (4:25; 7:27) to describe Antiochus, the second occurrence
involving the mother's speech to her last surviving son. However, the author of 4 Maccabees twice uses cognate adjectives to describe Antiochus
at precisely the same point in the story that Origen uses the noun form,
namely in relation to the first brother's contest. The first brother accuses
the "Greek" king of being, in fact, the ὠμόφρων, the "crude-minded," "savage," "uncivilized" one in the arena (4 Macc 9:15) rather than the young
Judeans, and the second brother spits this epithet in the face of the representative of Greek "culture" as he endures the tortures: "ὠμότατε τύραννε"
("most savage tyrant!", 4 Macc 9:30).

Origen says in regard to the youngest brother that Antiochus was
"persuaded that this one was indeed a brother (πεισθεὶς καὶ τοῦτον εἶναι
ἀδελφόν) of those who esteemed such sufferings in no respect, and had the
same resolve as they did" (*Exh.* 26 [PG 11:596]). Metcalfe observes that this
comment "may have been suggested by 2 Macc. vii. 29," where the mother
exhorts her youngest son to "prove worthy of [his] brothers," but refers the
interpreter also to 4 Macc 10:2, 12, 15.[31] Metcalfe might have done better
to refer us to 10:16 in lieu of 10:12, 15, as well as to have pressed further in
regard to the influence of 4 Maccabees on this point.

> Are you ignorant that the same father begot me as those who
> died, and the same mother gave me birth, and that I was nur-
> tured by the same teachings? I do not renounce the noble kin-
> ship of brotherhood. (4 Macc 10:2–3).

---

31. Metcalfe, "Origen's Exhortation," 269.

> Invent tortures, tyrant, in order that you may also learn through them that I am a brother to those who have been tortured beforehand. (4 Macc 10:16).

The notion that kinship will be manifested in a shared commitment to the Jewish way of life and in a common exhibition of courageous endurance is more directly expressed and more clearly underscored in this intermediate text.

The Mother

Although otherwise following the written text of 2 Maccabees closely throughout, Origen breaks with the sequence of his primary source in *Exhortation* 26 by choosing to defer giving attention to the mother of the seven brothers until after narrating the death of the seventh. His narrative thus aligns with the narration in 4 Maccabees, whereas 2 Maccabees interjects words of special admiration for the mother after narrating the death of the sixth brother but before narrating the ordeal of the seventh and last brother (2 Macc 7:20). This deviation is all the more striking in comparison with Cyprian's narration of the story in his own *Exhortation to Fortunatus, to Martyrdom* (11), in which he follows 2 Maccabees even at this point, making mention of the appropriateness of admiring the mother after narrating the death of the sixth son.

When he does finally come to speak of the mother's ordeal, Origen introduces topics that align with 4 Maccabees' presentation of her story, but which are absent (or, at least, much less developed) in 2 Maccabees. Commenting on the mother's endurance, Origen writes: "For the dews of piety ... did not permit the maternal fire (τὸ μητρικὸν πῦρ) that blazes in many women under the heaviest evils to flare up in her bowels (ἐν τοῖς σπλάγχνοις αὐτῆς)" (*Exh.* 27 [PG 11:596]). This comment, however, derives not from 2 Maccabees, but, as Metcalfe rightly suggested,[32] recalls the similar images used by the author of 4 Maccabees to comment upon the mother's struggle:

> Indeed, the lions around Daniel were not so wild nor the furnace of Mishael so kindled by exceedingly turbulent fire as the natural bent of parental love was burning that woman ... But by means of pious reasoning, the mother quenched so many and such great passions. (4 Macc 16:3–4)

There is a significant difference in that Origen claims that piety prevented the maternal fire from being kindled in the mother, while the author of 4

32. Metcalfe, "Origen's Exhortation," 269.

Maccabees speaks of the mother feeling the pain of this fire fully, but nevertheless "quenching" it by means of pious reasoning. This difference, however, pales before the commonalities: two authors speaking about the same woman's trial and using the images of fire and the suppression of fire ("quenching") to describe both that trial and the mother's ability to endure.[33]

As part of the technique of "vivid description," the martyr accounts in both 2 and 4 Maccabees give specific attention to the body parts affected by the tortures applied by the tyrants' lackeys, whether the extremities, the tongue, the skin, and so forth. In 4 Maccabees, though not in 2 Maccabees, the author several times speaks of the mother's viscera (τὰ σπλάγχνα; see 4 Macc 14:13; 15:23, 29) as the focal point of her experience of suffering. Since the ancient Greeks commonly used τὰ σπλάγχνα ("the entrails") to denote the seat of emotions, the author is drawing attention to that which is most thematic for his oration: the mother's piety enabled her to resist acting in such a way as would relieve the painful yearning for her children's safety and her deep-seated emotional pain at viewing their torture.[34] The fact that Origen also specifies this as the physical locus where a mother would most feel pain when her children are made to suffer, speaking of the power of piety and holiness to guard against the assaults on *this* mother's will perpetrated through her "bowels" (ἐν τοῖς σπλάγχνοις αὐτῆς, *Exh.* 27 [PG 11:596]), also points to the influence of 4 Maccabees on his own re-imagining of the episode.

At the close of his treatment of the mother's successful endurance, Origen affirms the power of love for God (τὸ πρὸς θεὸν φίλτρον), which proves more powerful "than every other love charm" (παντὸς φίλτρου,

33. Noce (*Origene: Esortazione*, 173 n.53) also finds Origen to recall 4 Maccabees at this point, insofar as the mother's demonstration of love for God, confronting her natural affection for her sons, is an expression of rising above the natural, common feelings of human beings—a topic that is developed fully in 4 Macc 14:11—16:25.

34. It is tempting to consider that the author highlights τὰ σπλάγχνα in his description of the mother's torment because the lower viscera are also her point of strongest physical connection with her sons, who emerged therefrom (and that also with great pain to the mother). The use of τὰ σπλάγχνα, rather than the more common γαστήρ, for the womb is attested in several major Greek authors (Pindar, *Olympian Odes* 9.42; *Nemean Odes* 1.35; Sophocles, *Antigone* 1066; Aeschylus, *Septem contra Thebas*. 1036, according to Liddell and Scott, *A Greek-English Lexicon*, 1628 col. 1), and the context of its appearance in 4 Maccabees (15:23) may invoke this sense. The author speaks of the mother, watching her sons' torment, "now being tested by more bitter pains than the birth pangs suffered for them" (15:16), and will speak of the result of her endurance of her current pains as "giving birth anew unto immortality to the full number of her sons" (16:13). If this sense is secondarily invoked, it would lend added poignancy to the author's declaration that "pious reason, imparting manliness to her womb/seat of emotion in the midst of her sufferings, strengthened her to disregard her temporal love for her offspring" (15:23).

Exh. 27 [PG 11:596]). This term does not appear in 2 Maccabees at any point, but, as William Metcalfe had observed, recalls 4 Maccabees 13:19, 27; 15:13, where the word is used to speak of the deep power first of sibling love (13:19, 27) and then of maternal love (15:13). Since "the word is uncommon in Origen," it is more likely that it enters his vocabulary through acquaintance with this source rather than through Origen's own familiarity with the term.[35] This is in keeping with the usage of the term in 4 Maccabees to name the two other powerful loves overcome for the sake of love for God in the experience of these martyrs.

Beyond the Narrative

Traces of 4 Maccabees' vocabulary, imagery, subject matter, and even argumentation can be found at several points in Origen's *Exhortation* outside of those chapters specifically treating the martyrdoms of Eleazar, the seven sons, and the mother.

Shortly after opening his work, Origen speaks of life's contests for virtues using the four cardinal virtues also named in 4 Macc 1:18 (φρόνησις καὶ δικαιοσύνη καὶ ἀνδρεία καὶ σωφροσύνη) as he speaks of those who "contended for temperance, . . . died with courage, . . . shown concern for prudence, and . . . committed themselves to justice" (περὶ σωφροσύνης . . . καὶ μετὰ ἀνδρείας . . . φρονήσεως τε . . . καὶ δικαιοσύνῃ, *Exh.* 5 [PG 11:568]). Admittedly, the four cardinal virtues are so widely broadcast throughout Greek and Hellenistic Jewish ethical literature (including such texts as Wis 8:7) that this correspondence would not normally suggest a point of direct influence. Two additional considerations, however, point in this direction. First, 4 Maccabees prefaces its discussion of the tales of the martyrs with claims that followers of Torah fulfill these virtues commonly sought by all people of character, just as Origen also prefaces his elevation of the vocation of the martyr with this note concerning common ethical achievement. Second, Origen will immediately go on to elevate piety and dying for piety as the pinnacle of virtuous achievement ("But the elect alone contend for piety," *Exh.* 5), a topic that also dominates 4 Maccabees.

Origen names affection for offspring or for spouse among the forces that threaten to distract the disciple from giving his or her "all" to God, promoting a degree of commitment that does, in fact, resist any such diversion: "and still more, if we should not be dragged aside or distracted even by affection for children or for their mother or for some such one of those things considered to be most precious in life" (τῆς περὶ τὰ τέκνα, ἢ

35. Metcalfe, "Origen's Exhortation," 269.

τὴν τούτων μητέρα . . . φιλοστοργίας, *Exh.* 11 [PG 1:577]). The author of
4 Maccabees had previously cited the fact that the Jew trained by Torah
was not turned aside by even natural affections as a highwater mark of
Torah's moral formation: Torah, and, by extension, the mind trained by it,
"exercises control over love for one's wife (τῆς πρὸς γαμετὴν φιλίας), rebuk-
ing her on account of her transgression, and it masters love for children
(τῆς τέκνων φιλίας), chastening them on account of wickedness" (4 Macc
2:11–12). The author also underscores the brothers' mastery of fraternal affection (φιλαδελφία, 4 Macc 13:23, 26; 14:1; see, topically, 13:19–14:1) and
the mother's mastery of affection for offspring (φιλοστοργία, 4 Macc 15:6,
9; see, topically, 14:13–15:13, 23, 25; 16:3) in his reflections on the martyr
stories. Origen thus uses a topic highlighted by the author of 4 Maccabees
in regard to the general ethical achievement of the Torah-observant, and
the Maccabean martyrs in particular, to speak of an essential obstacle also
to be overcome by Christian martyrs in their effort to show God the full
measure of devotion God merits.

Origen speaks of the ordeal to be faced by the Christian martyr in terms
that combine athletic and judicial imagery: "a great spectacle is contrived as
we contend and are summoned to bear witness" (μέγα θέατρον . . . ἐφ᾽ ἡμῖν
ἀγωνιζόμενοις, καὶ ἐπὶ τὸ μαρτύριον καλουμένοις, *Exh.* 18 [PG 11:585]). While
the image of a "spectacle" is derived most directly from 1 Cor 4:9, a text that
is also recited immediately following, the idea of being summoned to bear
witness by contending in an arena of sufferings appears in no New Testament
text so clearly as in 4 Macc 16:16: "My sons, noble is this contest. Having been
called hereto on behalf of giving evidence (ὑπὲρ τῆς διαμαρτυρίας) on behalf
of the nation, contend (ἐναγωνίσασθε) zealously for the ancestral law." This
shared blending of the image of "contending" in an arena with "bringing forth
evidence" or "giving testimony" as a subpoenaed witness again suggests direct
influence rather than independent invention.

Finally, Origen specifically recommends remaining faithful to God to
the point of death as the best way in which to make a fair return to God, who
has so greatly benefitted the individual:

> A saint, being honorable and desiring to repay the benefactions
> falling upon him from God, seeks out what he might do on the
> Lord's behalf for all that he has received from him. And he finds
> nothing else so capable of being considered equally balanced to
> God's benefactions, to be given back to God from a person of
> good resolve, as perfection in martyrdom. (*Exh.* 28)

In martyrdom, one gives up one's life. Since God has given each person the
gift of life and all the good things that appertain to it, martyrdom emerges as

the most complete return of grace for grace, gratitude for favor.[36] This logic had been explicated, and elaborated particularly in the context of martyrdom, giving back one's life to God or using one's body in defense of God's honor, in the speeches of the martyrs to one another in 4 Maccabees:

> Let us consecrate ourselves from our whole heart to God, to the One who granted us our lives, and let us use our bodies for a guard post for the law. (4 Macc 13:13)

> Remember that you received a share of the world and enjoyed life because of God, and on account of this you are obliged to endure every pain for the sake of God. (4 Macc 16:18–19)

Also noteworthy here is the idea that martyrdom is the "perfection," "completion," or "consummation" (τὴν . . . τελευτήν, *Exh.* 28 [PG 1:596]) of the nobility of one's life (or, here, one's response of gratitude and piety toward God), an idea shared by the author of 4 Maccabees, who considers death to provide "the faithful seal" that "perfects" (ἐτελείωσεν) Eleazar's long life of virtue (4 Macc 7:15).[37]

Conclusion

While the value of any one of these pieces of evidence could be disputed, the accumulation of data strongly suggests that Origen read both 2 and 4 Maccabees, and that he incorporated a substantial amount of vocabulary, imagery, and thought from the latter both in his retelling of the story of 2 Maccabees 6–7 in particular and in his exhortation to Ambrose and Protoctetus in general.

Toward the end of his retelling of the story of the Maccabean martyrs, Origen speaks of having taken these powerful examples "from the Scripture" (ἀπὸ τῆς γραφῆς, *Exh.* 27 [PG 11:596]). Clearly, Origen regards

---

36. On the social logic of reciprocity and the moral weight attached to the same in the Greco-Roman world, see deSilva, *Honor, Patronage*, 95–119, and the literature cited therein.

37. Both observe that it is more prudent to fear God than to fear mortals (*Exh.* 4; 4 Macc 13:14–15), but Origen could just as easily have derived this from Matt 10.28; Acts 5.29. Additionally, in *Exh.* 28, Origen speaks of the παρρησία before God, the "special confidence" (O'Meara, *Origen: Prayer*, 168), that martyrdom confers. The word is not used in 2 Maccabees, but does appear in 4 Macc 10:5 in reference to the "freedom of speech" exercised by the third brother in the presence of the tyrant. Nevertheless, the fact that παρρησία is fairly common in the New Testament both in regard to openness before God and before human beings preempts the possibility of using this datum as part of the case for 4 Maccabees' influence upon Origen.

2 Maccabees, which he consistently recites throughout this section, as an authoritative sacred text worthy of being placed in the same category as the classical Hebrew prophets or the apostle Paul. But can we conclude with Metcalfe that the evidences of Origen's use of 4 Maccabees "suggest that 'Maccabees' in the Origenist list of books of the Bible included Fourth Maccabees"?[38] This conclusion, however attractive, may be too confident in light of the very different manner in which Origen handles the material from 2 and 4 Maccabees. When Origen recites portions of the story, he recites only portions of 2 Maccabees. He never actually *recites* 4 Maccabees, nor even recontextualizes phrases of any length. The influence of 4 Maccabees shines through only secondarily, informing Origen's commentary upon the story, but not as if it is an authoritative witness to the story. Demonstrating "influence" is not the same as demonstrating "canonicity" and, with Origen, we have not yet reached the point where 4 Maccabees' inclusion in the codices of the Septuagint is assured.

Nevertheless, 4 Maccabees has contributed to Origen's "pastoral" task in several significant ways, and thus can be said to have exercised "authority" as a witness to the rigors and meaning of martyrdom in the midst of a challenging situation. First, the attention given in 4 Maccabees to the human feelings of the martyrs for one another and their families reminds Origen of the very real personal losses and relational losses that martyrdom entails, so that he can address these feelings as they come to bear on Ambrose and Protoktetos as well. Second, through its own interpretation of resistance unto death as a "noble contest" as well as the death of the martyr as "perfection," it provides the interpretive images that help Origen position Ambrose and Protoktetos to face martyrdom not as an experience of being victimized, but as an opportunity for active resistance and witness. Origen can spur them on to martyrdom, not as the negation of the value of their lives, but as the consummation and completion of that which has made their lives valuable. Moreover, 4 Maccabees provides essential resources for reminding the disciples of the ethical context of martyrdom—in particular, how such a death is virtuous, rather than deviant or criminal. Particularly important in this regard is the interpretation of martyrdom as the just and gracious return to God for the gift of life received from God.

Origen is probably not the first Christian to read 4 Maccabees and to find it particularly helpful for addressing the prospect of martyrdom. Several studies have sought to demonstrate the influence of 4 Maccabees on Christian martyrology as early as Ignatius of Antioch and the *Martyrdom of Polycarp*. Scholars have found some truly impressive parallels at the level

---

38. Metcalfe, "Origen's Exhortation," 269.

of diction and precise imagery as well as at the broader level of plot outline and rhetorical convention, though not all are ready to concede direct influence.[39] Although recent studies have located 4 Maccabees more securely in the region of Antioch,[40] the unresolved issue of its date remains a perpetual stumbling block to demonstrating Ignatius's knowledge of 4 Maccabees (though the *successful* demonstration of the latter could also provide leverage for the debate concerning date).[41] The definitive study on the question of 4 Maccabees' influence on Ignatius and the *Martyrdom of Polycarp* has yet to be undertaken. Such a study might significantly advance establishing the starting point of 4 Maccabees' route to success, at least in the ante-Nicene and post-Nicene churches of the third through fifth centuries.

Fourth Maccabees would exercise ongoing influence on Christian martyrology, as seen in the *Martyrdom of Pionius*, the *Martyrdom of Montanus and Lucius*, the *Passion of Saints Perpetua and Felicity*, and the *Martydom of Habbib the Deacon*.[42] It remains an enduring testimony to the freedom and dignity of the human being, who is reminded by the story of the Maccabean martyrs that he or she need never submit to any external or internal compulsion that would compromise his or her self-respect. If the blood of the martyrs provided the seed for the church, 4 Maccabees was an important resource when it came to exhorting Christian disciples to bear witness in the spilling of their own blood, and to celebrating the virtuous achievement of the same, so that others would join in emulating them. Meeting such a significant need in the early church during its greatest distresses, 4 Maccabees found at least one path from obscurity toward the prominence it would enjoy in the century after Constantine.

---

39. See especially Perler, "Das vierte Makkabäerbuch," 47–72; Klauck, *4 Makkabäerbuch*, 671 n.116; van Henten, "Zum Einfluß"; van Henten, "Martyrs as Heroes," 305–10, 312–13; deSilva, *4 Maccabees*, 149–51; Hilhorst, "Fourth Maccabees."

40. See especially van Henten, "Jewish Epitaph." For a fuller discussion of the various positions and arguments advanced, see deSilva, *4 Maccabees: Introduction and Commentary*, xvii–xx.

41. Scholarship is divided on the issue of date, some preferring an earlier date of 19–72 CE, others placing the composition of the book at the start of the second century CE, and still others looking to the period of the Bar Kochva Revolt as the likeliest setting. Either of the first two positions would allow, theoretically, for influence upon Ignatius; the last position would still allow for the possibility of influence on the composition of the *Martyrdom of Polycarp*. See the review of the various arguments in deSilva, *4 Maccabees: Introduction and Commentary*, xiv–xvii.

42. See deSilva, *4 Maccabees: Introduction and Commentary*, xxxvi–xxxvii; Hilhorst, "Fourth Maccabees," 115, 118–19.

9

Ambrose's Use of 4 Maccabees
in *De Jacob et Vita Beata*

The influence of 4 Maccabees in the early church did not by any means
diminish after the Edict of Toleration. In the latter half of the fourth
century, Gregory Nazianzen composed an encomium on the Maccabean
martyrs (*In Maccabaeorem Laudem* or εἰς τοὺς Μαχχαβαίους πανηγυρικός,
PG 35:911–34). Gregory leaves no doubt about whether he draws upon
2 or 4 Maccabees as his principle source, referring specifically to "the
book concerning the [martyrs] . . . which philosophizes concerning reason's exercise of complete mastery over the passions" (*Or.* 15.2).[1] John
Chrysostom preaches two sermons on the Maccabean martyrs that betray
knowledge of 4 Maccabees in addition to the more "visible" 2 Maccabees
(*De Maccabaeos homiliae*, PG 50:617–28, and *De Eleazaro et de septum pu-
eris*, PG 63:523–30). These eastern fathers also avidly promoted the commemoration of these martyrs as part of the Christian liturgical calendar,
together with the veneration of their remains, particularly in Antioch. If
the situation of persecution initially brought attention to 4 Maccabees as a
useful resource in Christian circles, the dramatic change in the Christians'
situation after Constantine resulted in 4 Maccabees being read and used
in ways more directly in keeping with the author's own purposes: as an
encomium for the remarkable achievement of nine pious Jews, and as an
exhortation to pursue reason's mastery of the passions by means of one's
commitment to live piously before God.

The thorough and beautifully-executed monograph by Raphaëlle Ziadé has left little more to be said about these works.[2] This essay, therefore,

1. Slightly later, Jerome invokes 4 Maccabees as proof that reason can "subdue and
rule the perturbations of the soul," an ethical goal of perennial importance quite apart
from the situation of martyrdom (*Dialogus adversus Pelagianos* 2.6).

2. Ziadé, *Les martyrs Maccabees.*

focuses on the reception of 4 Maccabees in the work of the western father, Ambrose of Milan (ca. 339–397). Ambrose composed a series of writings on the patriarchs. The third of these, *On Jacob and the Happy Life* (*De Iacob et vita beata*, 386 or 387 CE), most concerns us. These texts reflect the preaching Ambrose prepared each year for those seeking baptism and membership in the Catholic Church, a service that would take place at the Great Vigil of Easter.

De Jacob et vita beata is somewhat inappropriately named, as Jacob does not emerge as a focal topic until the beginning of Book Two and disappears well before the end of the same. Ambrose opens his treatise with a free paraphrase of 4 Maccabees 1:1–3:18 (*De Jacob* 1.1.1–1.3.8). He treats the order of material fluidly and makes some interesting alterations to his source material—all the more interesting since clearly intentional. He could not have reproduced this much of 4 Maccabees, following its details so closely, without having access to the text itself, perhaps even open before him at (or soon before) the time of writing.

Ambrose commends "sound instruction" as that which equips the mind that "excels in virtue and restrains its passions" (*De Jacob* 1.1.1; cf. 4 Macc 1:1, 15–17). He agrees with the author of 4 Maccabees, against the more hardline view of Stoics like Cicero, that sound reasoning does not eliminate emotions or desires, but equips the will to withstand these impulses and to choose the course of action in keeping with virtue instead:

> Reason . . . is able to mitigate [concupiscence] but not uproot it, because the soul that is capable of reason is not the master of its passions but can only restrain them. And it is not possible that the irascible man not get angry, but only that he restrain himself through reason, check his indignation, and withdraw from punitiveness. (*De Jacob* 1.1.1; see also 1.1.2).[3]

> None of us can eliminate . . . emotion, but right thinking makes it possible for us not to be slaves to our emotions. None of you can eliminate anger from your soul, but right thinking can help you deal with your anger. (4 Macc 3:2–3)

Ambrose incorporates the example of David's irrational thirst. He follows some of the details from the version in 2 Samuel 23:13–17 but clearly depends on 4 Maccabees's interpretation of the story and uses it to the same end (*De Jacob* 1.1.3; 4 Macc 3:6–18). He affirms on this basis that "the prudent mind can restrain and keep in check the assaults of the passions . . . and cool all

---

3. Translations of Ambrose are taken from McHugh, *Saint Ambrose*. I have occasionally edited them for inclusive language.

the heat of the most burning concupiscence" (*De Jacob* 1.1.4), reflecting the conclusion that the author of 4 Maccabees reached on the basis of the same episode: "The sensible mind is able to overcome the pressures of the emotions and to put out the flames of frenzied desires" (4 Macc 3:17).

Ambrose further regards reason's restraint (rather than extirpation) of the passions as the proper internal hierarchy intended by God in creation, incorporating at this point the anthropological model articulated in 4 Macc 2:21–23.

> Indeed, when God created human beings and implanted in them moral laws and feelings, at that time He established the royal rule of the mind over the human being's emotions, so that all their feelings and emotions would be governed by its strength and power. (*De Jacob* 1.1.4).

> When God shaped humankind, God planted emotions and inclinations within them. At that time, he also set the mind on the throne in the midst of the senses, to serve as a holy ruler over them all. (4 Macc 2:21–22)[4]

Ambrose then defines and enumerates the major passions using the taxonomy found in 4 Maccabees (*De Jacob* 1.2.5; 4 Macc 1:20–27). Ambrose's debt to 4 Maccabees at this point is not typically acknowledged. Marcia Colish, for example, writes that

> Ambrose proceeds to analyze the passions under three headings. Some passions arise in the body. The examples he gives are gluttony and wantonness. Some passions arise in the soul. Under this rubric, his examples are pride, envy, avarice, ambition, and strife. There are also passions that, according to Ambrose, arise in both the body and the soul. In this third category he places the Stoic quartet of pleasure, pain, fear, and desire. But he alters this Stoic doctrine significantly. In the first place, the Stoics were monists. For them, the fabled mind-body problem did not exist . . .[5] Accordingly, the Stoics saw all four of the passions as arising from false rational judgments . . .

4. While Marcia Colish (*Ambrose's Patriarchs*, 102) correctly attributes to Ambrose the position "that passions are a feature of the human condition which, while they can be governed and redirected, cannot be excised from our nature," she does not explore the origins of Ambrose's position beyond positing a general view shared with "Plato and Aristotle, and Panaetian Middle Stoicism." It seems clear, however, that Ambrose has derived his own position more immediately from 4 Maccabees (see 2:21–23; 3:1–6).

5. Colish (*Ambrose's Patriarchs*, 100) rightly observes that the mind-body or soul-body contrast in Ambrose is not an ethical dualism where the mind/soul is good while the body tends toward evil: "our problem is not the body, which is the agent of the will,

In addition to departing from the Stoics on the sources of the passions, Ambrose also expands the number of the passions from four to seven and invokes his own set of principles for analyzing them. Ambrose's approach to the passions is developmental. He considers them in the light of the sequence in which we experience them. Unreasonable desire leads to pleasure, which leads to joy. Fear leads to pain, which leads to sadness. Ambrose adds another passion, mental agitation, to joy and sadness, as the common outcome, with them, of joy and pain. This theory of the passions is not just an amplification of the Stoic doctrine on this topic; it is an original Ambrosian interpretation of the origins of the passions.[6]

Ambrose's formulation of his taxonomy of the passions vis-à-vis traditional Stoic categories is, however, not nearly so original. Rather, Ambrose found almost every detail in 4 Maccabees.

The author of 4 Maccabees had written of "two general categories of emotions—pleasure and pain"—each of which "shows up in different ways in the body and in the soul" (4 Macc 1:20), as Ambrose also speaks of "pleasure and pain" in regard to the body and the soul.[7] The author of 4 Maccabees had also already dispensed with the Stoic quartet of grief, fear, desire, and pleasure (as reflected in Diogenes Laertius, *Vit.* 7.110; Cicero, *Tusc. Disp.* 4.9–22) in favor of a taxonomy of two emotions—"pleasure" and "pain," the two identified by Aristotle as the principal passions (*Rh.* 2.1.8; *Eth. Nic.* 2.5.2)—with four others listed as the "attendants" (ἀκολουθίαι) of these two, some preceding, some following.[8]

> The emotions of pleasure and pain are accompanied by several others. Desire comes before pleasure, and joy follows it. Fear comes before pain, and grief follows it. Anger is a mixture of both pleasure and pain, as anyone who thinks about the experience could agree. (4 Macc 1:21–24)

---

and which, accordingly, can be the instrument of either virtue or vice." This is also true in 4 Maccabees, where there is no hint of spirit-flesh or mind-body dualism, but rather a functional dualism of reason-passions (the latter arising from any component part of the human person, whether soul/mind or body; see 4 Macc 1:20–27).

6. Colish, *Ambrose's Patriarchs*, 103.

7. Against Colish, I do not find evidence that Ambrose intends to introduce passions arising "from both body and soul" as a third category. Rather, it is at this point that he begins a new line of thought, analyzing the basic types of passion—just as the author of 4 Maccabees does at precisely the same point in the development of his discourse.

8. DeSilva, *4 Maccabees: Introduction and Commentary*, 87–88.

Ambrose adopts this same *reduction* of the Stoic four, followed by the same *expansion* to six overall major headings for the passions. Thus Ambrose: "Standing as natural leaders, so to speak, among the passions are pleasure and pain, and the others," which he lists as desire and joy, fear and grief, "follow these" (*De Jacob* 1.2.5). Ambrose differs from his source merely in generalizing the seventh passion. The author of 4 Maccabees speaks of "anger" as a combination of pleasure and pain (see Aristotle, *Rh.* 2.2.1–2), where Ambrose broadens this to "mental agitation." Ambrose has thus, in the main, adopted his doctrine of the passions wholesale from 4 Maccabees' treatment of this subject.

Ambrose's debt to 4 Maccabees continues throughout the prologue to *De Jacob*: the divine Law exercises individuals in curbing gluttony and luxury (*De Jacob* 1.2.5; 4 Macc 1:31–35), lust (through the example of Joseph; *De Jacob* 1.2.6; 4 Macc 2:1–6), enmity (*De Jacob* 1.2.7; 4 Macc 2:14), and anger (through the example of Jacob's rebuke of Simeon and Levi; *De Jacob* 1.2.7; 4 Macc 2:19–20). In all these topics, he follows the content and order of the introductory section of 4 Maccabees (1:1–3:18).

Colish observes that "at the midpoint of Bk. 1 of *De Jacob*, Ambrose . . . no longer focuses on the need to disdain physical pleasures. Rather, he focuses on the constancy of the sage confronted by sufferings and misfortunes of all kinds."[9] This shift corresponds to the shift in 4 Maccabees between 1:1–3:18 (which Ambrose has been following closely in the opening of *De Jacob*) and the moral interpretation of the martyr narratives that follow in 4 Macc 3:19–18:24. Ambrose will return to this material at the end of Book 2. At this point, however, Ambrose turns to other resources—specifically, to resources that he calls "Scriptural"—to continue his theme.

About three-quarters through the second book (2.10.43) and continuing to the end of his treatise, Ambrose recounts the martyrdoms of Eleazar, the brothers, and the mother. For this, he turns again pre-eminently to 4 Maccabees, often treating the text quite loosely as the basis for his own more fully elaborated version of some aspects of their story. We find his paraphrase of the dialogue between Antiochus and Eleazar, the torture of the old man, and the proposed ruse by which Eleazar might have satisfied the king and saved his life (4 Macc 5:1–38; *De Jacob* 2.10.43–44); a summarized version of the exchange between Antiochus and the seven brothers, omitting the brothers' hypothetical response conceding to Antiochus (4 Macc 8:1–9:9; *De Jacob* 2.11.45); the seriatim torture of the seven brothers and their defiant words toward the tyrant, the latter significantly embellished by Ambrose at several points (4 Macc 9:10–12:19; *De Jacob* 2.11.46–11.52). For example, Ambrose

9. Colish, *Ambrose's Patriarchs*, 97.

represents the second brother saying in response to being scalped that he has "a spiritual helmet" that the tyrant cannot take away, which Ambrose further explicates as a reference to the headship of Christ (*De Jacob* 2.11.47). He also gives the third brother a lengthy speech concerning the proposed amputation of his tongue (2.11.48) and has the fifth brother meditate on verses pertinent to his experience of being burned with fire, interpreting it as that which tries and purifies him (2.11.50).

Ambrose, however, shows himself to be aware also of the account in 2 Maccabees, blending in material from the older account and shifting to its version at a critical moment. In 4 Maccabees, none of the brothers speaks of his sufferings as an offering made to God in the hope that God would become merciful to the people. Eleazar makes such a prayer at the end of his ordeal (4 Macc 6:28–29), and the author himself comments on their obedient deaths in such terms (17:21–22). Similarly, in 4 Maccabees the brothers do not speak of suffering for their own sins, but rather for the sake of piety and virtue. It is in 2 Maccabees, however, that the sixth and seventh brothers speak as does the sixth in Ambrose's conflated version:

> For we are suffering because of our own sins. And if our living Lord is angry for a little while, to rebuke and discipline us, he will again be reconciled with his own servants. (2 Macc 7:32–33, NRSV)

> I, like my brothers, give up body and life for the laws of our ancestors, appealing to God to show mercy soon to our nation and by trials and plagues to make you confess that he alone is God, and through me and my brothers to bring to an end the wrath of the Almighty that has justly fallen on our whole nation. (2 Macc 7:37–38, NRSV)

> Thanks be also to you, because you are so hard and cruel that the Lord, against whom we have sinned, may become merciful toward our people through such punishments as ours. (*De Jacob* 2.11.51)

Ambrose's version of the mother's exhortation to her last surviving son includes recitations and expansive paraphrases of 2 Maccabees 7:21–23, 27–28, but notably does not include the topics used by the mother to exhort her sons on to martyrdom in 4 Macc 16:16–23 (or 18:6–19, for that matter), such as the examples of Abraham, Daniel, and the three youths in Babylon or the notion that dying for God repays a debt to God. Ambrose also suggests that the youngest brother is tortured to death, perhaps more bitterly than his senior brothers (as in 2 Macc 7:39–40), not that he committed suicide (as in 4 Macc 12:19).

At this point, however, Ambrose returns to the topics, images, and language of 4 Maccabees as he praises the mother encircled by her sons like a chorus (*De Jacob* 2.11.53; 4 Macc 8:4); affirms her victory over maternal affection (*De Jacob* 2.12.54; 4 Macc 14:20; 15:8, 11–12); recalls the encouragement that the brothers gave to one another (*De Jacob* 2.12.55; 4 Macc 13:9–18); speaks of the "place filled with the corpses of her sons" (*De Jacob* 2.12.56; 4 Macc 15:20); compares the cries of the sons to the song of Sirens or dying swans (*De Jacob* 2.12.56; 4 Macc 15:21); compares the glory of that family favorably to the glory of the moon shining among the stars (*De Jacob* 2.12.56; 4 Macc 17:5); speaks of her soul as "adamantine" (*De Jacob* 2.12.57; 4 Macc 16:13); and compares the flood of passions that the mother withstood to the ark withstanding the great deluge (*De Jacob* 2.12.57; 4 Macc 15:31–32).

Traces of 4 Maccabees appear in incidental ways as well. For example, Ambrose praises the naked, fleeing Joseph using a contrast found in 4 Maccabees' encomium on Eleazar:

> Joseph was not naked even though he had thrown off his external clothing, as he possessed the safe covering of virtue. Therefore the wise person is never empty . . . His soul is filled, for it guards the garments of grace it has received. (*De Iacob*, 2.5.22)

> First they stripped the old man, though he remained adorned with the gracefulness of his piety. (4 Macc 6:2, NRSV)

Ambrose can be presumed to have been familiar with 4 Macc 6:2, since he incorporates the similarly ironic statement found in 4 Macc 6:3, that the aged priest kept his spirit upright even though his body was bent down to the ground, in his own treatment of Eleazar (*De Jacob* 2.10.44).

Similarly, Ambrose uses nautical imagery to decorate his discussion of the exemplary sage's resistance to the passions and of the destiny of the pious martyrs that closely resemble the use of nautical imagery in the encomium on Eleazar in 4 Maccabees:

> Like a pilot of foresight, [the sage] must steer his ship in the storm, and as he meets the mounting waves, he must avoid shipwreck by plowing through such waters rather than turning away from them. (*De Jacob* 1.8.36)

> How safe is that harbor of pious devotion! (*De Jacob* 2.11.53)

> Our father Eleazar's right thinking was like a skilled captain, steering the ship of godly reverence over the sea of the emotions. Although the storms of the tyrant beat against the ship and the powerful waves of the tortures crashed over its decks, he kept the rudder of godly reverence straight until he sailed into the harbor of immortal victory. (4 Macc 7:1–3)

Colish rightly observes that Ambrose is partial to nautical metaphors, attributing this to Ambrose's use of a rhetorical and philosophical commonplace rather than as a sign of his dependence upon Plato.[10] While she is correct that such metaphors have become a commonplace, it seems likely that Ambrose was reminded of the utility of this commonplace for his theme specifically by 4 Maccabees, where it is prominently used in the encomium on Eleazar (4 Macc 7:1–3) and the mother (4 Macc 15:31–32).

Ambrose moves freely and fluidly between 2 and 4 Maccabees, chiefly employing the latter, in his ethical treatise *On Jacob*. The latter is perhaps the greatest single literary influence on this two-part treatise outside of the Genesis narratives on Jacob's life. But how do these two texts function for Ambrose? I do not find evidence that he would have regarded 4 Maccabees as "Scripture," despite his obviously high regard for and extensive use of the work. He paraphrases it extensively, but he never speaks of it as he does the book of Job or the writings of Paul. Indeed, as he transitions from his paraphrase of the opening chapters of 4 Maccabees (*De Jacob* 1.1.1–1.3.8) into his further reflections upon the topics he has been raising, he writes:

> Moreover, Scripture gives witness that temperance, wisdom, and discipline are taught—in the law as regards temperance, but as regards the other virtues, in the book of Job, in which it is written, "Is it not the Lord who teaches understanding and discipline?" And in the Gospel the Lord Himself says, "Learn from me, for I am meek and humble of heart." (*De Jacob* 1.3.9)

Ambrose, however, has been discussing how "virtue is teachable" from the opening of this treatise (*De Jacob* 1.1.1). Does this suggest that he first used the material in the opening chapters of 4 Maccabees to develop his thesis, and then moved to books that he considered "Scripture" for more authoritative support and further elaboration? When he opens book two, he describes his approach here to be to take "the examples of famous men who were placed in the greatest dangers and yet did not lose happiness of life but gained it instead" (*De Jacob* 2.1.1). He proceeds, then, to speak of the example of Jacob (finally!) at length, briefly touching upon the examples of

---

10. Colish, *Ambrose's Patriarchs*, 98, against Courcelle, "De Platon," 22–23.

Joseph in prison, Isaiah being sawn in two, Jeremiah drowning, and Daniel in the lions' den (as recounted in Bel and the Dragon) as a segue into his second major example, the Maccabean martyrs. All of his examples could be said to be drawn from Scripture, all the more as Ambrose knows the last story from 2 Maccabees; his decision to use 4 Maccabees as a principal resource in developing their example says nothing about his view of its authority as canonical Scripture alongside 2 Maccabees, but merely his knowledge, positive evaluation, and use thereof.[11]

I would like to close by responding briefly to two issues that arise in scholarly conversations concerning the *De Jacob*. First, Daniel Joslyn-Siemiatkowski speaks pervasively of Ambrose (and others) "erasing the Jewish identity of the Maccabean martyrs" by positing connections between their contest and dying for Christ (e.g., through his interpretation of the scalped brother's spiritual helmet as Christ, *De Jacob* 2.11.47).[12] Ambrose, however, is not "erasing" the martyrs' Jewish identity, at least no more than Paul "erases" Jewish identity by speaking of the Rock, from which the Israelites were supplied with water during their wilderness wandering, as Christ (1 Cor 10:1–13) or by speaking of the "Gospel being announced beforehand to Abraham" (Gal 3:6–9), or than the author of Hebrews erases the Jewish identity of Moses because he endured "the reproach of God's Anointed" (Heb 11:24–27). Ambrose is not erasing the martyrs' Jewish identity so much as drawing on typical early Christian strategies for speaking of the *continuity* of the faith of pre-CE Israel with the faith of the post-resurrection Church. Ambrose no more "makes the Maccabees more Christian than Jewish for Ambrose's audience" than Paul does to Abraham for his.[13]

As evidence for this counterclaim, I would note that Ambrose specifically preserves the focal point of their contest as being, as Eleazar's speech

11. Colish (*Ambrose's Patriarchs*, 122) writes that "all versions of the Septuagint, the text of the Old Testament that Ambrose used, include 1 and 2 Maccabees. The Alexandrian version of the Septuagint includes all four books of the Maccabees as canonical. Jerome also includes these books as canonical in his Vulgate Bible, and 4 Maccabees forms part of the *Vetus Latina*." To the best of my knowledge, Jerome only included 1 & 2 Maccabees in his Vulgate; there is no evidence that the pre-Vulgate Latin Bibles included 4 Maccabees; Codex Vaticanus lacks all of the books entitled "Maccabees" while Sinaiticus includes 1 and 4 Maccabees, but not 2 or 3 Maccabees (hence, not "all versions of the Septuagint . . . include 1 and 2 Maccabees"). Moreover, we must question whether inclusion in a codex implies canonicity. If so, would we extend this to the Epistle of Barnabas and the Shepherd of Hermas, included in Codex Sinaiticus, or to 1 & 2 Clement, included in Codex Alexandrinus? It is likely that Ambrose would have regarded 1 and 2 Maccabees as part of his Old Testament, as would his disciple, Augustine. There is nothing to suggest that he so regarded 4 Maccabees.

12. Joslyn-Siemiatkoski, *Christian Memories*, 39.

13. Joslyn-Siemiatkowski, *Christian Memories*, 40.

expresses it, "respect for the law, which has taught that one must abstain from the flesh of swine" (*De Jacob* 2.10.43). This is underscored by a second statement: "But if you consider this a slight matter, the eating of the swine's flesh, how will the person who has shown contempt for the law in the smallest matters keep it in great matters?" (*De Jacob* 2.10.43; cf. 4 Macc 5:19–21). The audience is left in no doubt that these are Jewish martyrs, dying for the sake of obedience to the Mosaic covenant—and particularly for a practice that is a central boundary marker for Jewish identity, an aspect of the Mosaic law that is rejected within (most) early Christian practice. It is true, of course, that Ambrose takes care in his application of their example not to use them to promote Torah-observance, but an equal commitment to the law of God and the Gospel of Christ as brought together in Pauline theology.[14]

The second issue concerns the importance of Ambrose's conflicts with the emperor Valentinian II over possession of the Portian Basilica in 385–386 CE. Valentinian was himself an Arian Christian, seeking to establish a place for Arian worship in Milan. He (perhaps rather modestly) sought to seize the older and smaller of the two basilicas in the city for Arian use. Ambrose refused to acknowledge his right to appropriate property from the Catholic Church, and led non-violent demonstrations against Valentinian's actions (some violence *did* erupt, but Ambrose sought to curb it on his side).[15] The tendency in Ambrosian scholarship is to read *De Jacob* as a response to this crisis, hence dating its composition to Lent 387.[16]

This confrontation was clearly a tense one. Ambrose was personally threatened for his resistance, and both he and his followers proceeded at risk to life and limb (though the threats never eventuated in actual harm). It is quite possible that Ambrose himself turned to texts like 4 Maccabees during this time for his own encouragement and the encouragement of his followers, which might account for its freshness in his mind as he wrote *De Jacob* and, indeed, account for its substantial impact upon, even intrusion into, a treatise on the patriarch.

I would like, however, to caution scholars of Ambrose in regard to over-zealous "mirror-reading" of this one known situation into the composition

---

14. See Joslyn-Siemiatkowski, *Christian Memories*, 37–38, on the importance of Romans 7, and perhaps we might add Galatians 5, for transforming 4 Maccabees's endorsement of the Law which, according to Paul, only brings sin and death in its train into an endorsement of "the spirit of Christ that properly led the virtuous person to victory over the passions of the flesh."

15. On the two-year history of the confrontations (385–86 CE), see Ramsey, *Ambrose*, 25–29; McLynn, *Ambrose of Milan*, 170–96; Nauroy, "Le fouet et le miel."

16. So, e.g., Colish, *Ambrose's Patriarchs*, 94.

and impact of *De Jacob*.[17] Joslyn-Siemiatkowski writes that the martyrs offer "both an example of virtue and a righteous resistance of unjust imperial power," and that "Ambrose drew on his own experience of enduring the threat of persecution during the confrontation between Catholic Christians in Milan and imperial troops seeking to seize the Portian Basilica in Milan on behalf of the Arian emperor Valentinian II during Lent of 386."[18] It is striking to me, however, that Ambrose *at no point* refers to this historical event nor his part in it in the *De Jacob*.

Does Ambrose's sudden first-person-singular apostrophe to Eleazar— "I, who am a priest and will be helped by your prayers, O Eleazar, will not omit to mention you, who are a priest" (2.10.43)—indeed indicate that "Ambrose identified with Eleazar's opposition to Antiochus IV because, like Eleazar, he also had been forced to stare down an emperor"?[19] Or is Eleazar merely Ambrose's point of connection (as an aging priest himself) with the characters in the story?[20] I am struck by Ambrose's silence about any point of connection beyond what he explicates, and I do not get the impression that Ambrose was shy or subtle in his political speech. Can we rightly deduce that Ambrose's representation of Eleazar's speech to Antiochus IV (*De Jacob* 2.10.43) reflects Ambrose's historical situation?[21] This seems difficult to sustain when Ambrose simply presents here a paraphrase of 4 Macc 5:23–24 in his ongoing paraphrase of 4 Maccabees as a whole.

Colish (*Ambrose's Patriarchs*, 124) reads the peroration of *De Jacob* as another piece of evidence supporting a dating of the treatise as a response to the basilica crisis of 386. Ambrose "yokes the spiritual triumph of the Maccabees to that of his own Milanese audience: 'You have stood among the armies of the king, to which the whole world was subject—even India turned aside and fled from them into the remotest parts of the farthest sea—and you only, and without warlike combat, have achieved victory over the proud king'" (*De Jacob* 2.12.58). This passage is the closing part of Ambrose's apostrophe to the Maccabean martyrs, conflating Antiochus's armies' victories with those of his more illustrious predecessor, Alexander, who did rattle the inhabitants of India (see opening of 1 Maccabees for the establishing of an easy connection between the two). Do Ambrose's words

17. New Testament scholars have been well-cautioned in this regard in Barclay, "Mirror-Reading a Polemical Letter."

18. Joslyn-Siemiatkowski, *Christian Memories*, 35.

19. Joslyn-Siemiatkowski, *Christian Memories*, 36.

20. Colish (*Ambrose's Patriarchs*, 121) suggests that this is simply an expression of Ambrose's conviction that "the prayers of the departed saints help the living" (an idea found quite explicitly in 2 Maccabees).

21. Thus Joslyn-Siemiatkowski, *Christian Memories*, 38–39.

truly blend the horizons between the historical situation of the martyrs and his Milanese audience in their much milder struggle against a much less awesome king? Or is this nothing more than a supposition on the part of scholars who know of the events of 385–386 CE? Those years saw the possibility of renewed imperial violence against (Catholic) Christians which might, in turn, have been a factor in Ambrose's use of 4 Maccabees in the composition of *De Jacob*.[22] I would simply caution against over-reading or over-interpreting *De Jacob* in this direction. The crisis had been resolved; Ambrose and his community were unharmed; and *De Jacob* is, after all, about the mind's mastery of the whole range of passions that impede virtue, which was also the scope of 4 Maccabees. Like 4 Maccabees, *De Jacob* speaks as relevant a word to people in situations of social pressure as to people in situations of social ease.

The esteem in which Ambrose held 4 Maccabees and the extensive use to which he put this text in his own exhortations to his Christian congregations fade considerably in the works of his disciple, Augustine, who appears to have little use for the text (or even its contents as mediated through Ambrose). Among Augustine's surviving works, two sermons—Sermon 300 ("On the Solemnity of the Maccabee Martyrs," date uncertain) and Sermon 301 ("On the Feast of the Holy Maccabees," 417 CE)—are dedicated to the remembrance of the nine martyrs. For these sermons, Augustine returns entirely to the material from the account he considers canonical—2 Maccabees—and uses this as his starting and ending point for textual reflection on the martyrs, contributing to the eclipsing of 4 Maccabees in the West.

---

22. Colish (*Ambrose's Patriarchs*, 124) observes that "in *De Isaac*, Ambrose speaks of the age of the martyrs as now past . . . But in *De Jacob*, it appears as if religious persecution, of a highly specific sort and from a highly specific quarter, may well be at hand"—or, if not "at hand," a recently renewed possibility.

10

Beyond the Eclectic Text of 4 Maccabees

Reading 4 Maccabees in Codex Sinaiticus

T extual criticism, with its diligent and rigorous reconstruction of the
hypothetical "original" text, provides the foundation for the vast majority of scholarly investigations of the Jewish and Christian Scriptures, but
we are reminded from time to time that the "eclectic" text upon which our
commentaries, monographs, and articles are frequently based represents
at the same time *all* manuscripts and *none*. The eclectic text is an ideal
type, the hypothetical *Urtext* that theoretically lies behind all the extant
witnesses but is nowhere evidenced in the form of an actual manuscript
that we know to have been read by ancient readers. However much we
depend upon the textual critics who have provided us with these critical
tools, the importance of actual manuscripts for the study of the reception
and impact of a particular book can never disappear from view.

A landmark achievement in weaving sinew and flesh over the dry bones
of the textual apparatus remains Bart D. Ehrman's *The Orthodox Corruption of Scripture*, a monograph that clearly demonstrated the importance of
what specific manuscripts can tell us about the concerns, interests, and even
power plays of the communities that produced and read these copies of texts.[1]
Scholarly results of this caliber no doubt gave impetus to the publication
of *The Complete Text of the Earliest New Testament Manuscripts*, edited by
Philip W. Comfort and David P. Barrett, who correctly remind us that "these
manuscripts were the 'Bible' they [Egyptian Christians of the second and third

---

1. Also noteworthy is Ehrman's slightly more recent exploration of the relationship
between the study of textual variants and the reconstruction of the social history of
early Christianity. See Ehrman, "Text as Window."

centuries] read and revered; to them, these manuscripts *were* the New Testament text," rather than the eclectic text derived from them.[2]

A massive project that reflects the importance of the particular manuscript as a witness to a text as it was read by real communities of faith is the emerging Septuagint Commentary Series published by Brill and edited by Stanley E. Porter, Richard Hess, and John Jarick, the first volume of which was published in late 2004.[3] Unlike most commentary series, contributors are tasked with providing translation and commentary based on a critical edition of a particular manuscript witness rather than the Rahlfs or Göttingen eclectic texts. While the series promises also to be of great use to students of the Septuagint who will be working from the eclectic text, it brings the added dimension of moving that reader beyond a hypothetical construct to a conversation about how the readers of a particular manuscript of a text as their "Scripture" would have experienced that text. It is from my research for the volume on 4 Maccabees that the current essay is derived, in an attempt to synthesize the data gathered and make preliminary observations about potential interests and emphases present in the Sinaiticus text (S) of 4 Maccabees that would be missed by the modern reader studying 4 Maccabees chiefly on the basis of the critical edition of Rahlfs—the text of 4 Maccabees to which most modern readers will have access, either directly or through the English translations based on the critical text like the main running text of the RSV, NRSV, ESV, and CEB (although the marginal notes help keep even the English reader aware of variant readings in unspecified "other witnesses").[4] From among these many variant readings in S, several noteworthy patterns emerge, suggesting how ancient readers would have experienced 4 Maccabees based on their reading of the S text differently from modern readers' experience of the book based on the eclectic text, and these shall occupy our attention here.

An Enhanced Philosophical Demonstration

Fourth Maccabees presents itself as a demonstration of a common philosophical thesis with a significant twist, namely that "pious reason is absolute

---

2. Comfort and Barrett, *Complete Text*, 13.

3. Auld, *Joshua, Jesus son of Naue*. As of 2020, sixteen volumes have appeared in print.

4. Significant differences in reading appear in 1:8, 20; 2:9, 15, 18, 24; 3:4, 8, 11, 13; 4:2, 9, 10; 5:9, 13, 23, 27; 6:14, 35; 7:14; 8:28; 9:1, 15, 21, 23, 28; 10:3, 14, 17; 11:2, 3, 4, 10; 12:1, 3, 6, 11, 13; 13:7, 21, 27; 14:3; 15:3, 5, 20, 24, 31; 16:3, 14, 23; 17:5, 17; 18:5, 7, 9, 23.

master of the passions" (1:1).[5] By this the author means that the person who
makes his or her decisions in line with the dictates of Torah and the requirements of piety will enact virtue rather than succumb to the power of the
desires, emotions, and sensations and their tendency to lead one away from
acting virtuously (1:15–18).[6] The martyrs provide the best examples from
which to prove his claim (1:7–9) because the passions to which they were
subjected were just about the most severe that could be suffered or even
conceived of in human experience. Thus any and all embellishment of the
passions experienced by the martyrs (the emotions of fear or compassion
that they felt for one another, the pain of the physical torments and of the
grief of watching beloved family members tortured) would in turn lead to
the amplification of their achievement as they mastered those passions and
of the value of Torah-observance as an educative process that fits people for
attaining such high ethical ideals. Several readings in S, but not accepted by
Rahlfs into the main text, would provide such embellishment.

In the context of the martyrdom of the seventh and last brother, S introduces a significant embellishment of the mother's contest with the emotions into the text.

---

5. The compound αὐτοδέσποτος is usually taken to signify "supreme ruler." Dupont-
Sommer (*Quatrième Livre*, 87) thus argues that "the prefix αὐτός reinforces the idea
expressed in the simple form of the word, giving it the sense of absolute, dictatorial, personal power" (my translation). This is confirmed in Liddell and Scott, *A Greek-English
Lexicon*, 280 col 1 (s.v. αὐτοδέσποτος), and additional support can be drawn from the fact
that its synonym, αὐτοκράτωρ (also used at 1:7), is the Greek equivalent for *imperator*
in the string of imperial titles (Hadas, *Maccabees*, 144). The term, however, might be
heard to denote "self-mastery," a meaning also consonant with the common usage of the
prefixed αὐτός, in the context of philosophical discussions of the mastery of the passions
(a meaning allowed in Montanari, *Lexicon*, 342 col. 2). Philosophers often name "self-
mastery" as the essential goal of ethical philosophy (see Cicero, *Tusc. Disp.* 2.22.53; *Let.
Arist.* 221). Plato promotes "self-mastery" as a desirable and praiseworthy state, in which
"the better part [of a human being] is master of the worse part," while the opposite is censurable (Plato, *Resp.* 431A; see also *Gorg.* 491). Plato asserts that mastering oneself is a
prerequisite for ruling others (*Gorg.* 491), a background that might give added moment
to the author's depiction of the martyrs as masters of themselves, but Antiochus as a slave
to his passions (Moore and Anderson, "Taking It Like a Man," 253–54). αὐτοδέσποτος
could be heard, then, in this context as a reference to that power of self-restraint over the
passions that pious reason confers upon its adherents, saving them from being mastered
by themselves, that is, made slaves of their passions and thus liable to lose their freedom
(see Shaw, "Body/Power/Identity," 277).

6. For a fuller analysis of the author's philosophical argument, see deSilva, *4 Maccabees*, 51–75. The landmark analysis of the author's relation to the various philosophical
schools remains Renehan, "Greek Philosophic Background."

ὅπως {ε}αὐτὴν ἐλεήσασα τοσούτων υἱῶν στερηθεῖ{σ}αν
παρορμήσειεν ἐπὶ τὴν σωτήριον εὐπείθειαν τὸν περιλειπόμενον
(12:6 S)[7]

. . . in order that, taking pity on herself as she was bereft of so
many sons, she might urge the remaining one on toward the
ready obedience bringing deliverance.

This is Antiochus's last chance, as it were, to achieve a victory over these
martyrs. To heighten his chances of success, he brings the mother, hoping
that she would help persuade her last surviving child to save himself from
martyrdom by eating the pork from the sacrifice. In Rahlfs's eclectic text,
which follows Alexandrinus here, it is Antiochus who is feeling compassion
for the mother and, acting on this impulse, gives her a chance to save her
last son on account of his own pity (αὐτὴν ἐλεήσας).[8] In S, however, bringing
the mother forward is part of his cold and calculated strategy for success.
He thinks to play upon the mother's weakness, inducing *her* to take pity
on herself ({ε}αὐτὴν ἐλεήσασα) and, breaking after so much stalwart resistance, plead with her last son to capitulate. The mother refuses, however,
to weaken in her resolve as she witnesses the eradication of her experience
of motherhood and her role as a woman, and therefore assumes a more
masculine role as she encourages even her last son to die.[9] The reading in S
accords well with the emphasis in 14:11—16:25 on the mother's mastery of
her own passions of maternal love, heightening the reader's appreciation for
her victory in the grueling final "test" of 12:6.[10]

　　The emotions of brotherly love are extremely important to the author
of 4 Maccabees, since these feelings played just as powerfully upon the
seven brothers as the physical assaults on their bodies and the resultant
pains (see 4 Macc 13:19—14:10). The opening sentences of this reflection
on the power of fraternal affection look at the ways in which fraternal love
grows from conception itself, through gestation in the womb and the common experience siblings have therein, drawing on one common life (the

　　7. Characters within angled brackets were supplied to the main text by a corrector.

　　8. Hadas (*Fourth Maccabees*, 206–7) also prefers this reading. It is probably this
shift in emphasis from the mother's inner contest to Antiochus's alleged act of "compassion" that makes this poignant verse drop from sight in discussions of the mother's
mastery of the passions, even in the excellent articles by Moore and Anderson ("Taking
It Like a Man") and Young ("Woman with the Soul of Abraham").

　　9. The author's belief in the immortality of the soul, however, allows him to "rein-
state" her as a mother—indeed, to "perfect" her as a mother who gives birth a second
time to all her sons for immortality (16:13).

　　10. Dupont-Sommer (*Quatrième Livre*, 131) and Klauck (*4 Makkabäerbuch*, 734)
favor this reading over the reading in Alexandrinus.

mother) for their own formation both before and after birth as they nurse. Sinaiticus brings this process to a more effective and appropriate climax by reading that the brothers were "compacted together" (συνστρέφονται, 13:21) by their early lives together, rather than simply being "nursed together" (συντρέφονται in Rahlfs), the latter reading being in fact redundant in context. In this way, the reading in S makes a greater impression upon the reader in regard to the unity, harmony, and solidarity shared among the brothers, a topic that the author invokes so heavily throughout this section. In regard to fraternal affection, S also calls greater attention to the emotional turmoil experienced—and overcome—by the brothers as they died for the sake of piety, thus again heightening the reader's appreciation for the power of pious reason:

> "for the sake of piety those left behind endured seeing the ones for whom they felt deep pity (τοὺς κατοικτιζομένους ὁρῶντες) being tortured to death" (13:27 S)

> "for the sake of piety those left behind endured seeing them mistreated (τοὺς καταικιζομένους ὁρῶντες), being tortured to death" (13:27 Rahlfs)

The first reading draws attention to the compassion felt by the brothers for each other at a crucial and climactic juncture in the discussion of their mastery of the passion of brotherly love. A variant in S 16:3, where the reader encounters αὐτήν in place of αὐτῆς, achieves a similar effect: "Indeed, the lions around Daniel were not so wild nor the furnace of Mishael so kindled by exceedingly turbulent fire as the natural bent of parental love was burning that woman as she herself (αὐτήν) saw the seven sons thus variously being tortured." The original reading in S placed more emphasis on the mother's own experience in her own "furnace of fire." Rahlfs, following the corrector of Sinatitus, reads αὐτῆς instead, a mere possessive form that somewhat diminishes the rhetorical force of the verse.

Finally, the reading of ἀσθενέστεραν in S at 15:5, in contrast with the reading of ἀσθενόψυχοι in Rahlfs, significantly affects how this verse is heard and how the author's understanding of a woman's moral constitution and capacity for displaying virtue is construed.

> ὅσῳ γὰρ καὶ ἀσθενέστεραν [corrector changes to ἀσθενέστεραι] καὶ πολυγονώτεραι ὑπάρχουσιν αἱ μητέρες τοσούτῳ μᾶλλόν εἰσιν φιλοτεκνότεραι (15:5 S)

> For insofar as mothers are both *weaker* and more productive in childbearing, so much more are they more affectionate toward their offspring.

ὅσῳ γὰρ καὶ ἀσθενόψυχοι καὶ πολυγονώτεραι ὑπάρχουσιν αἱ μητέρες τοσούτῳ μᾶλλόν εἰσιν φιλοτεκνότεραι (15:5 Rahlfs)

For insofar as mothers are both *weak-souled* and more productive in childbearing, so much more are they more affectionate toward their offspring.

The author seeks to argue that a mother's love does not diminish for each of her children the more numerous those children become, as if there were a limited amount of love to be shared by a growing number, but actually augmented. Dupont-Sommer and Hadas find the placement of ἀσθενέστεραι difficult, transposing it conceptually to stand outside and prior to the ὅσῳ clause.[11] The author's rather clear conjunction of the two comparative adjectives (καὶ . . . καί . . .) shows, on the contrary, his desire to forge a link between the mother's constitution as she endures increasing numbers of pregnancies and deliveries and her love for her offspring.

Pregnancy and childbirth posed serious threats to the health and life of a mother. The author creates a proportional relationship between the degree to which mothers pour out their own life and strength (i.e., through multiple births) and the resulting love that they feel for their offspring, in whom they have invested so much of themselves. The reading in S is careful to present a strictly physiognomic evaluation of maternity that cannot be construed as an evaluation of the mother's psychological or moral capacity, something to which the reading in Rahlfs (ἀσθενόψυχοι, "weak-souled") might easily be susceptible.

The reading in S will, in turn, lend clarity to the meaning being conveyed in the concessive clause of 16:5 as the author moves from his acclamation of the mother's achievement to his imaginative reconstruction of what her response might have been, had she been "fainthearted": δειλόψυχος εἰ ἡ γυνή, καίπερ μήτηρ οὖσα, ὠλοφύρετο ἂν ἐπ' αὐτοῖς (16:5 S, "if the woman [were] fainthearted, although being a mother, she would have lamented over them"). Hadas understands the concessive καίπερ— quite against its natural, concessive sense—to introduce a factor that is complementary to a woman's proving fainthearted, providing something of a rationale for why she might have indeed proven fainthearted ("being, as she was, a mother").[12] Such a sense could be defended by invoking the particular vulnerability to which motherhood exposes women, who are weakest there where their offspring are threatened. This is clearly the case in the parallels from classical literature that are echoed so unmistakably in

---

11. Dupont-Sommer, *Quatrième Livre*, 140; Hadas, *Fourth Maccabees*, 221.

12. Hadas, *Fourth Maccabees*, 227.

the "fainthearted speech" of 16:6–11.[13] Dupont-Sommer had previously supported this reading, arguing against Deissmann's insistence on taking the καίπερ in its concessive sense (Deissmann indicating thus that the author would not expect a mother to be fainthearted) that the author has already called women "weak-spirited" in 15:5.[14] This evidence, however, does not exist in S, where, as we have seen, mothers are described as "weaker" (ἀσθενέστεραι, 15:5), not "weak-souled" or "weak-spirited" (ἀσθενόψυχοι). The reader of S would thus naturally come to Deissmann's conclusion as well: having faced and survived childbirth, any woman who is a mother has already proven herself to possess a clear measure of courage and would not be expected to prove fainthearted. The "weaker" vessel is thus not less capable of moral strength, as indeed the mother of the seven proved, being "more manly than men in regard to endurance" (15:30).

A More Vivid "Narrative Demonstration"

The reader of 4 Maccabees as it stood in the original hand of S would have experienced the text as slightly more vivid and dramatic than does the modern reader of the eclectic text. For a start, there are two examples of what appear to be an intentional doubling of rhetorically evocative words in the text. In 9:1, the seven brothers spit out the vocative ὦ τύραννε twice rather than once, as in Rahlfs, which omits the second occurrence:

τί μέλλεις, ὦ τύραννε; ἕτοιμοι γάρ ἐσμεν, ὦ τύραννε, ἀποθνῄσκειν ἢ παραβαίνειν τὰς πατρίους ἡμῶν ἐντολάς[15] (9:1)

What are you about to do, O tyrant? For we are prepared, O tyrant, to die rather than transgress our ancestral commandments.

Similarly, in 17:5 the initial adverbial phrase is doubled in S:

οὐχ οὕτως, οὐχ οὕτως σελήνη κατ᾿ οὐρανὸν σὺν ἄστροις σεμνὴ καθέστηκεν . . . (17:5)

Not so, not so seemly has the moon been set in heaven among the stars . . .

13. On these parallels, see Klauck, 4 Makkabäerbuch, 747–48; deSilva, 4 Maccabees, 73. These are also discussed in chapter 5 above.

14. Dupont-Sommer, Quatrième Livre, 145; see Deissmann, "Das vierte Makkabäerbuch," 172.

15. Quotations from the S text have been regularized with conventional spellings in regard to itacismus and other orthographic peculiarities.

The doubling of οὐχ οὕτως in 17:5 might well be dismissed as nothing more than a dittography originating with the scribe of S, following as it does immediately upon the heels of the first, and could have been quickly corrected by the next reader. It is interesting to observe, however, that, though the scribe[16] was given to dittography, he usually stopped himself before reproducing entire words or phrases (see, for example, the dittography in 9:17, ἰσχυρό{τερο}ς ὑμῶν ἰσχυρ, where the scribe recognizes his own mistake and stops the doubling in the middle of the word). The reduplication of ὦ τύραννε in 9:1, however, does not have the same random character, being rather far removed from the first occurrence and appropriately placed to break up the second part of the verse, and may have a stronger claim to representing the way the text was known in the community of the scribe prior to the work of the corrector who eliminated the second instance. These doublings could signal that the scribe of S was trying to provide a rhetorically more effective presentation of the work. The reader experiences the repetition of ὦ τύραννε as embellishing the vituperation of Antiochus (who, being Greek, would surely have rejected the title) and clarifying its character more as a curse to be thrown out than a political title. The repetition of οὐχ οὕτως—and one can almost hear the dramatic pause after the first—also potentially contributed to the evocation of pathos. This, in turn, would enhance the reader's appreciation particularly of the mother's ethical achievement (which we have already seen to be more prominently displayed and more carefully nuanced in S than in the readings chosen for the eclectic text).

The S text contains several additional verbs and more colorful vocabulary when compared alongside the eclectic text, the effect of which is to enhance the drama and emotional impact of the respective scenes in which they appear. In 3:8, S adds the verb ἔσπευδεν, underscoring the wearying efforts put forth by David and the fact that he had reached his limits of endurance (τότε δὴ γενομένης ἑσπέρας ἔσπευδεν ἱδρῶν καὶ σφόδρα κεκμηκὼς ἐπὶ τὴν βασίλειον σκηνὴν ἦλθεν, 3:8; "then when evening came, *he pressed on*, perspiring heavily, and came, exceedingly wearied, into the royal tent"). Similarly, in 9:28 we find the addition of the verb εἵλκυσαν in the disturbing description of the second brother's torture:

ὡς δ' εἰ φαγεῖν βούλοιτο πρὶν βασανίζεσθαι πυνθανόμενοι τὴν εὐγενῆ γνώμην ἀκούσαντες, εἵλκυσαν ἀπὸ τῶν τενόντων ταῖς σιδηραῖς χερσὶν . . . (9:27–28).

---

16. Or, better, scribes, since there appear to have been two different hands in the production of the main text of 4 Maccabees in S (Metzger, *Manuscripts*, 77).

> When inquiring whether he might be willing to eat before being tortured, and having heard his noble decision, *they tore out* his sinews with the iron gloves . . .

The additional verb εἵλκυσαν simplifies the structure of this sentence considerably at the same time that it adds an additional image to the verbal depiction of the scene. More vivid verb tenses in S (involving present tense verbs or verbs with μέλλω) invite the hearer more fully and with greater immediacy into the unfolding of the drama (ἦσαν γὰρ μέλλοντες περίφρονες, "for they were about to be despisers," rather than ἦσαν γὰρ περίφρονες, "for they were despisers" in 8:28; the present infinitive ἐκτεμνεῖν, "to proceed to cut out," rather than the aorist ἐκτεμεῖν, "to cut out," in 10:17; the present participle οἰκοδομουμένην, "being built up," in place of the perfect ᾠκοδομημένην, "built up," in 18:7). For native Greek hearers and readers sensitive to verbal aspect, such vivid aspect would likely have exerted a subtle effect on their experience of the drama that is lost to modern readers of the eclectic text.

An ambiguous textual variant that nevertheless heightens the vividness of the story either way the ambiguity is resolved is found in 15:20, where S reads χόριον ("afterbirth") or possibly χορεῖον ("dancing area") if the iota be understood as an instance of itacismus. Rahlfs has chosen χωρίον (merely "place") for the eclectic text (a reading with which the corrector of S would essentially agree, using the diminutive form χορίδιον [sc. for χωρίδιον] to describe the scene viewed by the mother). If this is not simply an error on the part of the original scribe of S, hearing χόριον as "afterbirth" here would introduce a poignant image given the descriptions of biological waste laying around the site (the contents of 15:15, 20 could hardly be described otherwise). The mother has witnessed her children being turned into the dead waste matter of pregnancy by Antiochus's soldiers. Reading this variant in context, we find that it is meant to "rename" πολυάνδριον: πολυάνδριον (πολυανδρεῖον?) ὁρῶσα τῶν τέκνων χωρίον διὰ τῶν βασάνων οὐκ ἐδάκρυσας ("seeing the mass grave, the afterbirth of her children by means of the tortures, she did not cry," 15:20). The word πολυάνδριον could be construed as "a place where many people assemble,"[17] hence "when you saw the χόριον/χορεῖον crowded with people by virtue of the tortures of the children." This word, however, can also be read as πολυανδρεῖον,[18] "mass grave," a sense that is certainly more in keeping with the emphasis on carnage (especially "corpse upon corpse," ἐπὶ νεκροῖς νεκρούς) in the preceding phrases (see also

---

17. Liddell and Scott, *A Greek-English Lexicon*, 1436 col. 2; so Dupont-Sommer, *Quatrième Livre*, 142; Hadas, *Fourth Maccabees*, 223.

18. Liddell and Scott, *A Greek-English Lexicon*, 1436 col. 2. Itacismus would make it indistinguishable in S in any case (so, rightly, Klauck, *4 Makkabäerbuch*, 745).

the use of the word in the author's source, 2 Macc 9:4). The S text, then, could invite its readers to perceive the mother's experience as witnessing her children transformed into their own afterbirths (i.e., biological waste matter) and her environment becoming their mass grave (even though it would not be their *final* resting place). This reading is admittedly uncertain (see below), but the tendency in S to elevate the presentation and heroic triumph of the mother recommends at least the possibility that the ambiguity should be resolved in this direction. If, however, we hear χόριον as χορεῖον (as does LS 1998 col. 1), a different but still appropriate image is introduced, naming the place of the martyrs' torture and death their "dancing place" in keeping with the choral imagery used in association with the brothers in 13:8; 14:3, 7,[19] a dance that has now become a place of death.

Several other distinctive readings are noteworthy in their contribution to a more dramatic experience of 4 Maccabees. The use of μιαροφαγεῖν ("to eat defiling foods") rather than ἐσθίειν (merely "to eat") in 5:27 and κόλασιν ("fury/vengeance") rather than ἀκολασίαν ("intemperance") in 13:7 both enhance the telling of the story, the first by keeping the repugnance of the food and its consequences for the eater in view, the second by displaying the "antagonist" in the martyr's contest in stronger terms. In 11:10, the reader encounters the more specific detail that the fifth brother is "bent back up to the neck" (τράχηλον) rather than simply "bent back upon the wheel" (τροχόν); similarly, in 12:13 the reader of S is reminded by the seventh brother of the specific pains of fire endured by the previous martyrs (κατακαύσας) rather than the more general reference to "ill-treatment" (καταικίσας in Rahlfs) that does not evoke specific images in the reader's mind.

The reader of S also experiences a sharpening of the tone of several incidences of direct address. At one point, the audience is challenged directly, should any of them hold to what is perceived as an erroneous view (εἴποιτε ἤ, "you might perhaps say") rather than distanced from the challenge lodged against the third person interlocutor (εἴποι τις ἄν εἰ, "if anyone might say," 2:24). Within the narrated dialogue, moreover, Eleazar's peers challenge him more directly with the "folly" of his actions as S omits the τί in 6:14, turning a question into an indictment:

τί τοῖς κακοῖς τούτοις σεαυτὸν ἀλογίστως ἀπόλλεις Ελεαζαρ; ("why are you irrationally destroying yourself by means of these evils?"; Rahlfs and the corrector of S)

τοῖς κακοῖς τούτοις σεαυτὸν ἀλογίστως ἀπόλλεις Ελεαζαρ. ("you are irrationally destroying yourself by means of these evils"; original reading of S)

19. Townshend, "Fourth Book," 681.

Further, S keeps the focus of the brothers' resistance more intently on Antiochus himself, maintaining the sense of "one-on-one combat" between the
king and the philosopher-subjects, when the fourth brother answers Antiochus (αὐτῷ) rather than the taunting torturers who actually initiate the challenge in that scene (hence αὐτοῖς in the Rahlfs text of 10:14). To this list could
be added 5:13, in which Antiochus would be heard to pronounce a wish over
Eleazar (συγγνωμονήσειεν, "may [God] pardon") rather than merely suggest
a possibility (συγγνωμονήσειεν ἄν, "[God] may pardon").

The penchant for dramatic flair may even be observed in the peculiar
line breaks present before 14:2, which marks the transition from discursive
reflection to encomium (here, an apostrophe), and 14:3, which separates the
first apostrophe from a second. Although not in keeping with "paragraphing"
in any modern sense, this double break makes the reader pause longer at the
triumphant moment of acclaiming victory for the seven brothers, signaling to
him or her to linger there at the end of so long a struggle.

An Enhanced Encomiastic Emphasis
on Virtue and Victory

A second cluster of distinctive readings in S draws the reader into a portrayal of the martyrs that emphasized their "nobility and goodness" and their
"virtue" slightly more than the readings chosen for the critical text do. As
is well known, depicting these martyrs as the paragon of "moral excellence"
(ἀρετή) and of "nobility and goodness" (καλοκἀγαθία) is an important feature of the author's proptreptic goal, as he promotes rigorous observance
of the Law of Moses as the path to the manifestation of the virtuous ideal
lauded by the Greco-Roman culture that, irrationally, denigrated the Jewish
way of life.[20] Sinaiticus introduces καλοκἀγαθία as early as 1:8 in the exordium, where Rahlfs follows Alexandrinus in reading ἀνδραγαθία ("heroism,"
"manly virtue"), a term of slightly lesser distinction:

πολὺ δὲ πλέον τοῦτο ἀποδείξαιμι ἀπὸ τῆς καλοκἀγαθίας τῶν ὑπὲρ
ἀρετῆς ἀποθανόντων (1:8 S)

---

20. See deSilva, *4 Maccabees*, 46–49, 80–81. Antiochus exemplifies the dominant
culture's misapprehension of the nature of the Jewish philosophy and the resultant failure to respect it as a viable and virtue-producing way of life. This is the main topic of
4 Maccabees 5, where the author creates an opportunity to refute common objections
against the Jewish way of life in the mouth of Eleazar. See, further, Redditt, "Concept of
Nomos," 260–62; Hadas, *Fourth Maccabees*, 169–76; Dupont-Sommer, *Quatrième Livre*,
106–9; Klauck, *4 Makkabäerbuch*, 709–14; deSilva, *4 Maccabees*, 103–11.

But I might prove this much better from the *nobility and goodness* of those who died on behalf of moral excellence.

πολὺ δὲ πλέον τοῦτο ἀποδείξαιμι ἀπὸ τῆς ἀνδραγαθίας τῶν ὑπὲρ ἀρετῆς ἀποθανόντων (1:8 Rahlfs)

But I might prove this much better from the *bravery* of those who died on behalf of moral excellence

Similarly, in the midst of the peroration, S holds up the martyrs' "virtue" (τὴν ἀρετήν) as well as their "endurance" (τὴν ὑπομονήν) as objects of the spectators' admiration, where Rahlfs places only the latter in the main text:

αὐτός γέ τοι ὁ τύραννος καὶ ὅλον τὸ συμβούλιον ἐ{ξε}θαύμασαν αὐτῶν τὴν ἀρετὴν καὶ τὴν ὑπομονήν (17:17 S)

Indeed, the tyrant himself and his whole council marveled at their *moral excellence and endurance.*

αὐτός γέ τοι ὁ τύραννος καὶ ὅλον τὸ συμβούλιον ἐθαύμασαν αὐτῶν τὴν ὑπομονήν (17:17 Rahlfs)

Indeed, the tyrant himself and his whole council marveled at their *endurance.*

The words ἀρετή and καλοκἀγαθία sum up the Greek ideal of the good and honorable person.[21] These terms reappear throughout the oration with notable frequency (καλοκἀγαθία and cognates: 1:8, 10; 3:18; 11:22; 13:25; 15:9; ἀρετή and cognates: 1:2, 8, 10, 30; 2:10; 7:22; 9:8, 18, 31; 10:10; 11:2; 12:14; 13:24, 27; 17:12, 23), especially in connection with the examples of the martyrs. The effect of this is to grace those who most strenuously resisted Hellenization where fidelity to the Jewish Law would be compromised—and those who continue to do so—with the highest terms of distinction offered by the Greek culture. That καλοκἀγαθία and its cognates appear only in 4 Maccabees among all the books of the Septuagint underscores the particular interest of its author to honor pious Jews as the perfection of Greek values. The additional occurrences of καλοκἀγαθία in the exordium and ἀρετή in the peroration, therefore, underscore at rhetorically strategic places the claims being made on behalf of the martyrs and the way of life for which they stand.

21. Danker, *Benefactor*, 319.

Sinaiticus reads εὐγένειαν in 10:3 (whereas Rahlfs has elected to read συγγένειαν), placing thereby a double emphasis on the "nobility" or "noble birth" of these martyrs:

οὐκ ἐξόμνυμαι τὴν εὐγενῆ τῆς ἀδελφότητος εὐγένειαν (10:3 S)

I do not renounce the well-born noble birth of brotherhood.

οὐκ ἐξόμνυμαι τὴν εὐγενῆ τῆς ἀδελφότητος συγγένειαν (10:3 Rahlfs, following Alexandrinus)

I do not renounce the well-born kinship of brotherhood.

This reading is probably due to a scribal error at some point in the transmission process, the scribe having mentally transferred the beginning of εὐγενῆ to the beginning of συγγένειαν (an easy mistake, given the orthographic similarity of sigma and epsilon), thus turning the latter into a cognate of the former. Nevertheless, the reading in S now underscores the third brother's claim that the standard of honor to which he must live up is set by his pious kin and that his own honor consists of remaining steadfast to the way of life that defines their kinship—adherence to the Torah.

A second variant that underscores this same point is the reading of the intensifier αὐτός in 12:1 S (where Rahlfs has chosen to read οὗτος), which brings an added dimension to the sixth brother's noble death:

ὡς δὲ καὶ αὐτὸς μακαρίως ἀπέθανεν καταβληθεὶς εἰς λέβητα (12:1 S)

And when he himself also died honorably, having been thrown down into a cauldron . . .

ὡς δὲ καὶ οὗτος μακαρίως ἀπέθανεν καταβληθεὶς εἰς λέβητα (12:1 Rahlfs)

And when this one also died honorably, having been thrown down into a cauldron . . .

In S, it is not merely that "this one" also died in a state of special distinction,[22] but that he "himself" lived up to the noble mark previously set by his predecessors, who had likewise died nobly. The intensifier recalls the standard being set for the sixth brother by the noble steadfastness of his brothers, and the rule that their own honor would be preserved only insofar as they each

---

22. Recalling K. C. Hanson's important article that μακάριος is a term that ascribed honor or special favor to someone or some group ("How Honorable! How Shameful!").

lived out their noble bonds of kinship through commitment to the same values (hence 10:3 above).

Also related to the increased elevation of the nobility of the martyrs is the greater attention given to their combat, victory, and resultant honor. Sinaiticus includes an epithet for the mother in one of the encomiastic apostrophes in chapter 16 that is absent from the eclectic text:

> ὦ μῆτερ δι᾽ εὐσέβειαν θεοῦ, μῆτερ καὶ εὐσεβοῦς στρατιᾶς, στρατιῶτι πρεσβῦτι καὶ γύναι (16:14 S)

> O mother on account of reverence for God, *mother indeed of a pious host*, solider, elder, and woman!

> ὦ μῆτερ δι᾽ εὐσέβειαν θεοῦ στρατιῶτι πρεσβῦτι καὶ γύναι (16:14 Rahlfs)

> O mother on account of reverence for God, solider, elder, and woman!

Within the panegyric on Eleazar, S also reads ἐνίκησεν rather than ἠκύρωσεν ("he conquered the many-headed torment" rather than "he nullified the many-headed torment," 7:14), adding yet another incident of that frequently used verb to the hearing of the story (see also 1:11; 3:17; 6:10, 33; 7;4, 11; 8:1; 9:6, 30; 11:20; 13:2, 7; 16:14; 17:15, 24). Finally, the martyrs are said to have received "victorious" or "prize-winning" souls (ψυχὰς . . . ἀθλοφόρους, 18:23 S, rather than the more static ἀθανάτους preferred by Rahlfs) from God, applying to them the quality that had just been applied to their "prize-bearing mother" (τῇ ἀθλοφόρῳ μητρί, 18:23). They are also "announced" (εὐαγγελίζονται, 18:23 S) to the chorus of the ancestors, that is, as victors in the games would be given recognition, rather than simply "gathered" (συναγελάζονται, 18:23 Rahlfs) to the ancestors, a common passive—and not particularly honorific—idiom for dying.

The author uses military metaphors and athletic imagery throughout his oration, these bodies of imagery providing a way strategically to turn passive "endurance" into a form of "manliness" or "courage."[23] When, for example, the eldest brother incites his younger siblings not "to leave [their] post," but rather to "wage the noble and sacred battle for piety" (9:24), the military/agonistic imagery is a means by which to focus attention on resistance as the courageous path to a victory and a praiseworthy remembrance—in stark contrast to how Antiochus intended these tortures and

---

23. Moore and Anderson, "Taking It Like a Man," 259–261. On athletic imagery in 4 Maccabees, see Pfitzner, *Paul and the Agon Motif*, 57–64; deSilva, *4 Maccabees*, 92–93.

executions to be understood. The reader of S, then, experiences this facet of the rhetorical strategy of 4 Maccabees slightly more forcefully than the modern reader of the eclectic text.[24]

Additional Variants Affecting Meaning

A few other variant readings produce subtle shifts of meaning, even though they do not fall into one of the aforementioned patterns. In S, the reader encounters φιλαργυρίας ("love of money") in a list of the "more violent passions" where Rahlfs has elected to read φιλαρχίας ("love of offices," 2:15). The reader of S encounters the more mundane economic cravings among two lists of vicious and debasing traits (φιλαργυρία also appears at 1:26), something that might have convicted a broader segment of the readership than would have been the case for readers of those ancient manuscripts (preferred by Rahlfs) naming the "love of offices" that suggests the ambitious social climbing along the *cursus honorum* (a preoccupation limited to the elite).

In the scene of the public supplication that accompanied Apollonius' attempted seizure of the private funds deposited in trust in the Temple treasury, the reader of S finds "old men" (γεραιῶν) joining the women and children in prayer (4:9; the modern reader of the eclectic text encounters "priests" [ἱερέων] in place of "old men"). Not only is "old men" (γεραιῶν) a more emotionally-charged and evocative image (hence possibly belonging to the second class of variants described above), it also artfully intimates the contests for piety by an old man, a woman, and a group of children about to be narrated.

The reading Αβρααμ υἱός ("son of Abraham") in the S text of 9:21, rather than Αβραμιαῖος ("Abraham-like one," the reading preferred by Rahlfs), runs counter to the general tendency in 4 Maccabees to replace categories of genealogical descent with terms more suggestive of imitation of an archetype (see also 18:20, 23).[25]

Finally, in the S text of 12:3 one reads that Antiochus considered the deaths of the first six brothers to be a result of their "faithlessness" or "distrust" (ἀπιστίαν) rather than their "disobedience" (ἀπείθειαν, as in Alexandrinus and selected by Rahlfs), although the latter is still represented elsewhere in the text as an attribute of the martyrs in the eyes of the king (e.g., 9:10).

---

24. One reading in S, however, actually works against this overall tendency, namely the appearance of αἰῶνα rather than ἀγῶνα in 9:23, no doubt the result of a scribal error (either the scribe of S or his exemplar mistaking the gamma in ἀγῶνα for an iota).

25. Seim, "Abraham, Ancestor or Archetype," 30.

This variation subtly underscores the significance of Antiochus's invitation to the brothers to take him for their patron and, therefore, "trust" him (8:7), and the dangers of arousing the dominant culture's ire by refusing such relationships (so also in 9:10).[26] The reader of S thus has the two alternatives of remaining faithful to God (16:22) or breaking faith with God for the sake of networking with the representatives of the dominant culture placed before his or her eyes more starkly than the reader of the eclectic text.

Conclusion and Prospect

In this investigation, I have sought to illumine the ways in which the ancient or modern reader of 4 Maccabees as it stands in Codex Sinaiticus would experience the text differently from the modern reader of 4 Maccabees as it stands in the eclectic text of Rahlfs or in modern English translations. Even though the percentage of the overall text affected by these variants is small, and therefore the cumulative "difference" in that reading experience slight, several distinctive patterns have emerged. The S text of 4 Maccabees amplifies the reader's experience of the book in several ways: the philosophical demonstration is amplified by the embellishments of the force of the passions endured and withstood by the martyrs; the narrative itself, which is the principal medium of demonstration (3:19), is presented slightly more forcefully and vividly; the encomiastic elements, particularly those highlighting the nobility and the victory of the martyrs in their contest/battle, are heightened as well, and at strategic points in the rhetorical structure. One particular point that emerges more clearly for the reader of the S text is that women are not by nature weaker in their moral constitution, but only in their physiognomy. The fortitude showed in repeated endurance of gestation and childbirth is a token of fortitude, not a precursor of faintheartedness.

These observations, however, provide merely a starting point for further investigation, which might take the following form. A similar study of 4 Maccabees in Codex Alexandrinus has already been undertaken;[27] the partial text in Codex Venetus could also be examined to see if other patterns emerge. As textual data become more readily accessible (for example, with the long-awaited publication of the volume on 4 Maccabees in the Göttingen Septuagint), the important witnesses to the Lucianic recension could be added. For the purposes of my commentary, I examined the differences between one particular manuscript's readings and the critically-reconstructed *Urtext*, which could be profitably continued as

26. See deSilva, *4 Maccabees*, 111–13.
27. Adams, "Alexandrinus Text."

a kind of "baseline" point of reference, but as this line of inquiry moves forward it would also be important to compare each manuscript's readings more directly with the particular alternative readings available in the other witnesses (thus eliminating the dependence upon the eclectic—and always "hypothetical"—text as the baseline). This would be a desideratum because my study does not catch those places where the text of S has been affirmed to retain the "original" reading by Rahlfs, but still differs from the other available manuscripts. The final and most fruitful stage would come at the end of this longer process as the data from each study are collected and analyzed with a view to discovering, through these variants, what each manuscript can tell us about the interests, values, challenges, and group-maintaining strategies of the particular communities that produced and read them. How might such data contribute to our understanding of the social milieu, and reconstruction of the social history, of Hellenistic Judaism and Christianity in late antiquity (remembering that it is Christian scribes that are copying 4 Maccabees)? Needless to say, similar projects could also be profitably undertaken with any other Septuagint text, contributing to the revitalization of textual criticism by probing the potential contributions to our understanding of the history of interpretation and even the social and cultural milieu of the communities that preserved these manuscripts to be gained from the variants at the bottom of the page.

Conclusion

The Rhetorical and Ethical Achievement of 4 Maccabees

F ourth Maccabees represents a landmark achievement among the texts reckoned in the corpus of Apocrypha and Pseudepigrapha. Its author attained a level of competence in Greek language, composition, rhetoric, and cultural knowledge (including a more than passing acquaintance with philosophy and literature) unparalleled in these collections. He employed this linguistic and cultural facility, however, to make room at the table of elite Hellenistic discourse for the Jewish world view and way of life, which he thoroughly demonstrated to form the kind of person that embodies the highest ideals and achieves the most widely lauded goals of Hellenistic ethical philosophy, notably the self-control evident in reason's mastery of the passions. The ethical ideal articulated in the author's thesis is one of enduring value in and of itself. The experience of finding oneself torn between the expression of the virtues that one prizes (and that one's culture prizes) and alternately the gratification and alleviation of the feelings, desires, and sensations that are a constant facet of our human existence is common to many people across otherwise widely divergent cultures.

The author of 4 Maccabees has provided an interpretation of the value of the Torah as that which guides and empowers one to live out this ethical ideal—as opposed to, say, promoting the value of the Torah as a legislative system of social engineering that purposefully and positively creates barriers between a particular people and all the other peoples of the earth, because too free a social interaction with them would lead to being contaminated by their ignorance and error about divine matters (such as one finds in *Let. Aris.* 139-142).[1] He also does so in a way that resolves the tension between

---

1. This is not to say, however, that the author of 4 Maccabees promotes greater social

adhering to culturally affirmed virtues (i.e., those commitments and practices that make the individual a valuable member of the group) and answering the cry of the "passions" (i.e., those impulses that bend the individual to act in response to his or her pressing interests in the moment). The person who masters the passions and consistently chooses the path of virtue is the person who does not betray himself or herself, giving power over his or her choices neither to other people to control and to compel nor to those impulses within that are the more short-sighted when it comes to discerning one's own "good."

The author is, of course, not alone in his work within the Greek-speaking Jewish communities of the Hellenistic and Roman Diaspora. Well over a century before, the author of *Letter of Aristeas* pioneered the work of interpreting the Law that regulated Jewish practice in alignment with Greek philosophical discourse. Thus while he affirmed the social boundaries that the regulations of Torah fostered as a necessary and even providential insulation of the Jewish people and the distinctive insights into the divine to which they were heirs, he also probed the regulations themselves for the more universalist, moral principles that they encoded. It appears likely that he would have agreed with the author of 4 Maccabees concerning the principal aim of philosophy. During the seven-day symposium, King Ptolemy poses the question, "What is the highest rule?" The Jewish sage replies, "To rule oneself and not to be carried away by passions" (*Let. Aris.* 221-222).[2] The Law helps its devotees attain this end by means of the teaching it communicates symbolically.

---

interaction between Jews and Gentiles. Indeed, when the reader encounters his exclusivist claims on behalf of the Hebrew people (where they follow the Torah devoutly) rather than, say, invitations to people of all nations to take up this promising philosophy, he or she might justly suspect that the author of 4 Maccabees would, on some other occasion, also celebrate the social-engineering effects of Torah observance.

2. Translations from Hadas, *Aristeas to Philocrates*. Wright (*Letter of Aristeas*, 367) translates the question as "What constitutes the best way to rule?" He argues that "the Greek term ἀρχή in the context of government usually means power, sovereignty or majesty. It can also connote the method of government. In light of the present answer, I have translated 'way to rule' as a means of getting at this connotation, which I think is operative here" (Wright, *Letter of Aristeas*, 377). I agree with Wright (against Hadas's translation) that the question is best heard in the context of a king asking about government, but not that the word, and therefore the question, connotes *manner* of government. "What is the most noble dominion" or "magistracy" or "office in which to exercise authority?" would be an entirely appropriate question for a king to pose, and the response that governing oneself well is the noblest exercise of authority a deliciously subversive answer, since it puts the exercise of this highest authority within reach of every individual. The answer is not "You will be the best king that you can be if you master yourself," though that is a good answer, but rather "the noblest authority that a person can exercise is found in mastering one's impulses and passions."

The author of *Letter of Aristeas* reads the dietary laws as if Moses framed them employing the same technique attributed to Pythagoras, who forbade his disciples to eat certain foods based on the immoral attitudes or practices each animal symbolized.[3] Moses was not concerned to promote superstitious taboos concerning the flesh of certain animals, but to communicate guidelines concerning the boundaries of virtuous practice and the disciplines that maintain them. Thus Jews abstain from eating predatory and carrion birds that "are wild and carnivorous and with their strength oppress the rest and procure their food with injustice at the expense of the tame fowl" as a reminder of their own commitment to "practice righteousness in spirit and oppress no one, trusting in their own strength, nor rob anyone of anything" (*Let. Aris.* 146-147). Positively, Jews consume land animals that have cloven hooves and ruminate as a symbol of their larger commitment to "discriminate in each of our actions with a view to what is right" (*Let. Aris.* 150) and to ruminate upon the great and marvelous deeds of the Lord and, thus, the practical devotion due God (*Let. Aris.* 153-55). The dietary regulations—frequently the butt of Gentile disdain—are seen, when interpreted in Pythagorean fashion, to be entirely "directed toward justice and just intercourse" among people (*Let. Aris.* 169).

Alongside promoting the Greek translation of the Jewish Law as a reliable basis for Jewish identity and practice in a Greek setting, the goals of the author of *Letter of Aristeas* were "to encourage Jews to maintain their traditional ways and to live *as Jews* in Hellenistic Alexandria [and] to convince Jews that they could do so *and* participate fully in Alexandrian society at large."[4] Like the author of 4 Maccabees, the author of *Letter of Aristeas* "uses his Greek education and cultural position to argue for Judaism as consistent with elite Greek culture, but he also refuses to compromise on certain distinctive elements of Jewish identity that in practice separate Jews from Gentiles. He implicitly combats the notion that Jews are barbarians, particularly by employing Greek methods of interpretation to show that the laws that set off Jews from Greeks actually embody 'impeccable Hellenistic morals.'"[5] What appear to be the peculiar customs of a non-Greek (i.e., barbarian) people group encode moral precepts that are also thoroughly

---

3. Berthelot, "L'interprétation symbolique," 260-61.

4. Wright, *Letter of Aristeas*, 276.

5. Wright, *Letter of Aristeas*, 277, quoting Barclay, "Using and Refusing," 20-21. Both Jewish authors stand apart from the strategy found in the fragments of Artapanus, where the value of the Jewish people and Jewish practice is bolstered by making the (indemonstrable) claim that revered figures from the ancient heritage of Israel like Abraham, Joseph, and Moses were responsible for many of the inventions foundational to Egyptian and other Gentile cultures.

at home in Greek ethical discourse. Even as Jews continue to live by those laws that generate a visible, even a palpable, barrier between them and non-Jews—the "impregnable palisades and . . . walls of iron" that set Jews safely apart "from vain opinions" by setting them apart from those of other nations that hold to these "vain opinions" (*Let. Aris.* 139)—there is an underlying consonance between that manner of life and the moral principles to which (philosophically reflective) Greeks are also committed. The "barrier" of the Law becomes, at the same time, a bridge.

The aims of the author of 4 Maccabees align fairly well with those of the author of *Letter of Aristeas*, though he does not find it either useful or necessary to employ figurative methods of interpreting texts such as tropological or allegorical readings in order to achieve his ends.[6] The Torah's regulations concerning diet simply constrain one to restrain desire—to master it when it craves what is forbidden, perhaps for no other reason than the exercise itself, which develops the moral and intellectual reflexes that will serve the individual well in the face of more strenuous challenges. He also appears to be less concerned to encourage the full

6. Philo of Alexandria, an older contemporary of the author of 4 Maccabees, sets the highwater mark for the philosophical interpretation of Judaism in the Second Temple Period. He draws on multiple approaches across the extensive corpus of his writings. At points he is as practical in regard to Torah's legislation as the author of 4 Maccabees. The dietary restrictions keep Jews away from the most succulent meats that are most apt to excite and strengthen desire and that would eventually give it the upper hand (*Spec. leg.* 4.100-102). The rules concerning lending without charging interest, not harvesting in the sabbatical year for the sake of the poor who glean, and not destroying the fruit trees of one's enemies all constrain adherents of the Law to learn the virtues of being humane and generous (*Virt.* 84-85, 97, 150-52, respectively). Circumcision functions physically to eliminate "superfluous and excessive pleasure" such as can "delude the mind" (*Spec. leg.* 1.9), even while symbolizing a person's full commitment to restrain all forms of desire for the sake of retaining moral autonomy. The dietary laws are largely geared toward achieving "the extinction of [excessive] appetite" (*Spec. leg.* 4.118), even as the legislation of Torah as a whole has as its aim the restraint of "every immoderate and violent impulse and every irrational and unnatural emotion of the soul" that threatens to overthrow the rule of reason in the individual (*Spec. leg.* 4.79).

Alongside this, however, he gives a great deal of attention to the more Pythagorean, symbolic interpretation of the discrete regulations that one finds in *Letter of Aristeas*. Thus, for example, sea creatures lacking fins and scales are forbidden to Jews because they are (presumably) carried along with the current and lack the equipment to resist the force of the current, symbolizing the soul that is carried away by desire, while those sea creatures with both fins and scales are proper to ingest as they represent the soul equipped with the perseverance and temperance that masters the current of desire (*Spec. leg.* 4.110-112). Reptiles are forbidden because they represent a class of animals that gorge themselves indiscriminately, symbolizing the dangers of stimulating insatiable desires (*Spec. leg.* 4.113). And Philo retains the precise interpretation of permitting the ingestion of animals that part the hoof and chew the cud found long before in *Letter of Aristeas* (*Spec. leg.* 4.107-108).

participation in Greek society that Wright identifies as one of the goals of *Letter of Aristeas*. Indeed, the author of 4 Maccabees portrays Jews and Gentiles in a far more hostile situation than does the author of *Letter of Aristeas*. In the latter, Jews demonstrate the rationality and virtue of their way of life in a lengthy response to polite inquiry (in the case of the high priest Eleazar's explanation primarily of the dietary regulations in the Law of Moses) and—in an even friendlier setting of royal entertainment—over the course of a seven-day symposium (in the case of King Ptolemy posing questions to probe the wisdom of the seventy-two translators after their arrival in Alexandria). These are very different social interactions from what we find in the ad hoc torture chamber before Antiochus, reflective of the very different levels of social antagonism that the respective authors of *Letter of Aristeas* and 4 Maccabees choose to project.

Since neither text was likely to have been written during a period in which Jews were subject to any persecution beyond occasional reminders of the general disdain in which many of their Gentile neighbors held them, the choice of narrative setting holds both rhetorical potential and ethical implications. The author of 4 Maccabees implicitly suggests that the encounter between Gentile and Jew and the social dynamics within which Jews need to articulate the value of their ancestral traditions for themselves and others are characterized by antagonism. The author of *Letter of Aristeas* implicitly suggests that a far greater openness on both sides characterizes—or, at least, could and should characterize—the encounter. The former positions his audience to hold their ground and to mount a successful defense (indeed, one that will prove their position to be not only tenable but superior). The latter positions his audience for a rapprochement that seems to be ready at hand, though it is one that also does not require the Jew to relinquish his or her commitment to the distinctively Jewish way of life. The former depicts the Gentile "other" as the malicious inquisitor; the latter depicts the Gentile "other" as benignly inquisitive. Gentile characters come to appreciate the philosophical value, virtue, and nobility of the Jewish way of life in the course of extended dialogue in *Letter of Aristeas*; in 4 Maccabees, they come to understand this only after they have tortured their Jewish interlocutors to death and tested their resolve to the end.

The depiction of Gentile-Jewish relations in 4 Maccabees is rhetorically supportive of the author's agenda in obvious ways. The narrative world of the Jewish heroes of 4 Maccabees strengthens the audience's inclination to regard the Gentile others as a "them" with whom genuine rapprochement is unlikely and, in the persons of Antiochus and his lackeys, even unattractive. The potential value of assimilation to any degree to achieve such rapprochement is thereby discounted significantly, while the value of resisting, of maintaining one's ancestral way of life, and of disregarding the opinion non-Jews might form of one's way of life increases. The portrayal of an antagonistic situation also increases loyalty, as it were, to one's own side and one's own position. It strategically orients the audience to value, even to prioritize, fighting to maintain that which defines them over against the Gentile others. In a situation of imperial domination, moreover, such a portrayal helpfully keeps the members of the subaltern culture aware of the political and military dynamics that have led to the *need* to resist assimilation, since their way of life is indeed in jeopardy as a result of (a long line of) other peoples' imperialist incursions. But it is also the case that the author purchases effective resistance at the cost of promoting genuine rapprochement—a price that the author of *Letter of Aristeas* did not think it necessary to pay, and he, too, lived in a situation of imperial domination.

While the author of 4 Maccabees was concerned to assure his audience that they could hold their own defending their distinctive way of life at the table of elite Hellenistic discourse, there were no actual members of the Hellenistic philosophical elite *at* the author's table. It was a *conceptual* table only, a Jewish *construct* of the table at which the author assured his Jewish audience that they *could* sit and hold their own for the purpose of encouraging them to remain committed to that which gave them "their own" to hold. A Gentile might at some point read 4 Maccabees. Indeed, within two centuries or so some Gentiles, like Origen, assuredly did. They were Gentile Christians, of course, and were generally disposed to see themselves as the spiritual heirs of the Jewish people and their conceptual heritage. But the non-Christian Gentile who somehow chanced upon and read 4 Maccabees would not read it as a presentation made at a common table at which he or she had been invited to sit. The work was best described by Hans-Josef Klauck as "an inner-directed defense."[7] Its goal was to provide its *Jewish* audience with the self-assurance that Gentile criticism and devaluation of their ancestral way of life—and, by extension, of their own life choices— lacked validity, for their ancestral way of life had allowed the people of their nation to rise to the level of the Greeks' highest ideals of the free person, the wise person, the person who had mastered all the internal and external forces that might undermine his or her commitment to virtue. The Jewish audience could affirm their own and one another's honor *on the Gentile's terms* and, thus, nullify the social pressure both of the Gentile's scorn and the Gentile's invitation to assimilate more fully.

The author's successful and rhetorically artful presentation of the Torah-driven life as the path to attain the Greek ideals of self-mastery and

---

7. Klauck, *4 Makkabäerbuch*, 665 (my translation).

freedom perennially attests to its own value for all who read 4 Maccabees. The author's legacy written in the works of the later authors who read him also bears perpetual witness to his achievement. During the organized persecutions of Christians during the third century, the "athletes of piety" in 4 Maccabees became a source of encouragement for their successors in the great relay race of witnessing to the value of a faith and vision that stood apart (and often in *critical* distance) from the legitimating mechanisms of the imperial regime. After the edicts of toleration, 4 Maccabees continued to hold before Christians the value of self-mastery so as to encourage further generations to choose virtue above self-gratification or self-interest. Both lessons remain highly relevant to Christian readers in the 21st century, the first particularly to Christians in repressive political and religious settings across the globe, the second to Christians particularly in Western settings that seem at many points to have reversed the values of self-gratification and self-interest, on the one hand, and virtue on the other. But the work continues to speak also to Jewish readers and on behalf of Jewish communities concerning the moral vision that several Jewish authors of the Second Temple Period, at least, perceived to lie behind the legislation of the Torah and to be realized through diligent devotion to the same.[8]

8. I was particularly delighted by the Jewish Publication Society's initiative in preparing the three-volume collection that was eventually published as *Outside the Bible: Ancient Jewish Writings Related to Scripture* (ed. by L. H. Feldman, *et al.*), making visible once again and commending to a Jewish readership a number of important Jewish texts that had been the focal concern of Christian readers only for much too long—including 4 Maccabees.

Bibliography

Adams, Marcus. "The Alexandrinus Text of 4 Maccabees." *JSP* 17 (2008) 207–31.

Adams, Sean A., and Seth M. Ehorn. "Composite Citations in the Septuagint Apocrypha." In *Composite Citations in Antiquity: Jewish, Graeco-Roman, and Early Christian Uses*, edited by Sean A. Adams and Seth M. Ehorn, 119–39. Library of New Testament Studies 593. London: Bloomsbury T. & T. Clark, 2016.

Adkins, Arthur W. H. *Moral Values and Political Behavior in Ancient Greece: From Homer to the End of the Fifth Century.* London: Chatto & Windus, 1972.

Anderson, Arnold A. *2 Samuel.* WBC 11. Dallas: Word, 1989.

Anderson, Hugh. "4 Maccabees (First Century A.D.). A New Translation and Introduction." In *The Old Testament Pseudepigrapha*, edited by James H. Charlesworth, 2:531–64. 2 vols. Garden City, NY: Doubleday, 1985.

———. "Maccabees, Books of: Fourth Maccabees." In *Anchor Bible Dictionary*, edited by David Noel Freedman, 4:452–54. New York: Doubleday, 1992.

Arnim, Hans F. A. von. *Stoicorum Veterum Fragmenta.* 4 vols. 1903–1905. Reprint, Stuttgart: Teubner, 1964.

Auld, A. Graeme. *Joshua, Jesus Son of Naue in Codex Vaticanus.* Septuagint Commentary Series. Leiden: Brill, 2004.

Aune, David C. "Mastery of the Passions: Philo, 4 Maccabees and Earliest Christianity." In *Hellenization Revisited: Shaping a Christian Response within the Greco-Roman World*, edited by Wendy Helleman, 125–58. Lanham, MD: University Press of America, 1994.

Barclay, J. M. G. "Mirror-Reading a Polemical Letter: Galatians as a Test Case." *JSNT* 31 (1987) 73–93.

———. "Using and Refusing: Jewish Identity Strategies under the Hegemony of Hellenism." In Matthias Konradt and Ulrike Steinert, eds., *Ethos und Identität: Einheit und Vielfalt des Judentums in hellenistisch-römischer Zeit.* Paderborn: Ferdinand Schöningh Verlag, 2002.

Begg, Christopher. "The Exploits of David's Heroes according to Josephus." *Liber annus Studii biblici franciscani* 47 (1997) 139–69.

———. *Judean Antiquities, Books 5–7: Translation and Commentary.* Flavius Josephus, Translation and Commentary 4. Leiden: Brill, 2005

Berger, Peter L. *The Sacred Canopy: Elements of a Sociology of Religion.* New York: Doubleday, 1967.

Berthelot, Katell, "L'interprétation symbolique des lois alimentaires dans la Lettre d'Aristée: une influence pythagoricienne." *JJS* 52 (2001) 253-268.

Bertram, Georg. "Παιδεύω, παιδεία, κτλ." In *TDNT* 5 (1967) 596–625.

Berve, Helmut. *Die Tyrannis bei den Griechen.* 2 vols. Munich: Beck, 1967.

Bickermann, Elias J. "The Date of Fourth Maccabees." In *Studies in Jewish and Christian History,* edited by E. J. Bickermann, 1:275–81. 3 vols. Arbeiten zur Geschichte des antiken Judentums und des Urchristentums 9. Leiden: Brill, 1976.

Braun, Roddy. *1 Chronicles.* WBC 14. Waco, TX: Word, 1986.

Breitenstein, Urs. *Beobachtungen zu Sprache, Stil und Gedankengut des Vierten Makkabäerbuchs.* Stuttgart: Schwabe, 1978.

Brueggemann, Walter. *First and Second Samuel.* Interpretation. Louisville: Westminster John Knox, 1990.

Colish, Marcia. *Ambrose's Patriarchs: Ethics for the Common Man.* Notre Dame, IN: University of Notre Dame Press, 2005.

Collins, John J. *Between Athens and Jerusalem: Jewish Identity in the Hellenistic Diaspora.* New York: Crossroad, 1983.

Comfort, Philip W., and David P. Barrett, eds. *The Complete Text of the Earliest New Testament Manuscripts.* Grand Rapids: Baker, 1999.

Courcelle, Pierre. "De Platon à saint Ambroise par Apulée." *Revue de philologie* 35 (1961) 15–28.

Croy, N. Clayton. *Endurance in Suffering: Hebrews 12.1–13 in Its Rhetorical, Religious, and Philosophical Context.* SNTSMS 98. Cambridge: Cambridge University Press, 1998.

D'Angelo, Mary R. "*Eusebeia*: Roman Imperial Family Values and the Sexual Politics of 4 Maccabees and the Pastorals." *Biblical Interpretation* 11 (2003) 139–65.

Danker, Frederick W. *Benefactor: Epigraphic Study of a Greco-Roman and New Testament Semantic Field.* St. Louis: Clayton, 1982.

Deissmann, Adolf. "Das vierte Makkabäerbuch." In *Die Apokryphen und Pseudepigraphen des Alten Testaments,* edited by E. Kautzsch, 2:149–76. 2 vols. 1900. Reprint, Hildesheim: Olms, 1962.

Boeft, Jan den, and Jan N. Bremmer. "Notinculae Martyrologicae IV." *VC* 45 (1991) 105–22.

deSilva, David A. *4 Maccabees.* Guides to Apocrypha and Pseudepigrapha. Sheffield: Sheffield Academic, 1998.

———. *4 Maccabees: Introduction and Commentary on the Greek Text of Codex Sinaiticus.* Septuagint Commentary Series. Leiden: Brill, 2006.

———. *Despising Shame: Honor Discourse and Community Maintenance in the Epistle to the Hebrews.* SBLDS 152. Atlanta: Scholars, 1995.

———. *The Letter to the Galatians.* NICNT. Grand Rapids: Eerdmans, 2018.

———. *Honor, Patronage, Kinship & Purity: Unlocking New Testament Culture.* Downers Grove, IL: InterVarsity, 2000.

———. "How Greek Was the Author of 'Hebrews'?" In *Christian Origins and Greco-Roman Culture: Social and Literary Contexts for the New Testament,* edited by Stanley E. Porter and Andrew Pitts, 1:629–50. Texts and Editions for New Testament Study 9. Early Christianity in Its Hellenistic Context 1. Leiden: Brill, 2012.

———. *The Hope of Glory: Honor Discourse and New Testament Interpretation.* Collegeville, MN: Liturgical, 1999.

———. *Introducing the Apocrypha: Message, Context, and Significance.* Grand Rapids: Baker Academic, 2002.

———. *Perseverance in Gratitude: A Socio-rhetorical Commentary on the Epistle "to the Hebrews."* Grand Rapids: Eerdmans, 2000.

———. "Using the Master's Tools to Shore Up Another's House: A Postcolonial Analysis of 4 Maccabees." *JBL* 126 (2007) 99–127.

Dodds, E. R. *The Greeks and the Irrational.* Sather Classical Lectures 25. Berkeley: University of California Press, 1966.

Dupont-Sommer, André. *Le Quatrième Livre des Machabées.* Paris: Librairie Ancienne Honoré Champion, 1939.

Ehrman, Bart D. *The Orthodox Corruption of Scripture: The Effect of Early Christological Controversies on the Text of the New Testament.* New York: Oxford University Press, 1993

———. "The Text as Window: New Testament Manuscripts and the Social History of Early Christianity." In *The Text of the New Testament in Contemporary Research: Essays on the* Status Quaestionis, edited by Bart D. Ehrman and Michael W. Holmes, 361–79. 1995. Reprint, Eugene, OR: Wipf & Stock, 2001.

Feldman, Louis H., James L. Kugel, and Lawrence H. Schiffman, eds. *Outside the Bible: Ancient Jewish Writings Related to Scripture.* 3 vols. Philadelphia: Jewish Publication Society, 2013.

Foucault, Michel. *Fearless Speech.* Edited by Joseph Pearson. Boston: Semiotext(e), 2001.

Freudenthal, Jacob. *Die Flavius Josephus beigelegte Schrift über die Herrschaft der Vernunft (IV Makkabäerbuch): Eine Predigt aus dem ersten nachchristlichen Jahrhundert.* Breslau: Schletter, 1869.

Früchtel, Edgar. *Origenes: Das Gespräch mit Heracleides und dessen Bischofskollegen über Vater, Sohn und Seele: Die Aufforderung zum Martyrium.* Stuttgart: Hiersemann, 1974.

Gilbert, Maurice. "4 Maccabees." In *Jewish Writings of the Second Temple Period*, edited by Michael Stone, 316–19. Compendium Rerum Iudaicarum ad Novum Testamentum II/2. Philadelphia: Fortress, 1984.

Greer, Rowan A. *Origen: An Exhortation to Martyrdom, Prayer, First Principles: Book IV, Prologue to the Commentary on the Song of Songs, Homily XXVII on Numbers.* New York: Paulist, 1979.

Grimm, Carl L. W. "Viertes Buch der Maccabäer." In *Kurzgefasstes exegetisches Handbuch zu den Apokryphen des Alten Testaments*, edited by Otto Fridolin Fritzsche, 283–370. Leipzig: Hirzel, 1857.

Hadas, Moses, ed., *Aristeas to Philocrates (Letter of Aristeas).* 1951. Reprint ed., Eugene, OR: Wipf & Stock, 2007.

———. *The Third and Fourth Books of Maccabees.* Jewish Apocryphal Literature. New York: Harper, 1953.

Hall, Edith. *Inventing the Barbarian: Greek Self-Definition through Tragedy.* Oxford: Clarendon, 1989.

Hamman, A.-G., ed. *Le Martyre dans l'Antiquité Chrétienne: Tertullien, Aux martyrs; Origène, Exhortation au Martyre; Cyprien, écrits aux martyrs, á Fortunatus.* Paris: Migne, 1990.

Hanson, K. C. "How Honorable! How Shameful! A Cultural Analysis of Matthew's Makarisms and Reproaches." *Semeia* 68 (1994[96]) 81–111.

Hartmann, Prosper. "Origène et la Théologie du Martyre d'après le ΠΡΟΤΡΕΠΤΙΚΟΣ de 235." *Ephemerides theologicae lovanienses* 34 (1958) 773–824.

Heininger, Bernard. "Der böse Antiochus: Eine Studie zur Erzähltechnik des 4. Makkabäerbuchs." *Biblische Zeitschrift* n.F. 33 (1989) 43–59.

Hengel, Martin. *Jews, Greeks, and Barbarians: Aspects of the Hellenization of Judaism in the Pre-Christian Period.* Philadelphia: Fortress, 1980.

———. *Judaism and Hellenism: Studies in Their Encounter in Palestine during the Early Hellenistic Period.* 2 vols. Translated by John Bowden. 1974. Reprint, Eugene, OR: Wipf & Stock, 2003.

Henten, Jan Willem van. "A Jewish Epitaph in a Literary Text: 4 Macc 17:8–10." In *Studies in Early Jewish Epigraphy,* edited by Jan W. van Henten and Piet W. van der Horst, 44–69. Arbeiten zur Geschichte des antiken Judentums und des Urchristentums 21. Leiden: Brill, 1994.

———. *The Maccabean Martyrs as Saviors of the Jewish People: A Study of 2 and 4 Maccabees.* Journal for the Study of Judaism Supplements 57. Leiden: Brill, 1997.

———. "The Martyrs as Heroes of the Christian People." In *Martyrium in Multidisciplinary Perspective,* edited by M. Lamberigts and P. van Deun, 303–22. BETL 117. Leuven: Leuven University Press, 1995.

———. "The Tradition-Historical Background of Romans 3.25: A Search for Pagan and Jewish Parallels." In *From Jesus to John: Essays on Jesus and New Testament Christology in Honor of Marinus de Jonge,* edited by Martinus C. De Boer, 101–28. JSNTSup 84. Sheffield: Sheffield Academic, 1993.

———. "Zum Einfluß jüdischer Martyrien auf die Literatur des frühen Christentums, II. Die Apostolischen Väter." In *ANRW,* Part II.27.1, edited by Hildegard Temporini and Wolfgang Haase, 700–723. Berlin: de Gruyter, 1993.

Henten, Jan Wilhelm van, and Friedrich Avemarie. *Martyrdom and Noble Death: Selected Texts from Graeco-Roman, Jewish and Christian Antiquity.* Context of Early Christianity. London: Routledge, 2002.

Hertzberg, Hans W. *Die Samuelbücher.* Das Alte Testament Deutsch 10. Göttingen: Vandenhoeck & Ruprecht, 1973.

Hiebert, Robert J.V. "4 Maccabees 18,6–19—Original Text or Secondary Interpolation?" In *Die Septuaginta—Texte, Kontexte, Lebenswelten,* edited by Martin Karrer and Wolfgang Kraus, 439–49. WUNT 219. Tübingen: Mohr/Siebeck, 2008.

———. "The Greek Pentateuch and 4 Maccabees." In *Scripture in Transition: Essays on Septuagint, Hebrew Bible, and Dead Sea Scrolls in Honour of Raija Sollamo,* edited by Anssi Voitila and Jutta Jokiranta, 239–54. Supplements to Journal for the Study of Judaism 126. Leiden: Brill, 2008.

Hilhorst, Ton. "Fourth Maccabees in Christian Martyrdom Texts." In *Ultima Aetas: Time, Tense and Transience in the Ancient World,* edited by Caroline Kroon and Daan den Hengst, 107–21. Amsterdam: VU University Press, 2000.

Japhet, Sara. *I & II Chronicles: A Commentary.* OTL. Louisville: Westminster John Knox, 1993.

Joslyn-Siemiatkowski, Daniel. *Christian Memories of the Maccabean Martyrs.* New York: Palgrave Macmillan, 2009.

Kennedy, George A. *New Testament Interpretation Through Rhetorical Criticism.* Chapel Hill: University of North Carolina Press, 1984.

———. *Progymnasmata: Greek Textbooks of Prose Composition and Rhetoric.* Writings from the Greco-Roman World 10. Atlanta: Society of Biblical Literature, 2003.

Klauck, Hans-Josef. *4 Makkabäerbuch*. Jüdische Schriften aus hellenistisch-römischer Zeit 3.6. Gütersloh: Mohn, 1989.

———. "Brotherly Love in Plutarch and in 4 Maccabees." In *Greeks, Romans, and Christians: Essays in Honor of Abraham J. Malherbe*, edited by David L. Balch et al., 144–56. Minneapolis: Fortress, 1990.

———. "Hellenistiche Rhetorik im Diasporajudentum: Das Exordium des vierten Makkabäerbuchs (4 Makk 1.1–12)." *NTS* 35 (1989) 451–65.

Knoppers, Gary N. *I Chronicles 10–29*. AB 12A. New York: Doubleday, 2004.

Koester, Helmut. *Introduction to the New Testament*. Vol. 1, *History, Culture, and Religion of the Hellenistic Age*. 2nd ed. Berlin: de Gruyter, 1995.

Lange, Armin. "'The Law, the Prophets, and the Other Books of the Fathers' (Sir., Prologue): Canonical Lists in Ben Sira and Elsewhere." In *Studies in the Book of Ben Sira*, edited by Geza G. Xeravits and Josef Zsengellér, 55–80.Supplements to the Journal for the Study of Judaism 127. Leiden: Brill, 2008.

Lauer, S. "*Eusebes Logismos* in IV Macc." *JJS* 6 (1955) 170–71.

Lebram, Jürgen C. H. "Die literarische Form des vierten Makkabäerbuches." *VC* 28 (1974) 81–96.

Liddell, Henry George, and Robert Scott. *A Greek-English Lexicon*. 9th ed. Oxford: Clarendon, 1940.

Lorde, Audre. "The Master's Tools Will Never Dismantle the Master's House." In *This Bridge Called My Back: Writings by Radical Women of Color*, edited by Cherrie Moraga and Gloria Anzaldua, 94–97. 4th ed. New York: State University of New York Press, 2015.

Mack, Burton L. *Rhetoric and the New Testament*. GBSNTS. Minneapolis: Fortress, 1990.

Malina, Bruce J., and Jerome H. Neyrey. "Conflict in Luke–Acts: Labelling and Deviance Theory." In *The Social World of Luke–Acts: Models for Interpretation*, edited by Jerome H. Neyrey, 97–124. Peabody: Hendrickson, 1991.

Marrou, Henri Irénée. *A History of Education in Antiquity*. Translated by George Lamb. New York: Mentor, 1964.

Mazar, B. "The Military Elite of King David." *VT* 13 (1963) 310–20.

McCarter, P. Kyle, Jr. *II Samuel*. AB 9. Garden City, NY: Doubleday, 1984.

McHugh, Michael P. *Saint Ambrose: Seven Exegetical Works*. Fathers of the Church 65. Washington, DC: Catholic University of America Press, 1972.

McLynn, Neil B. *Ambrose of Milan: Church and Court in a Christian Capital*. Berkeley: University of California Press, 1994.

Metcalfe, William. "Origen's Exhortation to Martyrdom and 4 Maccabees." *JTS* 22 (1921) 268–69.

Metzger, Bruce M. *Manuscripts of the Greek Bible*. Oxford: Oxford University Press, 1981.

Momigliano, Arnaldo. "Freedom of Speech in Antiquity." In *The Dictionary of the History of Ideas: Studies of Selected Pivotal Ideas*, edited by Philip P. Wiener et al., 2:252–63. 5 vols. New York: Scribner, 1973–1974.

Montanari, Franco. *The Brill Dictionary of Ancient Greek*. Edited by Madeleine Goh and Chad Schroeder. Leiden: Brill, 2015.

Moore, Stephen D., and Janice C. Anderson. "Taking It Like a Man: Masculinity in 4 Maccabees." *JBL* 117 (1998) 249–73.

Morgan, Teresa. *Literate Education in the Hellenistic and Roman Worlds.* Cambridge Classical Studies. Cambridge: Cambridge University Press, 1998.

Myers, Jacob M. *I Chronicles.* AB 12. Garden City, NY: Doubleday, 1965.

Nauroy, Gérard. "Le fouet et le miel: le combat d'Ambroise en 386 contre l'arianisme milanais." *Recherches Augustiniennes* 23 (1988) 3–86.

Noce, Celestino. *Origene: Esortazione al Martirio.* Studia Urbaniana 27. Rome: Pontificia Universitas Urbaniana, 1985.

O'Hagan, Angelo P. "The Martyr in the Fourth Book of Maccabees." *Studii biblici Franciscani liber annus* 24 (1974) 94–120.

O'Meara, John J. *Origen: Prayer, Exhortation to Martyrdom.* Ancient Christian Writers 19. Westminster, MD: Newman, 1954.

Pearson, Alfred C. *The Fragments of Zeno and Cleanthes.* New York: Arno, 1973.

Perler, Othmar. "Das vierte Makkabäerbuch, Ignatius von Antiochien und die ältesten Martyrerberichte." *Rivista di archeologia cristiana* 25 (1949) 47–72.

Pfitzner, Victor C. *Paul and the Agon Motif: Traditional Athletic Imagery in the Pauline Literature.* Supplements to Vetus Testamentum 16. Leiden: Brill, 1967.

Pitt-Rivers, Julian. "Honour and Social Status." In *Honour and Shame: The Values of Mediterranean Society,* edited by John G. Peristiany, 21–77. The Nature of Human Society Series. Chicago: University of Chicago Press, 1966.

Rabinowitz, Louis I., trans. *Ruth.* In *Midrash Rabbah.* Vol. 8, *Ruth–Ecclesiastes.* Edited by Harry Freedman and Maurice Simon. 13 vols. in 10. London: Soncino, 1961

Ramsey, Boniface, OP. *Ambrose.* Early Church Fathers. London: Routledge, 1997.

Redditt, Paul D. "The Concept of *Nomos* in Fourth Maccabees." *CBQ* 45 (1983) 249–70.

Renehan, Robert. "The Greek Philosophic Background of Fourth Maccabees." *Rheinisches Museum für Philologie* 115 (1972) 223–38.

Robbins, Vernon K. *Exploring the Texture of Texts: A Guide to Socio-rhetorical Interpretation.* Valley Forge, PA: Trinity, 1996.

Rost, Leonhard. *Einleitung in die alttestamentlichen Apokryphen und Pseudepigraphen.* Heidelberg: Quelle & Meyer, 1971.

————. *Judaism Outside the Hebrew Canon: An Introduction to the Documents.* Translated by David E. Green. Nashville: Abingdon, 1976.

Schaller, B. "Das 4. Makkabäerbuch als Textzeuge der Septuaginta." In *Studien zur Septuaginta: Robert Hanhart zu Ehren,* edited by Detlef Fraenkel et al., 323–31. MSU 20. Göttingen: Vandenhoeck & Ruprecht, 1990.

Schürer, Emil. *The History of the Jewish People in the Age of Jesus Christ (175 B.C.—A.D. 135). A New English Version.* Volume 3, part 1, edited by Geza Vermes et al. Edinburgh: T. & T. Clark, 1986.

Seeley, David. *The Noble Death: Graeco-Roman Martyrology and Paul's Concept of Salvation.* JSNTSup 28. Sheffield: Sheffield Academic, 1990.

Segovia, Fernando F. "Biblical Criticism and Postcolonial Studies: Toward a Postcolonial Optic." In *The Postcolonial Bible,* edited by R. S. Sugirtharajah, 49–65. The Bible and Postcolonialism 1. Sheffield: Sheffield Academic, 1998.

Seim, Turid Karlsen. "Abraham, Ancestor or Archetype? A Comparison of Abraham-Language in 4 Maccabees and Luke–Acts." In *Antiquity and Humanity: Essays on Ancient Religions and Philosophy Presented to Hans Dieter Betz on His 70th Birthday,* edited by Adela Yarbro Collins and Margaret M. Mitchell, 27–42. Tübingen: Mohr/Siebeck, 2001.

Shaw, Bart D. "Body/Power/Identity: Passions of the Martyrs." *JECS* 4 (1996) 269–312.

Smith, Henry P. *A Critical and Exegetical Commentary on the Books of Samuel.* ICC. New York: Scribner, 1902.

Stanley, Christopher D. *Paul and the Language of Scripture: Citation Technique in the Pauline Epistles and Contemporary Literature.* SNTSMS 69. Cambridge: Cambridge University Press, 1992.

Stowers, Stanley K. "4 Maccabees." In *The HarperCollins Bible Commentary*, edited by James L. Mays, 844–55. Rev. ed. San Francisco: HarperSanFrancisco, 2000.

Sugirtharajah, R. S. "Biblical Studies after the Empire." In *The Postcolonial Bible*, edited by R. S. Sugirtharajah, 12–22. The Bible and Postcolonialism 1. Sheffield: Sheffield Academic, 1998.

———. "A Postcolonial Exploration of Collusion and Construction in Biblical Interpretation." In *The Postcolonial Bible*, edited by R. S. Sugirtharajah, 91–117. The Bible and Postcolonialism 1. Sheffield: Sheffield Academic, 1998.

Tcherikover, Victor. *Hellenistic Civilization and the Jews.* New York: Atheneum, 1977.

Thackeray, Henry St. John, and Ralph Marcus. *Josephus, with an English Translation. Volume 5.* LCL. Cambridge: Harvard University Press, 1966.

Townshend, Richard B. "The Fourth Book of Maccabees." In *The Apocrypha and Pseudepigrapha of the Old Testament.* Vol. 2, *Pseudepigrapha*, edited by R. H. Charles, 653–85. Oxford: Clarendon, 1913.

Williams, Sam K. *Jesus' Death as Saving Event: The Background and Origin of a Concept.* Harvard Theological Review Dissertation Series 2. Missoula: Scholars, 1975.

Winslow, Donald F. "The Maccabean Martyrs: Early Christian Attitudes." *Judaism* 23 (1974) 78–86.

Wright, Benjamin G., III, *The Letter of Aristeas.* Commentaries on Early Jewish Literature. Berlin: de Gruyter, 2015.

Young, Robin Darling. "The 'Woman with the Soul of Abraham': Traditions about the Mother of the Maccabean Martyrs." In *Women Like This: New Perspectives on Jewish Women in the Greco-Roman World*, edited by Amy-Jill Levine, 67–81. Early Judaism and Its Literature 1. Atlanta: Scholars, 1991.

Ziadé, Raphaëlle. *Les martyrs Maccabées: de l'histoire juive au culte chretien: Les homelies de Gregoire de Nazianze et de Jean Chrysostome.* Supplements to Vigiliae Christianae 80. Leiden: Brill, 2007.

Author Index

Scripture Index

Genesis

2:7–9	160
2:22	141
3:13	141, 168n17
3:23	150
4:1–10	40
4:1–8	143
6–9	40
6:1–4	167n16
22:1–19	40, 143
34:1–31	39
39:1–23	40
39:7–23	144
39:7–12	39
40:3	144
49:7	39

Exodus

20:17	28, 39
20:19	165
22:16	141
22:25	39
23:4–5	39
23:10–11	39
24:3	40
24:7	40

Leviticus

11:4–23	39
11:41–42	39
17:10–13	102
17:11–14	114
19:9–10	39

Numbers

16:1–35	39
16:41–50	40, 168
25:1–9	40
25:6–13	145
25:11	145n24

Deuteronomy

4:9	143
5:21	28, 39, 165
6:7	143
11:19	143
12:23–24	102
13:6–11	39
14:4–21	39
15:1–2	39
15:9	39
20:19–20	39
20:24	39
21:10–14	110
22:25–27	141, 168n17
23:19–20	39
27:15—28:68	171, 178
28:1–14	171
28:49–50	171
30:1–5	172
30:15–20	151n37